Ecce Scriptores Romani

A Selection of Latin Prose and Verse

PREPARED BY

The Scottish Classics Group

Oliver & Boyd

D0302178

This reader was prepared by the following members of the Scottish Classics Group:

Mary S. R. Burns   formerly Assistant Deputy Principal and Principal Teacher of Classics, The Mary Erskine School, Edinburgh

Iain R. Macaskill   Principal Teacher of Classics, Knox Academy, Haddington

M. Barclay Miller   formerly Depute Rector and Principal Teacher of Classics, Perth Academy

Richard M. Orr   Adviser in Classics, Strathclyde Region

Henry L. Philip   formerly H. M. Inspector of Schools and Headmaster, Liberton High School, Edinburgh

William F. Ritchie   formerly Depute Rector and Principal Teacher of Classics, Arbroath High School

Kenneth G. Silver   formerly Rector, Jedburgh Grammar School and Principal Teacher of Classics, Falkirk High School

Geoffrey Suggitt   formerly Headmaster, Stratton School, Biggleswade, and Principal Teacher of Classics, George Watson's College, Edinburgh

Cover   Alexander Mosaic from "House of the Fauns" in Pompeii

Illustrated by Peter Dennis and Gillian Glen

Photo Acknowledgements

We are grateful to the following for permission to reproduce photographs;
Ancient Art and Architecture Collection, pages 77, 130, 223 and 251; Ashmolean Museum, Oxford, page 171; Photographie Giraudon, pages 48 and 246; Sonia Halliday Photographs, page 157; Mansell Collection, pages 9, 13, 14, 24, 25, 30, 36, 78, 91, 100, 110, 113, 122 and 230; Museum of London, page 142.

Cover photograph by courtesy of Interdi Press, Naples

Oliver & Boyd
Addison Wesley Longman Limited
Edinburgh Gate
Harlow
Essex CM20 2JE England
An Imprint of Longman Group UK Limited

© The Scottish Classics Group 1993

First published 1993
Fifth Impression 1996

The publisher's policy is to use paper manufactured from sustainable forests.

ISBN 0 05 005042 7

Set in 10/12 pt Times
Produced through Longman Malaysia, CL

Contents

Notes for the Teacher

Substantial changes have taken place in national examinations over the past few years. One of the major challenges now facing the teacher of Latin is how to create a meaningful course within the greatly curtailed time available for teaching the subject. Examination Boards have generally recognised this fact and have amended their examinations accordingly. In particular, pupils are now expected to have an active knowledge of far fewer grammatical constructions and of a much smaller vocabulary. Considerable editing of texts is also required so that pupils do not have to face a level of Latin which is too demanding. Few texts of the required standard exist, and it can be very confusing for pupils if they are expected to use a traditional text from which only a small part is prescribed.

The Scottish Examination Board has undertaken to produce for schools a plain text of the prescription for Standard Grade for each year. While this is helpful, pupils and teachers still face the difficulty of having to use the notes and vocabulary of an existing reader, whose text may not correspond with the text of the prescription. The Scottish Classics Group has therefore prepared a reader which contains the forthcoming prescription for Standard Grade, together with almost the whole of the current prescription and additional passages which are of the level of difficulty faced in Standard Grade. Although we initially set out to provide material for Scottish schools, we have also studied the syllabuses and examination papers set by the Examination Boards in England and Wales, and we are encouraged to think that *Ecce Scriptores Romani* could be equally useful south of the border.

In the selection of reading passages, one has to make a choice – either to draw, from a restricted range of authors, material which requires only a limited vocabulary, or else, by extending the variety of authors and topics, to produce passages which are intrinsically much more interesting, even though this greatly increases the number of words used. We have adopted the latter course, believing emphatically that, while the traditional Latin diet may have been chosen for its obvious literary merit, much of it was too difficult for the pupils, even with the much greater allocation of time which Latin enjoyed in the past. We believe that our approach will help pupils to realise how alive Latin really is: it did not die with the fall of Rome but continued to have a powerful influence over the centuries and, indeed, dealt with a whole range of topics and problems which are still relevant today.

Our aim is to encourage the rapid reading of passages so that pupils understand the message the author is trying to convey rather than to promote a knowledge of syntax. In the notes which are printed opposite the text, therefore, we have kept the explanation of Latin grammar to a minimum and have concentrated instead on giving a good English translation of any difficult words and phrases, together with a literal translation which should explain how the final version was arrived at. Those who wish to pursue grammatical points in more detail are referred to *The Latin Language*, a handbook of the Scottish Classics Group published by Oliver and

5

Boyd, in which the explanation of Latin syntax and accidence is designed to improve students' ability to read Latin rather than to help them with Latin composition. This book is referred to as "LL" in the notes.

Likewise, since knowledge of vocabulary is one of the greatest stumbling blocks for most pupils, extensive word lists are provided on the same page as the text. In deciding which words to exclude from these word lists, we have been guided by the list of approximately 1000 common words which the Scottish Examination Board produced after studying various commercial lists (see footnote) as well as *Ecce Romani* and the *Cambridge Latin Course*. Since we have no way of knowing which passages pupils will read, each passage has been viewed independently as far as these special vocabularies are concerned. It will be found therefore that some words appear in the lists of several stories. The general vocabulary at the back contains all the words used in the book, and they are given in their full form. The words listed beside the Latin text are given in the simplest form possible.

Although a great deal of assistance has been given in the notes and in the special vocabularies, it is to be hoped that pupils will not simply accept the translation which has been given but will make use of the fuller vocabulary at the end of the book in order to extend their vocabulary knowledge. Indeed, time could profitably be spent periodically in examining such things as groups of words which have the same root, words beginning with the same prefix and words in which consonants are assimilated (e.g. **adfero/affero**). Further suggestions and practice can be found in *The Latin Language*, pages 78–87.

It is unlikely that many teachers will wish pupils at this stage to make a detailed study of the metres used. Nevertheless, we have included some basic notes on these (pp. 253–258) so that the essential information is there if required. We wish to emphasise how important it is to read the Latin passage aloud.

Brief notes on the main authors are to be found on pages 8–15. We would have preferred to use the latter as introductions to the reading passages, but the thematic approach we have adopted makes this impossible.

Comprehension and Interpretation now feature prominently in teaching and assessment. We have not included many straightforward comprehension questions, since it is relatively easy for teachers to devise these for themselves. Instead, we have concentrated on interpretation questions, many of them open-ended, which we think will provoke thought and class discussion, thus further indicating to pupils that what they are reading has a great deal of relevance to their own lives and times. It is our own experience that it is not always the ablest Latin pupils who contribute or gain most in these discussions. It is quite often the case that pupils who find the Latin difficult can nonetheless provide sensible and shrewd comments on the human issues once they have grasped the meaning of the Latin. In the sections headed "Points for Discussion", the more straightforward language and comprehension questions generally come first in the order in which they occur in the passage. The questions designed to promote open-ended discussion are usually arranged according to level of difficulty.

Behind our decision to arrange the passages thematically was the hope that pupils might be encouraged to draw comparisons between passages. Since pupils will be able to tackle only a limited number of the passages in Latin, teachers may wish pupils to study some of the other passages in an English translation in order to extend the scope of these comparisons. One theme which cuts across several of our themes is man's relations with the animal world – Arion and the Dolphin and Pliny's Dolphin; Androcles; Lesbia's pet bird and Martial's Issa. Again, Erotion and Androcles might be taken with the section on Slavery, while "The Songbird Dies" offers some comments on attitudes to death.

There are, no doubt, more questions than teachers will have time to use. Some of the questions are quite demanding, and many of them have no right or wrong answers. It will be for teachers to make their own selection from what is offered.

*The commercial lists studied by the Scottish Examination Board included: Masterman's *A Latin Word List*, *A Basic Latin Vocabulary* produced by the Orbilian Society, *A Basic Latin Vocabulary* compiled by Wilson and Parsons, and separate computer analyses of Latin vocabulary by Huchthausen and Kollmann.

Notes on Authors

Caesar

C. Julius Caesar was born about 100 BC. An ambitious politician, he won his way into high office through his ability as an orator and by courting the popularity of the people through lavish displays of generosity. To help his career, he also formed the First Triumvirate with two other powerful Romans, Pompey and Crassus, and married Pompey's daughter, Julia. The Triumvirate brought each of its members political gain. Caesar became consul in 59 BC and during his term in office forced through some important legislation, much of it designed to increase his popularity. At the end of his consulship he was rewarded with the governorship of the three provinces of Illyricum, Cisalpine Gaul and Transalpine Gaul. This five-year command was extended to ten when the Triumvirate came to a new agreement at Luca in 56 BC. As their rewards, Pompey and Crassus were to become consuls in 55 BC, followed by five-year governorships of Spain and Syria respectively. All three were granted funds for powerful armies.

During the period from 58 BC to 49 BC, Caesar extended his province by conquering and pacifying the whole of Gaul in a series of brilliant campaigns. He also crossed the Rhine into Germany and carried out two invasions of Britain in 55 BC and 54 BC. During his governorship he kept a kind of diary, called the *Commentarii de Bello Gallico*. In it he recorded not only details of his campaigns but also a range of other social and geographical information. These *Commentarii* were also skilful propaganda, for he seldom uses the pronoun "I", but describes all the events as performed by "Caesar". In this way he gives his exploits more credibility since they appear to have been written by a neutral observer. He does not falsify events, but he does interpret them in such a way as to justify his actions and describe them in the best possible light; thus he always seems to be defending Rome's interests rather than indulging in conquest for its own sake.

At the same time, however, he was creating enemies in Rome who tried to block his candidacy for the consulship by persuading the Senate to insist that he should first disband his army and come to Rome as a private citizen. By now, Crassus had been killed in Syria and Pompey had joined the Senate in its opposition to Caesar. (Julia had died in 54 BC.) Using as an excuse the fact that the Senate had acted unconstitutionally by passing its resolution in spite of opposition from two tribunes of the people, Caesar led his army across the Rubicon, the boundary of his province. Thus began the Civil War between Caesar and Pompey, recorded by Caesar in his *De Bello Civili*. Caesar drove Pompey and his other enemies from Italy and then pursued them to Greece where he defeated them at Pharsalus in 48 BC. Pompey fled to Egypt where he was assassinated; however, Caesar had to inflict further defeats on the Senatorial armies in Africa and Spain before he could regard himself as undisputed master of Rome.

Julius Caesar

During his few years as dictator, he brought much-needed stability to the empire after many years of conflict between ambitious generals who used their military might for their own advancement; and it had become clear that the republican constitution, which had worked well while Rome's power was confined to Italy, was no longer suited to an empire which extended over much of the known world. Caesar introduced several laws which improved the situation by providing stronger central government. He did not call himself "king" (a title detested by the Romans), but in the eyes of many influential Romans he was monarch in all but name. A plot was formed against him by some committed Republicans, and he was assassinated on the Ides (15th) of March 44 BC.

Cato

Born in 234 BC at Tusculum, which was about ten miles south of Rome, M. Porcius Cato the Elder devoted the early part of his adult life to military affairs, including distinguished service in the Second Punic War. In 191 BC, after twenty-six years of military service, he turned to civil and political activities in Rome and became famous for his strong opposition to the growing influence of Athenian culture, which he felt was undermining the traditional Roman virtues. His period as Censor, which began in 184 BC, was renowned for the severity with which he dealt with any form of corruption or decadence.

He mellowed somewhat in his old age and devoted himself partly to the study of Greek and partly to writing. Of his many works, only that on agriculture entitled *De Re Rustica* has survived. In the last year of his life, he was sent as an arbiter to settle a dispute between Carthage and one of its neighbours. The remarkable recovery made by Carthage in the half century following its defeat in the Second Punic War resurrected his narrow-minded nationalism and led him to the conclusion that Rome's future would never be secure as long as Carthage remained. On every occasion on which he spoke in the senate after that, therefore, no matter what the subject, he concluded his speech with the words **delenda est Carthago** (*Carthage must be destroyed*). He died at the age of 85 in 149 BC.

Catullus

Horace

Catullus

C. Valerius Catullus was born at Verona in Cisalpine Gaul about 84 BC. We know very little about his life – even the dates of his birth and death are guesswork. From his poetry, however, we glean that he came to Rome as a young man, joined a group of fashionable men-about-town, had a tempestuous love-affair with a woman whom he calls Lesbia, joined for a time the staff of the governor of Bithynia in Asia Minor, and died when he was only about thirty years old, possibly from tuberculosis.

Catullus had wealth, wit and worldliness – all the qualifications to commend him to the sophisticated and amoral (if not immoral) stratum of Roman society in his time. Known to his fellow poets as **doctus** (*accomplished*) because of his skill in recreating in Latin the metres and stanzas of Greek verse, he expresses his own feelings strongly on many topics – people, politics and the social scene. But possibly he makes his greatest impact in the many poems which trace the history of his love-affair with Lesbia (probably Clodia, the notorious wife of Metellus Celer) – poems of starry-eyed love, of bitter disillusionment, of reconciliation, of despair, of final rejection and parting. Equally tender, however, and displaying a different kind of love, are the lines which he wrote after visiting the tomb of his brother who had died in Asia Minor.

His poems almost died with him. It is thought that perhaps some friend, acting as literary executor, published his poems posthumously, under the title *Liber Veronensis*. But his manuscripts were never numerous and in the Middle Ages he was virtually unknown. It was only in the late thirteenth century that someone spotted the *Liber Veronensis* being used, according to one account, as a bung for a wine barrel. Fortunately, one or two copies were made from this; but the original vanished once more and all our texts are derived from copies of that original.

Curtius

The dates of the birth and death of Q. Curtius Rufus are unknown, but it is possible that he lived in the second half of the first century AD. He wrote a history of Alexander the Great in ten books, but the first two of these are lost, and there are considerable gaps in the others. His style tends to be anecdotal and is designed to attract the reader by means of its human interest rather than by its historical accuracy.

Eutropius

Eutropius was a Roman historian who lived in the fourth century AD. What he wrote was not so much a history as a summary of the main points in Roman history from its beginnings to his own time. In the main, he confined himself to brief statements about the most important facts, but occasionally he wrote more expansively about an episode which caught his interest. One such episode was the invasion of Italy by Pyrrhus, King of Epirus.

Gellius

Aulus Gellius was a Roman lawyer and writer who lived from about AD 123–165. After completing an education in language and literature in Rome, he went on to study philosophy in Athens, in Attica. While there, he kept himself busy during the long winter nights by writing *Noctes Atticae* – a collection of stories about all sorts of interesting things which he had seen, read or heard, including the tales of *Arion*, *Androcles* and *A Wise Bird*.

Horace

Q. Horatius Flaccus was born the son of a freedman in 65 BC. He received a good education and joined the Roman civil service. When his father lost his small farm, Horace was driven by poverty to turn his hand to the writing of verse. He was sufficiently successful in this to attract the attention of Maecenas (the "talent spotter" for the Emperor Augustus), who introduced him into the imperial circle in 38 BC; and, along with Virgil, he was made the equivalent of our Poet Laureate. As such, he was an eminently "safe" poet, well suited by nature to the task. He wrote nothing that was controversial. His *Satires*, for example, are conversational pieces which contain good-humoured comments on the social scene rather than biting criticism; and his later *Epistles*, though still critical of contemporary attitudes, are versified essays on moral and literary themes.

Horace himself wondered if these works merited the name "poetry", but he had no doubt about the poetic accomplishment of his four books of *Odes*, in which he felt he had naturalised in Latin the metres of Greek poetry. Posterity, however, has valued Horace not just for his metrical mastery, but for his wide range of subject-matter. There are many patriotic poems, interspersed with reflections upon such topics as friendship, love, rural life, religion and philosophy, all expressed with such melodious felicity of language that Horace has become the most widely quoted of all the Latin poets, and thus has achieved the claim which he makes in the poem with which we close our selection of passages – **exegi monumentum aere perennius**. He died in 8 BC.

Martial

M. Valerius Martialis was born in Spain around AD 40 and, after receiving a good education, he moved in his early twenties to Rome where his skill as a poet and the outrageous nature of his writings won him great popularity and the patronage of several rich men. He had a keen eye for the frailties of human nature, and he found many butts on which to exercise his clever wit and ridicule. In all, he wrote some 1200 epigrams or short poems, many of them giving us a good insight into every-day life in ancient Rome. Although he ridiculed other characters, including rich patrons, he was careful to write in flattering terms about the emperors Titus and Domitian while they were alive and so enjoyed many favours from them. This did not prevent him from lampooning the cruelties and vices of Domitian after his death. He did not find much favour with the new emperor Trajan, and in his late fifties he returned to Spain where he died in near poverty a few years later.

Ovid

Ovid

P. Ovidius Naso (43 BC–AD 17) belonged by birth to the upper classes of Rome. He studied rhetoric in preparation for a career in law; but, being too emotional by nature (on his own admission) to expect success in that sphere, he soon turned to writing verses of a somewhat satirical and sometimes scurrilous sort. Through these he fast found favour within an admiring circle of dilettante but perceptive and knowledgeable socialites who were fascinated by the many daring allusions and innuendos of his early poems on love-themes. After enjoying the favour of the Emperor Augustus, he was suddenly in AD 8 banished by the emperor to Tomi on the Black Sea. The official reason given for his banishment was his licentious poem on *The Art of Love*; but, as it had been written ten years before this, it is thought that his offence was probably some intrigue with the emperor's profligate daughter Julia. He hated life in Tomi but continued to write poetry, albeit of a more sorrowful nature. Although he wrote several poems in honour of the emperor, Augustus rejected his appeals to be allowed to return to Rome, and he died in Tomi at the age of sixty.

He was a prolific writer, and it is truly remarkable how many of his poems have survived. These include love poems (e.g. the *Heroides*, which deal with the tragic loves of heroines), the *Fasti* (a kind of poetic calendar describing the origins of famous festivals), the *Metamorphoses* (a collection of myths), and the *Tristia* (which bewail his fate in Tomi). He even wrote a tragedy, *Medea*, but it has not survived. He used only two metre forms – the Hexameter and the Elegiac Couplet (a hexameter followed by a pentameter). He is admired for his remarkable genius in the use of language, for his appropriate choice of words and the skilful way in which he arranges them, and for his equal skill in treating the frivolous and the serious, in creating the mock-heroic and in expressing genuine grief and tenderness.

Phaedrus

Phaedrus, who lived in the first century AD, was brought as a slave from northern Greece to Rome, where he learned Latin. He was later set free by the Emperor Augustus. Most of his poems were translations of the Greek fables of Aesop. His writings disappeared for many centuries and it was only in the sixteenth century that they were discovered in a library in Rheims.

Pliny the Younger

Pliny the Elder

Pliny

P. Caecilius Secundus was born in AD 61 at Novum Comum, modern Como, in north Italy. On his father's death, he was adopted by his uncle C. Plinius Secundus and, as was the custom, he took his adoptive father's name in its entirety, in addition to his own, and was then known as Gaius Plinius Caecilius Secundus. Since his uncle was himself a celebrated writer, being the author of a substantial encyclopaedia called *The Natural History*, it is usual to refer to the uncle as the Elder Pliny and to the nephew as the Younger Pliny.

The Younger Pliny is known to us chiefly as a letter-writer. He trained in oratory to prepare for a career in the law courts. Success in that brought him into public life where he passed through all the magistracies up to the consulship in AD 100, and eventually to the governorship of Bithynia in AD 111. It is thought that he died there in AD 113 or 114.

He knew all the great personalities of the day, and his letters afford us fascinating glimpses of contemporary people and events such as the eruption of Vesuvius in AD 79 (in which his uncle died) and the problems of governing a province, in which his correspondent is none other than the Emperor Trajan himself.

Seneca

Virgil and the Muses

Seneca

L. Annaeus Seneca, born in Spain around 4 BC, was brought to Rome by his parents when he was still a child. His education followed the normal lines, culminating in courses in rhetoric and philosophy. He was a keen student and quickly won distinction as a pleader of causes. At one stage in his career, he fell foul of both Caligula and Claudius; but, towards the end of the latter's reign, he became the tutor of the young Nero. When Nero succeeded Claudius as emperor, Seneca became one of his chief advisers and amassed considerable wealth. At first, he was successful in striking a balance between giving Nero support in his intrigues and trying to restrain him from his vicious treatment of opponents; but latterly Nero began to regard him as a thorn in his flesh. When he realised that Nero wished to get rid of him, he tried unsuccessfully to remove himself from the limelight; but this was not enough for Nero who ordered him to take his life, and this he did at the age of fifty-two.

Although he also wrote tragedies, it is for his writings on moral issues that he is best known. He was a Stoic and not a Christian, but many of his sentiments were in tune with Christian thinking and St Jerome (fourth to fifth century AD) included him in his list of Christian writers. Despite this, one cannot help feeling that, during his career, Seneca always had "an eye for the main chance".

Virgil

P. Vergilius Maro was born in fairly humble circumstances in a village in Cisalpine Gaul in 70 BC. His father owned only a small farm, but he was able to give his son a good education which culminated in the study of philosophy in Rome and Naples. The original intention had been that Virgil should pursue a career in law before entering politics, but his temperament was quite unsuited to this and he decided instead to devote himself to philosophy and poetry. Like Horace, he attracted the attention of Maecenas, the adviser of Octavian who was later to become the Emperor Augustus. His first important work was the collection of ten pastoral poems called the *Eclogues*.

After the civil war in which the murderers of Julius Caesar were defeated, the farm of Virgil's father was one of many confiscated for distribution among the soldiers of Octavian and the other victorious generals. With the help of influential friends, however, Virgil was able to have the farm restored, and for this he was eternally grateful to Augustus. His next work was the four books of the *Georgics* which, besides containing advice on agriculture and husbandry, extolled the virtues of the Italian countryside and tried to reinforce the attempts of Augustus to revive an interest in the simple way of life which had made Rome great in the past.

At Augustus' request, Virgil devoted the last ten years of his life to the writing of *The Aeneid*, a long epic poem modelled on Homer's *Iliad* and *Odyssey* and designed to celebrate Rome's achievements, to glorify the traditional Roman virtues (particularly that of **pietas**, dutifulness to one's country, the gods, one's parents and one's family), and to give thanks for the rule of Augustus himself which had brought peace and prosperity to an empire that had been torn repeatedly by civil strife for more than a century. The first six books of this national epic were devoted to the fall of Troy and to the wanderings of the Trojan hero Aeneas, who escaped from Troy with a small band of followers and was driven on by the gods to search for a new destiny in the promised land of Hesperia. The last six deal with the problems which Aeneas faced in establishing a settlement in Italy. Since the Julian family, to which Augustus belonged, claimed to be descended from Aeneas, the poem sought to identify the emperor with the original struggles from which the magnificence of Rome eventually emerged, as well as glorifying his present achievements in restoring Rome to all its glory.

Virgil had not finished the poem when he died at the age of fifty. He left instructions that it should be destroyed because he considered that it required three years' work to remove its imperfections. However, his literary executors decided that, even with the imperfections, it was such a brilliant work that it should be preserved.

Catullus: See Notes on Authors on page 10.
Metre: Hendecasyllabic (See page 258).

line

1   **cui dono**: *to whom do I dedicate*. In modern books, dedications are normally short and simple, along the lines of "to so-and-so, in memory of . . ." or "to so-and-so with love and thanks". Here, Catullus has chosen to write a rather elaborate dedication in verse to the historian Cornelius Nepos (line 3).

     libellum: *my little book*. The use of the diminutive **libellus** (from **liber**) does not necessarily indicate that the book was small in size; it probably indicates the poet's affection for his own newly-published work, and perhaps a degree of modesty too.

2   **pumice**: Books in Roman times were rolls (**volumina**) of "paper" (**charta**) made from the pith of papyrus reeds. Two layers of these were laid at right angles to each other and glued together. A pumice-stone (**pumex**) was then used to trim off the ragged edges of the roll, and the surface of the "paper" was smoothed (**expolitus**) so that it was suitable for writing on. A pumice-stone was also used to erase mistakes and remove blots.

3   **tibi**: This one word answers the question asked by **cui** in line 1.

4   **meas esse aliquid nugas**: This Accusative and Infinitive depends on **putare**.

     aliquid: *something*, i.e. *worth something* or *of some value*.

     nugas: *trifles, scraps (of verse)*.

5   **iam tum cum**: *even at the time when*.

     unus Italorum: *alone among Italians*. It appears that Nepos was the first Roman writer to attempt to write a complete world history (**omne aevum explicare**, *to unravel the whole of history*), although Greek writers had done so. Catullus finds it remarkable that his own small work should impress Nepos, who already had a three-volume history to his name.

6   **explicare**: *to unfold*, perhaps carrying the double idea of "explaining" the history and "unrolling" the scroll.

7   **Iuppiter**: *by Jove*, used as an exclamation to emphasise that these are indeed learned volumes.

     laboriosis: *elaborate*, i.e. *on which much effort has been spent*.

8   **habe tibi**: *please accept*, literally *have for yourself*.

     quidquid hoc libelli qualecunque: *this little book, such as it is, whatever it is worth*, literally *whatever this is of a book, whatever its nature*.

9   **patrona virgo**: Catullus appeals to his patroness (either Minerva, the maiden goddess of the arts, or Erato, one of the nine Muses) to secure the immortality of his poetry.

     quod maneat: *may it endure*, a wish which is reinforced by the adjective **perenne** (**per + annos**). (For the present subjunctive used in Wishes, see LL p. 107.)

10   **plus uno saeclo**: For Ablative of Comparison, see LL p. 16.

1 A Dedication

(Catullus 1)

cui dono lepidum novum libellum
arido modo pumice expolitum?
Corneli, tibi; namque tu solebas
meas esse aliquid putare nugas,
5 iam tum cum ausus es unus Italorum
omne aevum tribus explicare chartis
doctis, Iuppiter, et laboriosis.
quare. habe tibi quidquid hoc libelli
qualecunque; quod, o patrona virgo,
10 plus uno maneat perenne saeclo.

lepidus, charming, attractive
aridus, dry
modo, recently, only just
namque, for
aevum (*n*), age, generation

charta (*f*), sheet of papyrus, "volume"
quare, therefore
perennis, -is, -e, long-lasting, through the
  years
saeclum (*n*), generation

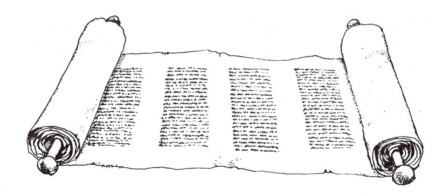

Points for Discussion

1 What words does Catullus use in this poem to point the contrast between his
   own book of poems and Nepos' history?

2 Do you think Catullus seriously thought that his poems were **nugae** (line 4)?
   Collect any evidence from the poem that seems to prove or disprove this
   view.

Gellius: See Notes on Authors on page 11.

line

1 **in Circo Maximo**: Although the Circus Maximus was built originally for chariot-racing, it was later used also for gladiatorial shows.

 venationis amplissimae pugna: *a lavish programme of wild beast fights*, literally *fighting (consisting) of a lavish wild beast hunt*. Besides contests in which various types of gladiators were pitted against one another, there were spectacles in which animals imported from overseas fought against each other or against men, some armed, some unarmed. To give an air of realism, the arena was filled with scenery to give the appearance of the animals' natural habitat.

2 **spectator fui**: *I (Apion) was an eye-witness*.

 ferae: Supply **erant** with **ferae** and **magnitudines**, corresponding to **erat** which goes with **forma** and **ferocia**.

3 **magnitudines bestiarum excellentes**: *beasts of exceptional size*, literally *exceptional sizes of beasts*.

4 **admirationi fuit**: *caused amazement*. (For Predicative Dative, see LL p. 13.)

5 **ceteros**: Supply **leones**.

6 **fluctuantibus**: The basic meaning of the verb **fluctuare** is *to move up and down like waves*. Here it is applied to the movement of muscles and of the lion's mane. English would probably require different verbs to describe these two movements.

8 **ad pugnam bestiarum datos**: *who had been provided to fight the wild beasts*.

9 **viri consularis**: *belonging to a man of consular rank*. Even after ending their year of office, those who had been consuls retained the rank, but not the power of consul.

 Androclus: Throughout the story, Gellius uses the Latin form of the name. The Greek form, Androcles, is more commonly used in English.

12 **crura** and **manus** are the direct objects of **demulcet**.

 eius: *of the man* (i.e. Androcles). **exanimati** (line 13) agrees with **eius**.

Circus and Arena

2 Androcles and the Lion

(Aulus Gellius, *Noctes Atticae* V. 14)

Gellius says that he heard the following story from a learned man, called Apion, who claimed he had actually seen the wonderful sight with his own eyes.

An amazing incident

in Circo Maximo venationis amplissimae pugna populo dabatur.   eius rei, Romae cum forte essem, spectator fui. ⌈multae ibi saevientes ferae, magnitudine bestiarum excellentes;   omniumque invisitata aut forma erat aut ferocia.   sed praeter alia omnia leonum immanitas admirationi fuit, praeterque
5 omnes ceteros unus.   is unus leo corporis impetu et vastitudine terrificoque fremitu et sonoro, toris comisque cervicum fluctuantibus, animos oculosque omnium in sese converterat.

introductus erat inter complures ceteros ad pugnam bestiarum datos servus viri consularis.⌉ ei servo Androclus nomen fuit.   hunc ille leo ubi vidit procul,
10 repente quasi admirans stetit, ac deinde sensim atque placide tamquam noscitabundus ad hominem accedit.   tum caudam more atque ritu adulantium canum clementer et blande movet, hominisque se corpori adiungit cruraque eius et manus, prope iam exanimati metu, lingua leniter demulcet.

saeviens, savage
fera (*f*), wild beast
invisitatus, not seen before,
  uncommon
ferocia (*f*), fierceness
praeter (+ *acc*.), beyond,
  more than
immanitas (*f*), vast size
impetus (*m*), power, strength
vastitudo (*f*), huge size
terrificus, terrifying
fremitus (*m*), roaring
sonorus, loud
torus (*m*), muscle, muscular body
comae (*f.pl*), hair, mane
cervices (*f.pl*), neck
sese = se
converto (3), to turn
introduco (3), to bring in
repente, suddenly

quasi, as if
admiror (1), to wonder, be amazed
ac, and
sensim, gradually
placide, quietly, gently
tamquam, as if
noscitabundus, recognising
accedo (3), to go towards,
  approach
cauda (*f*), tail
ritus (*m*), way, manner
adulor (1), to fawn (like a dog)
clementer, gently
blande, caressingly, in a
  fawning way
adiungo (3), to join, bring close to
crus, cruris (*n*), leg
exanimatus, petrified, paralysed
leniter, gently
demulceo (2), to stroke, lick

14   **amissum animum recuperat**: *regained his senses which had been paralysed.*

15   **ad contuendum leonem**: *to look at the lion.* (For use of Gerundive, see LL p. 61.)

16   **videres**: *you might have seen.* (For Potential Subjunctive, see LL p. 108.)

17   **accersitus**: This is another form of **arcessitus**.

      Caesare: This was the emperor Gaius Caesar, better known as Caligula.

      quaesita: Supply **est**.

18   **uni**: *alone.* By separating **uni** from **illi**, Gellius gives **uni** much more emphasis.

      parsisset is the pluperfect subjunctive of **parcere**.

19   **provinciam Africam**: The Roman province of Africa, roughly the northern part of modern Tunisia and Libya, was of vital importance to Rome because it was one of the main sources of her grain supply. For this reason, an ex-consul (**vir consularis**) was always chosen as governor, and he was given supreme power equivalent to that of a consul (**proconsulare imperium**). As proconsul, he had virtually unlimited power in his province.

21   **ut latebrae forent**: *so that my hiding-place would be.* The imperfect subjunctive **forent** (formed from the future infinitive **fore**) is sometimes used instead of the more regular **essent**.

      a domino: *from my master.* Take with **tutiores**.

22   **consilium fuit**: *I intended*, literally *my plan was.*

25   **edens**: This is the present participle of **edo** (**e + do**, *I give out*) and is not to be confused with **edere**, *to eat*, which appears in line 37.

26   **dolorem cruciatumque**: An idiomatic translation of these two nouns, which convey roughly the same idea (*pain and torture*), would be *excruciating pain.* (For Hendiadys, see page 259.)

      commiserantia: *seeking pity for.* This participle agrees with **murmura**, and it has two direct objects – **dolorem** and **cruciatum**.

27   **introgressus**: Supply **est**.

      ut re ipsa apparuit: *as became evident from what actually happened.* In English, we would probably use a free translation such as *which, in fact, turned out to be.*

      in habitaculum illud suum: Two ideas are compressed in this phrase – *into that dwelling-place* and *into his home.* Take the phrase closely with **ut re ipsa apparuit** and translate – *into that cave which, in fact, turned out to be his home.*

29   **ostendere** and **porrigere** both depend on **visus est**.

      quasi opis petendae gratia: *as if to ask for help.* (For use of Gerundive, see LL p. 61.)

30   **conceptam saniem**: *the pus that had gathered.*

31   **vulnere intimo**: *from deep within the wound.*

15 homo Androclus inter illa tam atrocis ferae blandimenta amissum animum recuperat, paulatim oculos ad contuendum leonem refert. tum, quasi mutua recognitione facta, laetos et gratulabundos videres hominem et leonem.

Androcles tells his story

accersitus est a Caesare Androclus, quaesitaque causa cur illi atrocissimus leo uni parsisset. ibi Androclus rem mirificam narrat atque admirandam.

20 "cum provinciam" inquit "Africam proconsulari imperio meus dominus obtineret, ego ibi iniquis eius et cotidianis verberibus ad fugam sum coactus; et, ut mihi a domino tutiores latebrae forent, in camporum et arenarum solitudines concessi ac, si defuisset cibus, consilium fuit mortem aliquo pacto quaerere. tum sole medio rabido et flagranti specum quandam nanctus remotam latebrosamque, in eam me penetro et recondo. neque multo post ad 25 eandem specum venit hic leo, debili uno et cruento pede, gemitus edens et murmura, dolorem cruciatumque vulneris commiserantia.

"postquam introgressus leo (ut re ipsa apparuit) in habitaculum illud suum, videt me procul delitescentem, mitis et mansues accessit et sublatum pedem ostendere mihi et porrigere quasi opis petendae gratia visus est. ibi ego 30 stirpem ingentem vestigio pedis eius haerentem revelli, conceptamque saniem vulnere intimo expressi, accuratiusque sine magna iam formidine siccavi penitus atque detersi cruorem.

---

atrox, -ocis, fierce
blandimentum (*n*), caress
paulatim, gradually
refero, to turn back
mutuus, mutual
gratulabundus, demonstrating
  their joy
mirificus, wonderful, strange
admirandus, surprising, wonderful
obtineo (2), to hold, be in charge of
iniquus, unjust, undeserved
cotidianus, daily
verber (*n*), whipping, flogging
arena (*f*), sand, desert
solitudo (*f*), solitude, lonely place
concedo (3), to withdraw to, take
  refuge in
desum, -esse, -fui, to fail, run out
aliquo pacto, somehow or other
sol medius, the mid-day sun
rabidus, raging, fierce
flagrans, scorching
specus (*f*), cave
nanciscor (3), **nanctus,** to find
latebrosus, providing a good
  hiding-place

me penetro, I make my way into, enter
recondo (3), to hide
debilis, lame
cruentus, blood-stained
gemitus (*m*), groan
murmur (*n*), growl, whimper
cruciatus (*m*), torture, pain
introgredior (3), to enter
delitesco (3), to hide, cower
mitis, gentle
mansues, tame
sublatus (from **tollo**), raised
porrigo (3), to stretch out
stirps (*f*), splinter, thorn
vestigium (*n*), pad (of his paw)
haereo (2), to stick
revello (3), **-velli,** to pull out
exprimo (3), **-pressi,** to squeeze out
accuratius, quite carefully, carefully
formido (*f*), fear
sicco (1), to dry
penitus, thoroughly
detergeo (2), **-si,** to wipe away
cruor (*m*), blood

33   **illa mea opera et medella**: *by the trouble I had taken in treating him,* literally *by that effort and treatment of mine.*

35   **et**: *also.*

    feras has been attracted into the relative clause. English would more naturally associate it with **membra** – *the joints of the beasts.*

39   **me damnandum curavit**: *he saw to it that I was condemned.* (For this use of the Gerundive, see LL. p. 61.)

40   **rei capitalis**: *to death*; the genitive expresses the charge on which he was condemned (literally *for a matter affecting my head*).

    hunc leonem . . . referre: Accusative and Infinitive depending on **intellego**.

41   **me tunc separato captum**: *captured after I was separated from it in the way I have described* (**tunc**, literally *at that time*).

43   **videbamus**: Four Accusative and Infinitive clauses depend on **videbamus**.

44   **donari** and **spargi** are present infinitives passive.

45   **obvios**: *who met them.*

Points for Discussion

1   Gellius is fond of using pairs of words, e.g. **aut forma aut ferocia** (line 3) and **impetu et vastitudine** (line 5). Gather five examples from lines 19–26, and state what, if anything, the second word adds to the description.

2   Give two ways of translating **fluctuantibus** as used in line 6, one to describe the lion's muscles, the other to describe its mane. What translations would be appropriate if this word was used of (*a*) the sea, (*b*) a pond, (*c*) hills, (*d*) sand-dunes, (*e*) sound?

3   Do you think that Androcles deserved (*a*) his punishment and (*b*) his reward?

4   What difficulties do you think the Emperor's gift might create (*a*) for Androcles and (*b*) for the rest of the Romans?

5   Do you think this story is true? Give reasons for your answer.

His life with the lion

"illa tunc mea opera et medella levatus, pede in manibus meis posito, recubuit et
quievit; ⌈atque ex eo die triennium totum ego et leo in eadem specu eodemque
35 et victu viximus. nam, quas venabatur feras, membra opimiora ad specum
1998 mihi subgerebat, quae ego, ignis copiam non habens, meridiano sole torrens
edebam. sed ubi me vitae illius ferinae iam pertaesum est, leone in venatum
profecto, reliqui specum et, viam ferme tridui permensus, a militibus visus
adprehensusque sum et ad dominum ex Africa Romam deductus.⌉ is me statim
40 rei capitalis damnandum dandumque ad bestias curavit. intellego autem hunc
quoque leonem, me tunc separato captum, gratiam mihi nunc beneficii et
medicinae referre."

A happy ending

*When an account of what Androcles had said was written down and passed
round the spectators, they insisted that both he and the lion should be set free,
and that the lion should be given to him as a gift. Apion concludes by saying
that he personally has seen the two of them walking through the streets of Rome
together.*

postea videbamus Androclum et leonem, loro tenui revinctum, urbe tota
circum tabernas ire, donari aere Androclum, floribus spargi leonem, omnes
45 ubique obvios dicere: "hic est leo hospes hominis, hic est homo medicus leonis."

levo (1), to relieve
recumbo (3), to lie down
quiesco (3), to rest, go to sleep
triennium (*n*), (period of) three years
victus (*m*), food
venor (1), to hunt
membrum (*n*), limb, joint
opimus, rich, fat, choice
subgero (3), to bring, supply
copia (*f*), supply, source
meridianus, mid-day
torreo (2), to dry, bake
ferinus, wild
me pertaesum est, I became weary, bored
venatus (*m*), hunting

ferme, almost, approximately
triduum (*n*), (period of) three days
permensus, having travelled
adprehendo (3), to seize, arrest
gratiam referre (+ *dat.*), to thank
medicina (*f*), (medical) treatment
lorum (*n*), leather lead, leash
tenuis, thin, fine
revincio (4), to tie
taberna (*f*), shop
dono (1), to present
aes, aeris (*n*), money
spargo (3), to shower
medicus (*m*), doctor

Fighting wild beasts – 4th century mosaic

3 Back to the Wild

(Martial, *Epigrams* II. 75)

A tame lion, which used to endure its master's blows without a murmur and actually allowed him to put his hand in its mouth, suddenly unlearned its peaceful ways and became even fiercer than you would have expected it to be on its native hills of Africa; for the deadly beast savaged to death two of the young boys who were raking over the blood-stained sand. The arena has never seen a greater crime, and you might well exclaim: "Cruel, treacherous robber, learn from our she-wolf how to show mercy to boys!"

She-wolf suckling Romulus and Remus, Capitoline Museum, Rome

Points for Discussion

1 In what ways were the above lion and Androcles' lion similar/different?

2 Do you think it is fair for Martial to call the lion "treacherous"? Justify your answer.

3 Why do you think this "tame" lion turned on the boys in the arena?

4 In the last sentence, why do you think Martial says "*our* she-wolf"? To what story is he referring? What would the she-wolf have taught the lion mentioned by Martial?

Seneca: See Notes on Authors on page 14.

line

1   **tam damnosum ... quam ...**: *so damaging ... as ....* (For Correlatives, see LL p. 63.)

3   **immo vero** suggests that the previous reply is either wrong or has not been strong enough. Translate *no, in fact*.

     inhumanior: There is more than a touch of irony in the fact that Seneca feels he becomes *more inhuman* as a result of associating with human beings.

5   **casu incidi**: *I happened to drop in*, literally *by chance I came in*.

     meridianum spectaculum: *a mid-day show*. The savagery of the arena reached its peak with the blood-bath created by the mid-day fighters (**meridiani**), who were usually condemned criminals.

     aliquid laxamenti: *some relaxation*. (For Partitive Genitive, see LL p. 9.)

6   **quo** here introduces a Purpose clause. Translate *with which (they might ...)*. (See LL pp. 44 and 103.)

     contra est: *it was the very opposite*.

7   **quidquid ante pugnatum est**: *all the fighting beforehand*, literally *whatever was fought previously*.

     misericordia: *kid-glove stuff*, literally *pity, compassion*.

8   **quo tegantur**: *to protect themselves with*, literally *with which they may be protected*.

9   **manum mittunt**: *aim a blow*.

10   **ordinariis paribus et postulaticiis**: *the regular pairs and challenge matches*.

     quidni praeferant? *why should they not prefer it?* (For Deliberative Subjunctive, see LL p. 38.)

11   **quo munimenta?** *what's the point of having protection?*, literally *for what purpose defences?*

13   **interfectores** is accusative case. Note the clever juxtaposition of **interfectores** (*those who have killed*) and **interfecturis** (*those who are going to kill*).

     in: *for*.

14   **exitus pugnantium**: *the only way out for the fighters*.

     res geritur: *the show is kept moving*. If it was felt that any of the combatants were not putting sufficient effort into their fighting, killing or dying, or if any of them tried to leave the arena, attendants would use pikes, whips, clubs and firebrands to urge them into action.

     dum vacat harena: literally *while the arena is empty*, i.e. *between the main shows* which took place during the morning and afternoon sessions. There was a break for lunch when the amphitheatre had far fewer spectators, and only the real enthusiasts, the connoisseurs of butchery, were present.

4 Seneca Condemns the Games

(Seneca, *Epistolae Morales* VII. *i*.7)

In his *Epistolae Morales* Seneca raises a whole range of moral issues. It should not be assumed that many Romans would have agreed with what he says in this letter. By and large, the masses were thrilled by the games which the rulers in the city staged to keep them contented.

nihil vero tam damnosum bonis moribus quam in aliquo spectaculo desidere. tunc enim per voluptatem facilius vitia subrepunt. quid me existimas dicere? avarior redeo, ambitiosior, luxuriosior? immo vero crudelior et inhumanior, quia inter homines fui.

5 casu in meridianum spectaculum incidi, lusus exspectans et sales et aliquid laxamenti quo hominum oculi ab humano cruore adquiescant. contra est: quidquid ante pugnatum est misericordia fuit; nunc, omissis nugis, mera homicidia sunt; nihil habent quo tegantur; ad ictum totis corporibus expositi numquam frustra manum mittunt.

10 hoc plerique ordinariis paribus et postulaticiis praeferunt. quidni praeferant? non galea, non scuto repellitur ferrum. quo munimenta? quo artes? omnia ista mortis morae sunt. mane leonibus et ursis homines, meridie spectatoribus suis obiciuntur. interfectores interfecturis iubent obici et victorem in aliam detinent caedem; exitus pugnantium mors est. ferro et igne res geritur. haec fiunt dum
15 vacat harena.

1998

mores (*m.pl*), character, morals
aliqui, -qua, -quod, some
spectaculum (*n*), a show
desido (3), to sit down, settle down
tunc, then
voluptas (*f*), enjoyment, pleasure
vitium (*n*), fault, defect (of character)
subrepo (3), to creep up on, sneak up on
avarus, greedy
ambitiosus, ambitious, self-seeking
luxuriosus, self-indulgent
lusus, -us (*m*), sport, entertainment
sales (*m.pl*), fun, amusement
cruor (*m*), bloodshed
adquiesco (3), to take a rest
omitto (3), to set aside, abandon
nugae (*f.pl*), frivolity, childish sports

merus, pure, unadulterated
homicidium (*n*), murder, slaughter
ictus (*m*), blow
expono (3), to expose, leave exposed
plerique, most people
ordinarius, ordinary, regular
praefero (3), to prefer
galea (*f*), helmet
repello (3), to repel
ars (*f*), skill
iste, that
ursus (*m*), bear
meridie, at mid-day
obicio (3), to throw to
detineo (2), to hold back, retain
vaco (1), to be empty
harena (*f*), arena

16   **sed latrocinium fecit aliquis**: *but he committed robbery.* Seneca quotes the likely response of the person to whom he is writing. He uses **aliquis** (literally *someone*) to indicate the idea: *Take any of them, and you will find that he is a criminal who is only getting what he deserves.*

    quid ergo? *so what?*

17   **tu**: Note the emphatic position – *what have **you** done to . . . .* The criminal deserved his fate, but what had the unfortunate spectator done to be subjected to such a sight?

18   **occide! verbera! ure!**: Compare line 14.

    parum audacter: *not sufficiently boldly*, i.e. *so reluctantly.*

19   **agatur**: *let him be driven.* (For the present subjunctive to express a Wish or Command, see LL p. 107. Compare **excipiant** in line 20 and **iugulentur** in line 21.)

    in vulnera: *into (inflicting and receiving) wounds.*

20   **intermissum est spectaculum**: A break in the official programme prompts the crowd to shout for more blood, *just to keep things going* (**ne nihil agatur**), literally *so that not nothing* (i.e. *something*) *may be happening.*

22   **ne hoc quidem intellegitis**: *don't you understand even this?* The Accusative and Infinitive (**mala exempla redundare**) explains **hoc**. Seneca is referring here to the corrupting influence of cruelty and violence.

23   **eum ... qui**: *someone who.*

"sed latrocinium fecit aliquis, occidit hominem." quid ergo? quia occidit, ille meruit ut hoc pateretur; tu quid meruisti miser ut hoc spectes?

"occide! verbera! ure! quare tam timide incurrit in ferrum? quare parum audacter occidit? quare parum libenter moritur? plagis agatur in vulnera,
20 mutuos ictus nudis et obviis pectoribus excipiant." intermissum est spectaculum: "interim iugulentur homines ne nihil agatur!"

age, ne hoc quidem intellegitis mala exempla in eos redundare qui faciunt? agite dis immortalibus gratias quod eum <u>docetis</u> esse crudelem qui non potest <u>discere.</u>

---

merere ut (+ *subj.*), to deserve to
miser, poor wretch
verbero (1), to beat, lash
uro (3), to burn
quare, why
timide, timidly
incurro (3), to run on
parum, too little, not enough
plaga (*f*), a blow

mutuus, mutual, from one another
nudus, bare, naked
obvius, exposed
excipio (3), to receive
intermitto (3), to interrupt
iugulo (1), to cut the throat
redundo (1), to come flowing back, rebound

Gladiators – 4th century mosaic

Points for Discussion

1 What reasons does Seneca give for going to the arena? In what ways were his expectations not fulfilled?

2 To what does **hoc** (line 10) refer?

3 What are the "means of delaying death" referred to in line 12?

4 Who are the subject of **iubent** and **detinent** in line 13?

5 Who are shouting the words quoted in lines 18–20?

6 The last sentence in the passage means: "You are trying to teach someone to be cruel who is not able to learn how to be cruel."

To whom do you think "someone" refers? Do you think it is a spectator, a fighter or Seneca himself?

What does he mean by "is not able to learn"? Do you think he means that the "someone" lacks the intelligence, the time, the opportunity or the will?

7 With which of the following statements do you agree? Give reasons for your answers.

(a) Seneca was moved not so much by revulsion at the slaughter as by contempt for the spectators.

(b) Seneca was less concerned by pity for those slaughtered than by apprehension over the harmful effect upon the Romans of watching the games.

(c) Seneca had no stomach for watching the bloodshed, but found excitement in describing the gory details.

If you agree with none of these statements, suggest your own interpretation of his attitude.

8 Do you agree with what Seneca says in line 22 about the corrupting influence of cruelty and violence (**age... faciunt**)? Quote some examples from your own knowledge and/or experience to support or disprove what he says.

5 Addicted to the Games

(Augustine of Hippo, *Confessions* Book VI. 7–8)

The name Augustine is commonly associated with Saint Augustine of Canterbury, who in the sixth century AD brought Christianity to England. However, the St Augustine who was the author of the passage below, which is translated and adapted from the Latin original, is the North African St Augustine of Hippo, whose famous *Confessions* tell of his conversion to Christianity – how, after being a pagan philosopher and professional teacher of oratory, he became a great defender of the Christian faith. In one of his episodes of personal reminiscence, he tells the story of Alypius, one of his students who, at the time when he came to Augustine's oratory classes in Carthage, was a victim of a mania for watching the chariot-races in the Circus and betting on these.

One day when I was sitting in my usual place with my students before me, Alypius came in, greeted me, took a seat and listened attentively to what we were discussing. It happened that the passage I had in hand was one which lent itself to an illustration from chariot-racing in the circus – an illustration which was not only apt and pointed in itself, but which gave me the opportunity to ridicule those enslaved by that form of madness. I had, God knows, no thought of curing Alypius' affliction by those words of mine. He, however, believed that I directed them expressly at him, for thereafter he heaved himself out of that deep pit into which he had wilfully plunged; and, with an effort of will, he gave up that evil habit and never went back to the Circus again!

Augustine later left Carthage for Rome to continue his career there as a teacher of oratory.

Alypius had preceded me to Rome to study law, and there, believe it or not, he was smitten by another incredible passion – this time for the games in the arena.

At the outset, he was opposed to such shows; in fact, he detested them. However, on one of the days when these brutal and bloody games were taking place, he happened to meet some of his fellow-students as they were returning from lunch; and, in spite of strong resistance on his part, his friends dragged him off, more or less bodily, to the arena.

"You may drag my body there," he said to them, "but you certainly cannot make me take any interest in the proceedings or even look at what is going on. I'll be absent even when I am present. In this way, I'll get the better of you *and* your games."

When they heard him say this, his friends were all the more determined to take him along with them, doubtless to find out if he could make good his boast. When they arrived at the arena and found what seats they could, the excitement was already running high. Alypius shut his eyes tight and made a firm resolve to take no part in such wickedness. Ah, if only he could have stopped up his ears as well!

For when the fighting reached a crisis and everyone around him was shouting like mad, his curiosity got the better of him. He was determined, of course, to reject whatever he saw; but, when he opened his eyes, he suffered a more serious wound to his soul than the fighter sustained on his body. His fall was more pitiable than that of the man whose fall had brought the shouting to a climax; for, at the moment when Alypius saw the blood, he drank deep of savagery. He gazed in fascination at the sight, soaking in the frenzy without realising it. He exulted in the wickedness of the contest; he was drunk with the lust for blood. He was no longer the same man; he had become one of the crowd, a fellow-enthusiast with those who had brought him along. He never took his eyes off the arena; he joined in the shouting; he burned with excitement; he took away with him from the arena the madness which doomed him to keep coming back, not just in company with the friends who had dragged him there in the first place, but even running on ahead of them and dragging others along with him.

But you, Lord, with your all-powerful and all-merciful might, tore him free and showed him how to have faith and confidence not in himself, but in You – but that happened much later. . . .

Points for Discussion

1 What do you think Augustine was trying to achieve by telling this story?

2 Imagine you are Alypius. Give your version of what happened.

3 Imagine yourself to be one of the writers whom you have read in this section of the book. Choose a present-day, widespread "addiction" to any sport or to some other popular entertainment and, in 150–200 words, describe the "addicts" in the way you think your chosen author would have done. Then state whether you yourself would regard their "addiction" as demoralising.

Pliny: See Notes on Authors on page 13.

line

1   S. is a shorthand form of **salutem (dicit)**, *sends greetings.*

   Calvisius Rufus was a rich friend of Pliny. Both of them came from Comum (modern Como) in northern Italy.

3   **circenses**: Supply **ludi.** These were the chariot races held in the Circus Maximus.

   quo genere spectaculi: *but by this kind of show*, literally *by which kind of show.* (For Linking Relative, see LL p. 26.)

4   **nihil quod non semel spectasse sufficiat**: *nothing that anyone would want to watch more than once*, literally *nothing which it is not enough to have watched once.*

5   **quo magis miror**: *I am therefore all the more amazed*, literally *by which I wonder more.* (For ablative expressing Amount of Difference, see LL p. 16.)

6   **currentes equos** refers to the teams of four (sometimes two) horses which pulled the chariots.

   insistentes curribus: Here, the participle **insistentes** contains two notions, one of the charioteer *standing on* the chariot, the other of him *urging on the horses.* Translate *hunched over their chariots* to produce the necessary picture.

7   **esset**: *there would be.* (For this Conditional use, see LL p. 54.)

8   **nunc**: *as it is, as things stand.* The word is used to contrast what has been said in the previous sentence and almost means *but, in fact.*

   panno: *the (colour of the) cloth.* Four rival companies (**factiones**) employed the charioteers and owned the horses and chariots; and these were distinguished by the colours worn by the charioteer – just like jockeys of the present day. There were the Reds, the Blues, the Whites and the Greens, and there was intense rivalry among these four "teams". Each had its fanatical following among the spectators, including leading public figures and sometimes even emperors. For example, Caligula was an ardent supporter of the Greens. There may also have been some betting on the results, although that was officially forbidden by law.

   si ... transferatur: *if (the colour) were to be transferred.* The present subjunctive implies that it is a supposition which is unlikely to become a reality. (See LL p. 54.)

9   **ille**: Supply **color.**

   transibit: *would cross over.* The use of the future indicative instead of the present subjunctive (which would be more normal in this type of conditional sentence) emphasises that the transfer of support would be inevitable. (Cf. **relinquent** in line 11.)

11   **auctoritas**: Supply **est.**

   in: *vested in.*

   mitto apud vulgus quod vilius tunica: *I do not mean* (**mitto** means literally *I pass over*) *in the eyes of* (**apud**) *the mob, which is even more worthless than the tunic.*

6 At the Races

(Pliny, *Letters* IX. 6)

C. Plinius Calvisio Suo S.

omne hoc tempus inter pugillares et libellos iucundissima quiete transmisi.
"quemadmodum" inquis "in urbe potuisti?" circenses erant, quo genere spectaculi ne levissime quidem teneor. nihil novum, nihil varium, nihil quod non
5   semel spectasse sufficiat. quo magis miror tot milia virorum tam pueriliter
identidem cupere currentes equos, insistentes curribus homines videre.

1999

si tamen aut velocitate equorum aut hominum arte traherentur, esset ratio
non nulla; nunc favent panno, pannum amant; et, si in ipso cursu medioque
certamine hic color illuc ille huc transferatur, studium favorque transibit, et
10   repente agitatores illos, equos illos, quos procul noscitant, quorum clamitant
nomina, relinquent. tanta gratia, tanta auctoritas in una vilissima tunica, mitto

pugillares (*m. pl*), writing-tablets	**ratio** (*f*), reason, justification
libellus (*m*), book	**non nullus**, some
iucundus, pleasant	**faveo** (2) (+ *dat.*), to favour,
transmitto (3), to spend (time)	support
quemadmodum, how	**cursus** (*m*), race, course
ne ... quidem, not even	**certamen** (*n*), contest, race
leviter, slightly	**favor** (*m*), support
teneo (2), to hold, attract	**repente**, suddenly
spectasse = spectavisse	**agitator** (*m*), driver
sufficio (3), to be sufficient	**procul**, from a distance
pueriliter, childishly	**noscito** (1), to recognise
identidem, repeatedly, over	**clamito** (1), to keep shouting
and over again	**gratia** (*f*), support, appeal
velocitas (*f*), speed	**auctoritas** (*f*), prestige, significance
ars, artis (*f*), skill	**vilis**, cheap, worthless
traho (3), to draw, attract	

12 **quos ... desidere**: an Accusative and Infinitive depending on **recordor**. **quos** is a Linking Relative (see LL p. 26).

13 **in re**: *in an activity*. Note how Pliny attaches three adjectives to **re** to emphasise how strongly he feels about the utter futility of the games. The verb **desidere** continues the same theme. Literally it means *to settle down*, but here it is close to our slang expression "hooked on".

14 **quod**: *from the fact that*.

   per hos dies: *during these past few days*.

Chariot racing – an engraving from a Roman relief

apud vulgus quod vilius tunica, sed apud quosdam graves homines; quos ego cum recordor in re inani frigida adsidua tam insatiabiliter desidere, capio aliquam voluptatem quod hac voluptate non capior. ac per hos dies libentissime
15 otium meum in litteris colloco, quos alii otiosissimis occupationibus perdunt. vale!

gravis, important, influential	**aliqui, -qua, -quod**, some
recordor (1), to recall, consider	**voluptas** (*f*), pleasure
inanis, empty, pointless	**litterae** (*f. pl*), studies
frigidus, boring, trivial	**colloco** (1), to spend, employ
adsiduus, constant, repetitive	**otiosus**, idle
insatiabiliter, insatiably, endlessly	**perdo** (3), to waste, squander

Points for Discussion

1   What is implied in the direct question in line 3?

2   In line 4, Pliny repeats the word **nihil** to produce a climax and make his words more pointed. From lines 7 –15, quote three similar examples of repeated words and suggest the effect he is trying to achieve.

3   What effect do you think Pliny is trying to create by placing **virorum** and **pueriliter** (line 5) so close together?

4   Discuss Pliny's attitude to the races. Is he an intellectual snob (e. g. lines 13 –14)? Do people spend too much time and money on trivial pursuits? Is it surprising that some people in important positions become just as infatuated with sport as ordinary people? Quote from the passage to support your answers.

5   Pliny says it was the *colour* that was important to the crowd, not the drivers or the horses. Can you think of any modern parallels, sporting or otherwise?

6   The poet Juvenal tells us that the rulers of Rome provided free bread and amusements (**panem et circenses**) for the masses in order to win favour with them and to keep them contented with the government's policies. Do you think this is a legitimate practice for rulers to adopt? Can you think of any modern parallels?

7   "Seneca objected to the games on moral grounds; Pliny rejected them on intellectual grounds." Do you agree with this statement? Collect evidence from "Seneca Condemns the Games" and from "At the Races" to support or disprove the statement.

Catullus: See Notes on Latin Authors on page 10.
Metre: Sapphic Stanza (See page 258.)

line

1 **ille**: *that man*, not a specific person but anyone lucky enough to enjoy Lesbia's company.

2 **si fas est**: *if it is lawful (in the eyes of the gods)*, i. e. if it is not blasphemous to say so.

   superare, like **esse** (line 1), depends on **videtur**.

5 **dulce ridentem**: *your sweet laughter*, literally *(you) laughing sweetly*.

   misero agrees with **mihi** in line 6: *wretch that I am*.

   quod: *something which*. The relative pronoun sums up what he has said in lines 3 – 5.

6 **eripit mihi**: *snatches away from me*, i. e. *robs me of*. The dative case can denote **from whom** something is taken away as well as **to whom** something is given. (See LL p. 10.)

7 **nihil est super mi vocis in ore**: *no voice remains in my mouth* (**est super = superest**).

8 **vocis in ore**: Before the printing press was invented, all manuscripts were written by hand. When copies were being made, mistakes often occurred; and further copies might later be made from these faulty copies. The best scribes were those who simply copied what was in front of them; but some scribes, realising that a mistake had been made, tried to correct the mistake without knowing what the original text had been, and so several different "corrections" were produced. Further copies would be made incorporating these "variant readings", as they are called, so that many different versions of the same text could appear in different manuscripts. Since all original manuscripts of ancient authors have been lost and only a fraction of the imperfect copies has survived, modern scholars have had to use their knowledge and expertise to decide which version is most likely to be the correct one. Line 8 has disappeared from all the surviving manuscripts of this poem, although the shape of the stanza clearly demands a line of five syllables. By studying what Sappho wrote in her poem, most scholars agree that the words omitted were either **vocis in ore** or **Lesbia, vocis**.

9 **sub artus**: *down through my limbs*.

10 **sonitu suopte**: *with their very own sound*, i. e. a sound that only his ears can hear.
   suopte, an archaic form of **suo**, is used for greater emphasis.

11 **gemina teguntur lumina nocte**: Scansion shows that the final **-a** of **gemina** is long, making it ablative agreeing with **nocte**. The literal meaning is *my eyes are covered in twin darkness*: this is a poet's way of saying *both my eyes are veiled in darkness*. (For Transferred Epithet, see page 261.)

Points for Discussion

1 Describe the four sensations Catullus feels in lines 9–12. In what sorts of words are these feelings conveyed in modern songs and poems?

2 Besides unhappiness (**misero**, in line 5), what other feelings does Catullus openly express or hint at? Justify your answer by reference to the Latin.

Love and Devotion: Love's Joys

7 The Power of Love

(Catullus 51)

It is possible that the following poem was the first that Catullus wrote to Clodia, wife of Metellus Celer. There was a convention in Roman love poetry that the lady's real name was never mentioned; and, in particular, it would have been very improper to name a married lady in such a poem. This poem is a free translation into Latin of a Greek poem written by the poetess Sappho of Lesbos (sixth century BC), and it may have been this that made Catullus think of using the pseudonym Lēsbĭă, which has the same metrical pattern as Clōdĭă (see "An Introduction to Latin Metres" on page 253). By using the pseudonym, Catullus also avoids saying directly that it is Clodia with whom he is in love; and, if she does not respond to his poetic "advances", he can save face by claiming that it was, after all, only a literary exercise.

> ille mi par esse deo videtur,
> ille, si fas est, superare divos,
> qui sedens adversus identidem te
>   spectat et audit
>
> 5 dulce ridentem, misero quod omnes
> eripit sensus mihi: nam simul te,
> Lesbia, aspexi, nihil est super mi
>   vocis in ore.
>
> lingua sed torpet, tenuis sub artus
> 10 flamma demanat, sonitu suopte
> tintinant aures, gemina teguntur
>   lumina nocte.

mi = mihi
supero (1), to surpass, be superior to
divus (*m*), god
adversus (+ *acc.*), opposite
identidem, repeatedly, over and over again
sensus, -us (*m*), feeling
simul = simulac, as soon as

aspicio (3), to look at, catch sight of
torpeo (2), to be numb, paralysed
tenuis, fine, delicate
demano (1), to spread (down)
tintino (1), to ring, buzz
auris (*f*), ear
lumina (*n. pl*), eyes

Catullus: See Notes on Authors on page 10.
Metre: Hendecasyllabic (See page 258.)

line

1   **passer**: Vocative case. The word **passer** is normally translated as *sparrow*, but ornithologists point out that the sparrow is not an easily domesticated bird. Lesbia's pet is therefore more likely to be a finch of some kind.

2   After addressing the bird in line 1, Catullus digresses to give us various pieces of information about it in lines 2–6. At **tecum** (line 7), he returns to the main point of the poem by again speaking directly to the bird: *I wish I could play with you.*

  ludere: *to play*. This infinitive depends on **solet** (line 4), *she is accustomed*, the subject "she" being understood from **puellae** in line 1. The other infinitives **tenere** (line 2), **dare** (line 3) and **incitare** (line 4) also depend on **solet**.

3   **primum digitum**: *the tip of her finger*.

  appetenti: *as you dab at it*, agreeing with **cui**.

5   **cum desiderio meo nitenti lubet iocari**: *when my radiant darling feels like playing*, literally *when it is pleasing to my shining desire to play*. Here, Catullus refers to Lesbia as **desiderium** – *the object of his longing* or *his heart's desire*.

6   **carum nescio quid iocari**: *to play some favourite game or other*.

7   **ipsa**: *(the mistress) herself.*

  possem: *I wish I could*, or *Oh, if only I were able*. (For Wishes expressed in this way, see LL p. 108.)

8   **tristes curas**: *tormenting pains (of love)*.

8 Lesbia's Pet

(Catullus 2)

> passer, deliciae meae puellae,
> quicum ludere, quem in sinu tenere,
> cui primum digitum dare appetenti
> et acres solet incitare morsus,
> 5   cum desiderio meo nitenti
> carum nescio quid lubet iocari:
> tecum ludere, sicut ipsa, possem
> et tristes animi levare curas!

deliciae (*f. pl*), darling, pet
quicum, with whom
sinus (*m*), lap
acer, acris, acre, sharp, sore
incito (1), to provoke

morsus, -us (*m*), bite
nescio quid, some ... or other
sicut, just like
animus (*m*), heart
levo (l), to lighten, relieve

Girl with a pet bird, from a 4th century BC oil flask

Point for Discussion

Do you think that the last two lines mean that Catullus really wants to play with the pet bird? Or is there more to it than that?

Catullus: See Notes on Authors on page 10.
Metre: Hendecasyllabic (See page 258.)

line

1   **o Veneres Cupidinesque**: *you gods and goddesses of love.*

2   **quantum est hominum venustiorum**: *all men of finer feelings*, i. e. who show more love and affection than the ordinary person. The literal meaning is *as big (a number) as there is of more sensitive men.* (For Partitive Genitive, see LL p. 9.) **venustus** is from the same root as the name Venus.

3   **passer**: See "Lesbia's Pet" (p. 41), line 1. After the dramatic opening two lines, the third line comes as an anticlimax!

5   **plus oculis suis**: *more than her own eyes.* (For Ablative of Comparison, see LL p. 16.)

6   **suam ipsam** *its own mistress.* The master and mistress of the household were commonly referred to as **ipse** and **ipsa**.

    norat: *it knew.* The form is contracted from **noverat**.

7   **tam bene quam**: *as well as.* (For Correlatives, see LL p. 63.)

8   **illius**: *her.* Note that the second -**i**- must here be scanned as short.

9   **modo huc modo illuc**: *now here, now there* – the sound of the words suggests the restless movements of the bird.

10 **usque pipiabat**: *it chirped continually.* (For Onomatopoeia, see page 260.)

11 **qui**: *it*, i. e. the bird.

    per iter tenebricosum: After the joyful picture of the sparrow and its mistress playing together, Catullus paints the sad picture of the poor little bird making its way down to the Underworld.

12 **negant quemquam**: *they say that no one.*

13 **at**: As used here, **at** marks an abrupt change of mood and there is probably no equivalent word in English. With this word, Catullus shakes himself out of his sad reminiscences and angrily curses the *evil darkness of Orcus* (**malae tenebrae Orci**) which has made his darling Lesbia so sad. Orcus was another name for Hades or the Underworld to which the souls of the dead were said to be conveyed by Mercury.

    vobis male sit: *a curse upon you* (literally *may it go badly for you*). Note the play upon the sound of the words **male** and **malae**.

14 **bella**: a colloquial word for *beautiful* or *pretty*, from which the French word *belle* is derived.

15 **mihi**: *from me.* (For this use of the dative case, see LL p. 10.)

9 The Songbird Dies

(Catullus 3)

lugete, o Veneres Cupidinesque,
et quantum est hominum venustiorum!
passer mortuus est meae puellae,
passer, deliciae meae puellae,
5   quem plus illa oculis suis amabat.
nam mellitus erat suamque norat
ipsam tam bene quam puella matrem;
nec sese a gremio illius movebat,
sed circumsiliens modo huc modo illuc
10   ad solam dominam usque pipiabat;
qui nunc it per iter tenebricosum
illud, unde negant redire quemquam.
at vobis male sit, malae tenebrae
Orci, quae omnia bella devoratis!
15   tam bellum mihi passerem abstulistis.

lugeo (2), to mourn
venustus, charming, lovable
deliciae (*f. pl*), darling, pet
mellitus, honey-sweet
sese = se
gremium (*n*), lap, bosom

circumsilio (4), to hop about
tenebricosus, shrouded in darkness, shadowy
devoro (l), to devour, swallow up
aufero, auferre, abstuli, ablatum, to take away

16   **o factum male!**: *what a wicked thing to do*! (For the Accusative of Exclamation, see LL p. 6.) Note that the **-e** of **male** is not elided, marking a heavy pause. (See An Introduction to Latin Metres on page 255.)

    miselle: *poor little*. The use of this diminutive form of **miser** adds to the pathos and tender affection. Compare the use of **turgiduli** (diminutive of **turgidus**, *swollen*) and **ocelli** (diminutive of **oculus**, *eye*) in line 18. Diminutives were common in colloquial speech.

18   **flendo:** *with weeping*. (For the Gerund, see LL p. 60.)

o factum male! o miselle passer!
tua nunc opera meae puellae
flendo turgiduli rubent ocelli.

tua opera, thanks to you
rubeo (2), to be red

Points for Discussion

1 In what ways do you think the sound of the words in lines 9–11 echoes the sense? Note in particular **pipiabat** and **it per iter**.

2 From the poem pick out other lines or phrases where you feel that the poet, by a careful choice of words, has succeeded, (a) in producing appropriate sound effects to match the context, and (b) in expressing particular emotions.

3 Do you think that Catullus really wants the reader to treat seriously his description of the bird's death? For example, do you think that lines 11–12 are serious or mock-serious? What other reason might Catullus have had for writing this poem?

4 Do we learn anything from this poem (especially lines 11–12) and from lines 5–6 of "Love and Kisses" (p. 47) about Catullus' view on what happens after death? Do the two poems present a consistent picture of death?

Catullus: See Notes on Authors on page 10.
Metre: Hendecasyllabic (See page 258.)

line

1   **vivamus**: *let us live*, i.e. *let us enjoy life*. (For the use of the present subjunctive to express a Wish, Command or Exhortation, see LL p. 107.) Compare **amemus** (line 1) and **aestimemus** (line 3).

2   **severiorum**: *too strait-laced* or *over-critical*. Criticism of the younger generation by their elders is nothing new!

3   **unius assis**: *worth only a single penny*, i.e. not worth bothering about. The **as** was a copper coin of very little value. (For the genitive used to express Price or Value, see LL p. 8.) By placing **unius** immediately after **omnes**, Catullus increases the emphasis on the worthlessness of the old men's criticism. Note that Catullus has allowed himself the licence of shortening the long **-i-** of **unius** to fit the metre.

4   **soles**: The plural indicates *each day's sun*.

5   **nobis**: *for us (mortals)*.

     brevis lux: *our brief light*. Catullus contrasts the shortness of human life with the never-ending sleep of death (line 6). Note the powerful effect of ending line 5 with **lux** and starting line 6 with **nox**.

6   **est dormienda**: *must be slept through*. (For the Gerundive of Obligation, see LL p. 61.)

     una: Again the position of **una** is emphatic, coming as it does immediately after **perpetua**.

10   **cum fecerimus**: *when we have reached a total of*. (For the use of the future perfect tense in Time clauses, see LL p. 52.) Note that the **-i-** is long.

11   **conturbabimus illa**: *we will muddle the numbers* – an accounting metaphor. To count one's wealth too accurately was thought both to tempt fate and to give dangerous information to one's enemies. Here the wealth is measured in kisses, not money; and Catullus' solution is to falsify the accounts by not counting the kisses.

12   **ne quis malus**: *so that no spiteful person*.

10 Love and Kisses

(Catullus 5)

vivamus, mea Lesbia, atque amemus,
rumoresque senum severiorum
omnes unius aestimemus assis!
soles occidere et redire possunt;
5 nobis cum semel occidit brevis lux,
nox est perpetua una dormienda.
da mi basia mille, deinde centum,
dein mille altera, dein secunda centum,
deinde usque altera mille, deinde centum.
10 dein, cum milia multa fecerimus,
conturbabimus illa ne sciamus,
aut ne quis malus invidere possit,
cum tantum sciat esse basiorum.

rumor (*m*), gossip, muttering
aestimo (l), to value
occido (3), to fall, set
semel, once
perpetuus, endless, unending
mi = mihi

basium (*n*), kiss
dein = deinde, then
usque, without a break, non-stop
invideo (2), to envy, cast the evil eye on
tantum (+ *gen.*), such a great number (of),
   so many

"L'amour menaçant" by Etienne Maurice Falconet

Points for Discussion

1 Which of the poems ("The Power of Love" and "Love and Kisses") appeals to you more as a love-poem? Give reasons for your answer.

2 The words **vivamus atque amemus** are often quoted by people nowadays. Why do you think this should be so?

3 The following poem by Robert Herrick (1591–1674), though different in several respects, has certain features in common with Catullus' poem. Gather the similarities; and comment, in particular, on the message and tone of the poems.

Counsel to Girls

1 Gather ye rose-buds while ye may,
   Old Time is still a-flying:
And this same flower that smiles today,
   Tomorrow will be dying.

2 The glorious Lamp of Heaven, the Sun,
   The higher he's a-getting,
The sooner will his race be run,
   And nearer he's to setting.

3 That age is best which is the first,
   When youth and blood are warmer:
But being spent, the worse and worst
   Times will succeed the former.

4 Then be not coy, but use your time:
   And while ye may, go marry:
For having lost but once your prime,
   You may for ever tarry.

4 Compare the first verse of Herrick's poem with the following, which are the last two lines of a 50-line poem in the *Appendix Vergiliana*, and identify the points of similarity and dissimilarity:

   **collige, virgo, rosas dum flos novus et nova pubes;
   et memor esto aevum sic properare tuum!**

colligo (3), to collect, gather
pubes (*f*), (vigour of) adulthood
memor esto! remember!
aevum (*n*), age, life
propero (1), to hasten

Catullus: See Notes on Authors on page 10.
Metre: Hendecasyllabic (See page 258.)

line

1 **basiationes tuae**: At first sight this would seem to mean *your kisses* but, in view of what is said in line 9, the meaning must be *kisses given to you* (literally *kissings of you*).

2 **satis superque**: *enough and more than enough* or *enough and to spare*, i. e. *to satisfy you fully*. It is likely that Lesbia was not as infatuated with Catullus as he was with her, and she may have peevishly asked him: "How many times must you kiss me to be really satisfied?" Catullus takes her question literally and goes on to produce this florid reply.

3 **quam magnus numerus harenae**: *as many as are the grains of sand*, literally *how great a number of sand*. In lines 3–10, to give an idea of how many kisses would satisfy him, Catullus draws a comparison with the sands of the desert and the stars in the sky which are too numerous to count. The balanced structure of the sentence is:

> **quam magnus numerus** – *as large as the number* ...
> **aut quam multa** – *or as many as* ...
> **tam multa** – *that's how many* ... (literally *so many*)

(For Correlatives in which the clauses are reversed in this way, see LL p. 64.) For the general theme, compare God's promise to Abraham in Genesis 22. 17: "I promise that I will give you as many descendants as there are stars in the sky or grains of sand along the seashore." (Good News Bible)

4 **lasarpiciferis Cyrenis**: *in Cyrene which produces asafoetida*. Despite the exotic sound of these words, asafoetida was a foul-smelling resin used for medicinal purposes. Cyrene, which exported it, was a Greek colony in North Africa.

5 **oraclum Iovis**: This refers to the temple of Ammon, the Egyptian equivalent of Jupiter and Zeus, situated in an oasis in the desert south-east of Cyrene. It was at this oracle that Alexander the Great was told that Zeus, not King Philip, was his father.

   inter governs both **oraclum** and **sepulcrum**.

   aestuosi: *hot and sultry*. The adjective is transferred from the oracle to Jupiter.

6 **Batti veteris**: Battus had been the first king of Cyrene, roughly six hundred years before Catullus' time. The distance between the oracle and the tomb was about 350 miles (560 km).

8 **vident**: The subject is **sidera**.

11 **quae** refers to **basia**.

   curiosi: *busybodies*.

12 **mala lingua**: *malicious tongue*. Scansion shows that the final **-a** in both words is short and therefore nominative – another subject of **possint**. For similar thoughts to those expressed in lines 11–12, compare the references to "the evil eye" and the mixing up of numbers in "Love and Kisses" (lines 11–13).

11 How Many Kisses?

(Catullus 7)

quaeris quot mihi basiationes
tuae, Lesbia, sint satis superque.
quam magnus numerus Libyssae harenae
lasarpiciferis iacet Cyrenis,
5   oraclum Iovis inter aestuosi
et Batti veteris sacrum sepulcrum;
aut quam sidera multa, cum tacet nox,
furtivos hominum vident amores:
tam te basia multa basiare
10 vesano satis et super Catullo est,
quae nec pernumerare curiosi
possint, nec mala fascinare lingua.

Libyssus, Libyan, African
sepulcrum (*n*), tomb
sidus, -eris (*n*), star
furtivus, secret
basium (*n*), kiss

basio (1), to kiss
vesanus, deranged, love-crazed
pernumero (l), to count
fascino (l), to cast a spell

Points for Discussion

1 Do you know of any other love songs or love poems which use the same type of imagery as is found in lines 3 and 7?

2 Consider this poem and the previous one "Love and Kisses". Which poem do you think is the more natural? Give reasons for your answer.

Catullus: See Notes on Authors on page 10.
Metre: Elegiac Couplet (See page 257.)

line

1 **se amatam**: Supply **esse** to complete the Accusative and Infinitive depending on **dicere**.

 tantum ... quantum ... : *as much as.* Compare **tanta ... quanta** (lines 3–4), *as great as.* (For Correlatives, see LL p. 63.)

4 **in amore tuo**: *in my love for you.*

 ex parte mea: *on my part.*

12 Constant Devotion

(Catullus 87)

nulla potest mulier tantum se dicere amatam
    vere, quantum a me Lesbia amata mea est.
nulla fides ullo fuit umquam in foedere tanta,
    quanta in amore tuo ex parte reperta mea est.

vere, truly   **foedus, -eris** (*n*), bond, pact

Points for Discussion

1 What do you think Catullus' purpose is in making these statements?

2 Suggest another title for this poem.

Catullus: See Notes on Authors on page 10.
Metre: Hendecasyllabic (See page 258.)

line

1   **puella**: vocative case. The reference is to Ameana, mistress of Mamurra. (See line 5.)

    nec minimo naso: *whose nose is not very small*, literally *with a not very small nose*. This is the first of a series of Ablatives of Description. (See LL p. 15.)

2   **bello**: a colloquial word for *beautiful* or *pretty*, from which the French word *belle* is derived. Used of a foot, it would mean *neat* or *dainty*.

4   **nec nimis elegante lingua**: *whose tongue is none too refined*, i.e. her speech is as bad as her looks.

5   **decoctoris amica Formiani**: *o mistress of the bankrupt from Formiae*. This refers to Mamurra, who was born in Formiae (on the coast between Rome and Naples). As one of Julius Caesar's officers in Gaul, he had amassed considerable wealth but, on returning to Rome, he squandered it on extravagant and dissolute living.

6   **ten = tene**: Note the emphatic position of this word and of **tecum** in the next line – *Is it you that ...?* and *Is it with you that ...?*

    provincia: This refers to Gallia Cisalpina (*Gaul on this side of the Alps*, as viewed from Rome), which corresponded roughly to that part of modern Italy which lies north of Florence. In Catullus' time, Gallia Cisalpina was not part of Italy proper; and Catullus, and others who like him had moved from there to live in Rome, used to refer to it as "the province". During his Gallic campaigns, Caesar established his winter quarters in Cisalpine Gaul to be as close to Rome as possible; and it was possibly there, in Verona, that Mamurra met his mistress, Ameana. According to Catullus, she may have been one of the beauties of the province, but she would have been rather ordinary in Rome.

13 No Comparison

(Catullus 43)

salve, nec minimo puella naso,
nec bello pede nec nigris ocellis
nec longis digitis nec ore sicco
nec sane nimis elegante lingua,
5   decoctoris amica Formiani.
ten provincia narrat esse bellam?
tecum Lesbia nostra comparatur?
o saeclum insipiens et infacetum!

ocellus = oculus (*m*), eye
digitus (*m*), finger
os, oris (*n*), mouth, lips
siccus, dry
sane, certainly, truly

comparo (l), to compare
saeclum (*n*), generation
insipiens, foolish
infacetus, coarse, lacking in good taste

Points for Discussion

1   Using the information given in the poem, describe what Catullus regards as the essential features of a beautiful woman.

2   What do you think was Catullus' main aim – to be critical of Ameana or to praise Lesbia?

3   Compare the above poem with the following compliment Robert Burns paid to his current sweetheart as he watched all the beautiful women dancing at a ball:

Tho' this was fair, and that was braw,
   And yon the toast of a' the town,
I sigh'd and said amang them a':
   "Ye are na Mary Morison!"

Both Catullus and Burns are making comparisons. In what ways are their methods of doing this similar/different? Which poem do you think pays the greater compliment? And why?

Catullus: See Notes on Authors on page 10.
Metre: Elegiac Couplet (See page 257.)

line

1   **iucundum ... perpetuumque**: Note how emphatic Catullus makes these adjectives by placing them at the beginning and end of the sentence. They describe **hunc nostrum amorem**.

    mea vita: He is addressing Lesbia.

    mihi proponis: *you declare to me* – the main clause on which the Accusative and Infinitive depends.

3   **facite ut ... possit**: *grant that she may be able.*

4   **ex animo**: *from her heart*, i. e. she really means it.

5   **ut liceat nobis**: *so that we may be permitted* (a Purpose clause).

    tota vita (ablative case) = **per totam vitam**.

6   **sanctae**: *inviolable*, because Catullus believed they had pledged their love (**amicitia**) for one another before the gods.

Love and Devotion: Love's Sorrows

14 Promises! Promises!

(Catullus 109)

> iucundum, mea vita, mihi proponis amorem
> > hunc nostrum inter nos perpetuumque fore.
>
> di magni, facite ut vere promittere possit,
> > atque id sincere dicat et ex animo,
>
> 5 ut liceat nobis tota perducere vita
> > aeternum hoc sanctae foedus amicitiae.

iucundus, pleasant, delightful
perpetuus, everlasting
fore, future infinitive of **esse**
vere, truly, truthfully, really

sincere, sincerely
perduco (3), to continue, prolong
foedus (*n*), bond, pact

Points for Discussion

1 Why does Catullus refer to Lesbia as **mea vita** in line 1? Collect from the other poems you have read other expressions Catullus uses in addressing Lesbia. Make a list of words and expressions used nowadays to refer to a girl-friend or boy-friend.

2 What effect is produced by using both **nostrum** and **inter nos** in line 2?

3 In lines 1–2, Catullus is addressing Lesbia. Why do you think he addresses **di magni** in lines 3–6? At what stage in the love-affair do you think this poem was written?

4 In lines 3–4, why do you think Catullus used **vere**, **sincere** and **ex animo**, all of which have roughly the same meaning?

5 Which expressions in this poem suggest that Catullus does not trust Lesbia?

Catullus: See Notes on Authors on page 10.
Metre: Elegiac Couplet (See page 257.)

line

1   **nulli = nemini**: Note the emphatic position – *There is no one at all ....*

   mulier mea: *my mistress*, a less affectionate expression than **mea puella** which he used when the love-affair was going well.   **dicit mulier mea** introduces an Accusative and Infinitive clause.

   nubere: *to marry*, used of a woman marrying a man. The verb is derived from the same root as **nubes** (*cloud* obscuring the sun, or *veil* obscuring the face). When about to marry, a Roman bride put on a veil *for* her future husband, which explains why the verb governs the dative case.

2   **non si**: *not (even) if.* Jupiter was the king of the gods.

   petat: *were to court or woo*, literally *were to seek.* (For Conditional sentences, see LL p. 54.)

3   **dicit**: *that's what she says.* The single word is very effective.

   mulier quod dicit: Supply **id** with **quod** – *what* (literally *that which*) a *woman* says. This clause is the object of **scribere oportet** in line 4. The normal order is changed to emphasise **mulier**. Similar emphasis is given to **cupido** by its separation from **amanti**.

15 Broken Promises

(Catullus 70)

> nulli se dicit mulier mea nubere malle
> > quam mihi, non si se Iuppiter ipse petat.
> dicit: sed mulier cupido quod dicit amanti,
> > in vento et rapida scribere oportet aqua.

malle quam, to prefer, like better than
amans (*m*), lover
rapidus, swift-flowing

oportet (+ *infinitive*), one ought (to)
aqua (*f*), water, stream

Points for Discussion

1 At what stage in the love-affair do you think this poem comes?

2 Sir Walter Scott has four lines very similar in content to lines 3–4 above:

> Woman's faith and woman's trust –
> Write the characters in dust,
> Stamp them on the running stream,
> Print them on the moonlight's beam.

Compare:

"I write the promises of woman on water" (translated from the Greek dramatist Sophocles)
varium et mutabile semper femina, "Woman is ever a fickle and changeable thing" (Virgil)
la donna e mobile, "Woman is changeable" (Italian saying)

What point is being made by these authors? Do you agree with the sentiments they express, or do you think that they are the product of male-dominated literature? Or is it simply in the nature of woman to claim that it is her prerogative to change her mind?

Catullus: See Notes on Authors page 10.
Metre: Choliambics (limping iambics) (See page 258.)

line

1   **miser**: *poor* – the stock epithet of the unhappy lover.

     desinas ineptire: *stop being foolish!* The present subjunctive may be used in poetry to express a command. (See LL p. 107.) Compare **ducas**, *consider!* or *reckon!* in line 2.

2   **quod vides perisse**: *what you see is lost.* **perisse** is the contracted form of **periisse** (*to have perished*). Note the deliberate juxtaposition of **perisse** and **perditum** (*lost for ever*), all the more effective since **perire** is often used as the passive of **perdo**. The metaphor (see p. 259) is from accountancy, in which bad debts are "written off".

3   **fulsere = fulserunt**: *shone.* The use of the perfect tense with **quondam** implies that they no longer shine. The love-affair is over and done with. The **-ere** form of the 3rd plural of the perfect tense gives the poet a useful alternative to the more usual **-erunt**, to help him meet the demands of the metre.

     soles: Although we may translate this as *suns*, the word is really equivalent to *days*. Catullus associates sunshine with happiness. Note the importance of the word **tibi**: because he was so happy in Lesbia's company, Catullus felt the sun was shining, whether it was actually shining or not. Note that Catullus is still addressing himself.

5   **amata nobis**: *loved by me*, **amata** agreeing with **puella** (line 4). For the dative case used to express the person "by whom" something is done, compare its use with the Gerundive. (For the Dative of Agent, see LL pp. 11 and 62.)

     In the opening lines of the poem, Catullus has been addressing himself and trying to give himself some objective advice. In line 5, the memory of his love gets the better of him and he now reverts from the 2nd to the 1st person (**nobis**).

     quantum ... nulla: Supply **tantum** before **amata** – literally *loved as much as no woman*, i. e. *loved more than any woman.* (For Correlatives, see LL p. 63.)

6   **ibi**: *then.*

     illa multa cum iocosa fiebant: *when all those pleasurable things happened.*

8   The repetition of line 3, with the emphatic **vere** (*without a doubt*) replacing **quondam**, serves as a kind of refrain to his reminiscences. Catullus can hardly believe that the love-affair is all over.

9   **nunc iam**: *as things stand now.* The mood of the poem changes from idle daydreaming to the stark reality that now faces him. In a series of short, sharp commands, Catullus tries to shake himself out of his folly.

     tu quoque impotens noli: *you too, you weakling, do the same!* (literally *be unwilling*). **tu** is contrasted with **illa** (his girl-friend); and **impotens** is vocative, addressing himself.

10   **quae**: Supply **eam** as the antecedent, *her who* ... (i. e. Lesbia).

     sectare: an imperative (deponent verb).

     vive is deliberately stronger than the simple imperative **es** (*be*): *go on living.* In this context, English would probably translate the adjective **miser** by *a miserable life.*

16 Vale, Puella!

(Catullus 8)

miser Catulle, desinas ineptire,
et quod vides perisse perditum ducas.
fulsere quondam candidi tibi soles,
cum ventitabas quo puella ducebat
5 amata nobis quantum amabitur nulla.
ibi illa multa cum iocosa fiebant
quae tu volebas nec puella nolebat,
fulsere vere candidi tibi soles.
nunc iam illa non vult: tu quoque impotens noli,
10 nec quae fugit sectare, nec miser vive,

quondam, once (upon a time)
candidus, bright, dazzling
ventito (1), to keep going

impotens, weak
sector (l), to pursue

14   **nulla**: Coming at the end of the sentence, **nulla** is a very strong negative – *when you are not courted at all*. Note that the future **rogaberis** is translated by a present tense in English.

15   **scelesta**: *poor wretch* rather than *wicked woman* in this context. This adjective was commonly used in Latin comedy of people who brought bad luck upon themselves.

    vae te!: *alas, for you!*

17   **cuius esse diceris?**: *whose lover will they say you are?*, literally *whose will you be said to be?*

18   **cui labella**: *whose lips*. (For Dative of Possession, see LL p. 11.)

19   **at tu**: The questions (lines 15 –18) have the effect of stirring up in Catullus a sense of longing for the past. He therefore shakes himself out of his reverie with the words **at tu obdura**.

    destinatus: English would probably translate this adjective (meaning literally *fixed, firm*) as a second imperative along with **obdura**: *be resolute and stand firm.*

sed obstinata mente perfer, obdura!
vale, puella! iam Catullus obdurat,
nec te requiret nec rogabit invitam.
at tu dolebis, cum rogaberis nulla.
15 scelesta (vae te!), quae tibi manet vita?
quis nunc te adibit? cui videberis bella?
quem nunc amabis? cuius esse diceris?
quem basiabis? cui labella mordebis?
at tu, Catulle, destinatus obdura!

obstinatus, stubborn
mens (*f*), spirit, resolve
perfero, –ferre, to endure
obduro (1), to be firm, resolute

requiro (3), to seek out
bellus, beautiful, pretty
basio (1), to kiss
mordeo (2), to bite

Points for Discussion

1 Why do you think Catullus wrote **amabitur** (line 5) rather than **amata est**? Which would be the greater compliment to Lesbia?

2 In line 7, what do the words **tu volebas** and **nec puella nolebat** reveal about the different attitudes of Catullus and Lesbia towards the love-affair? What shift does **non vult** (line 9) suggest in Lesbia's attitude?

3 In the above poem, Catullus sometimes talks to himself, sometimes to Lesbia. Identify the points at which he changes from one to the other. What effect do you think he is trying to create by these means?

4 What purpose do you think Catullus has in asking all the questions in lines 15–18? For example, is he being spiteful in reminding her that her attractiveness to men will soon disappear? Or is he being conceited in reminding her of what she will be losing by rejecting himself? Or is he using a kind of blackmail to win her back? Do you think line 19 has any bearing on the matter?

Catullus: See Notes on Authors on page 10.
Metre: Elegiac Couplet (See page 257.)

line

2   **nescio**: *I cannot explain it*, literally *I do not know*. Note that the **-o** must be scanned as short.

    fieri sentio: *it is a very real feeling*, literally *I feel that it is happening*.

17 Torment

(Catullus 85)

odi et amo. quare id faciam, fortasse requiris.
  nescio, sed fieri sentio et excrucior.

odi, I hate
quare, why
fortasse, perhaps

requiro (3), to ask
excrucio (1), to torture

Points for Discussion

1 What kind of torment is the poet experiencing when he says **odi et amo**?

2 Describe a situation in which you yourself might experience conflicting feelings.

Catullus: See Notes on Authors on page 10.
Metre: Elegiac Couplet (See page 257.)

line

2   **efficias:** In poetry, the present subjunctive is often used instead of an imperative – *you must achieve*. (See LL p. 107.)

3   **una:** Note the emphatic position of **una** – *the one and only*.

     hoc est tibi pervincendum: *this is something you must get the better of*, literally *this must be completely conquered by you*. When the Gerundive is used, the dative regularly expresses the person by whom something must be done. (For Dative of Agent, see LL p. 62.) The spondee + spondee ending of the line, instead of the normal dactyl + spondee, stresses the immense effort he must make.

4   **facias:** Compare **efficias** in line 2.

     non pote: Supply **est** – *it is impossible* (**pote** + **est** = **potest**).

5   **si vestrum est:** *if it is in your power*.

6   **extremam:** Catullus has placed considerable emphasis on this word by separating it from **opem** and by reinforcing it with the phrase **iam ipsa in morte**. Translate *at the end*.

8   **hanc pestem perniciemque:** *this disease which is destroying me* (i.e. his obsession with Lesbia), literally *this plague and destruction*. (For Hendiadys, see p. 259.) The medical metaphor (see p. 259) is taken up again in line 13. Note also the effect of the repeated "p" sound. (For Alliteration, see p. 259.)

9   **imos in artus:** Great care should always be taken in translating the adjective **imus**. Its most common meanings are *lowest, deepest, bottom of*, i.e. something which is at the opposite end of a line from **summus** (*highest, top of*). When applied to something three-dimensional (e.g. bones, limbs, heart), it refers to the part farthest from the surface, e.g. *innermost* or *the very heart of*. Translate *deep into my limbs*.

     ut torpor: *like a paralysis*.

10   **ex omni pectore:** *completely from my heart*.

11   **contra me ut diligat illa:** an Indirect Command depending on **quaero** and explaining **illud**. **contra** is an adverb (*in return*), and **me** is the object of **diligat**. Note the emphatic position of **illa**.

12   **aut . . . velit:** Another Indirect Command depending on **quaero** – *or that she should want . . . .*

     quod = id quod.

14   **pietate: pietas** covers a range of dutiful qualities – reverence for the gods, love for one's parents, wife and children, loyalty to one's country, scrupulousness in one's dealings with others. In addressing this prayer to the gods, Catullus reminds them how punctilious he has been in worshipping them and now asks them to keep their side of the bargain.

18 Free Me from this Torment!

(Catullus 76. 13–26)

difficile est longum subito deponere amorem.
    difficile est, verum hoc qua lubet efficias.
una salus haec est, hoc est tibi pervincendum,
    hoc facias, sive id non pote sive pote.
5   o di, si vestrum est misereri, aut si quibus umquam
    extremam iam ipsa in morte tulistis opem,
me miserum aspicite et, si vitam puriter egi,
    eripite hanc pestem perniciemque mihi,
quae mihi subrepens imos ut torpor in artus
10   expulit ex omni pectore laetitias.
non iam illud quaero, contra me ut diligat illa,
    aut, quod non potis est, esse pudica velit:
ipse valere opto et taetrum hunc deponere morbum.
    o di, reddite mi hoc pro pietate mea.

depono (3), to forget, discard
verum, but
qua lubet, in any way you can
salus (*f*), safety, means of survival
sive ... sive ..., whether ... or ...
potis, pote, possible, able
misereor (2), to feel pity
si quis, if anyone
opem ferre, to give help
aspicio (3), to look at, take notice of

vitam agere, to spend one's life
puriter, without fault, blamelessly
eripio (3) (+ *dat.*), to take away (from)
subrepo (3) (+ *dat.*), to creep up (on)
laetitia (*f*), pleasure, joy
diligo (3), to love
pudicus, chaste, pure
taeter, -tra, -trum, foul, loathsome
mi = mihi
pro (+ *abl.*), in return for

Points for Discussion

1 In line 4 Catullus says "whether it is impossible or possible" (**sive id non pote sive pote**), whereas in English the normal expression is "whether it is possible or not". What does Catullus' expression reveal about his feelings?

2 List the words and phrases through which Catullus likens his love to an illness.

3 Compare the tone of the three poems: "Vale, Puella!" (page 61). "Torment" (page 65) and "Free Me from this Torment!". Do you detect any change in Catullus' attitude? Has he accepted Lesbia's rejection of him? In your opinion, which of his remarks ring true? What advice would you give him, and why?

Martial: See Notes on Authors on page 12.
Metre: Elegiac Couplet (See page 257.)

line

1   Martial addresses these four lines to his former lady-love, Lycoris, who has been replaced by Glycera as the object of his affections. The poem achieves its impact through the clever use of word repetition and contrasting tenses – past with present and present with future. All that Lycoris was to him in the past, Glycera is to him now.

3   **haec**: (twice in this line) refers to Glycera. Translate both uses as *she*. Compare **hanc** (*her*) in line 4.

     hoc quod tu: Supply **es** - *what you are now*, literally *this thing which you (are)*.

4   **quid** introduces an exclamation, not a question. The plural **tempora** indicates all the moments which build up into *the passage of time*. Translate **tempora quid faciunt!** as *such is the effect of time!* (For a similar sentiment, compare **tempora mutantur, nos et mutamur in illis**, *times change and we change with them*.)

     volo: *I want* or *I desire*.

19 Passing Fancy

(Martial, *Epigrams* VI. 40)

femina praeferri potuit tibi nulla, Lycori:
   praeferri Glycerae femina nulla potest.
haec erit hoc quod tu: tu non potes esse quod haec est.
   tempora quid faciunt! hanc volo, te volui.

praefero, to prefer

Points for Discussion

1 What effect does Martial achieve by separating **femina** and **nulla** in line 1?

2 What point is Martial making in the first half of line 3?

3 Is "Passing Fancy" a suitable title for this poem? What does it imply? Is it fair to the poet? Can you suggest and justify another title?

4 Compare Martial's attitude to his broken romance with that of Catullus when his love-affair with Lesbia ended.

Catullus: See Notes on Authors on page 10.
Metre: Elegiac Couplet (See page 257.)

line

1   **multas per gentes**: literally *through many peoples*, but English would more naturally say *over many lands*. On an ancient map, areas were indicated by the name of the people who lived there rather than by the name of the country.

2   **advenio**: Although this is present tense, the more natural translation in English would be *I have come*.

    miseras ad inferias: *to (make) these sad offerings*, i.e. to pay his last respects to his dead brother.

3   **ut te donarem**: The imperfect tense is unusual since this Purpose clause depends on the present tense verb **advenio**; but the thought is clear enough – I planned my journey here *so that I might give you*, literally *present you (with)*.

    mortis: *due to the dead*, literally *of death*.

4   **mutam cinerem**: *your silent ashes*, i.e. they can make no reply to Catullus.

    nequiquam: *in vain*, for he had no hope of receiving a reply.

5   **mihi tete abstulit ipsum**: *has robbed me of your very presence*, literally *has taken away you yourself from me*. As usual, the dative case is used to indicate the person *from whom* something is taken away. (See LL p. 10 and compare **mihi** in line 6.) The word **tete** is a stronger form of **te**, and the addition of **ipsum** emphasises the fact that the brother no longer physically exists.

6   **adempte**: *taken away*, vocative case agreeing with **frater**.

7   **nunc tamen interea**: *yet, for all that*, i.e. despite the hopelessness of the offering and the unfairness of his brother's death, Catullus will do all he can in the circumstances.

    haec: *these gifts*. The relative clause which follows (**prisco quae ... inferias**) separates **haec** from the verb which governs it – **accipe**.

8   **tradita sunt tristi munere ad inferias**: *are traditionally handed over as a funeral offering in sad tribute (to the dead)*. In ancient times, these offerings consisted of such things as flowers, wine, milk, honey and locks of hair. The modern equivalents are flowers and wreaths.

9   **multum manantia**: *all wet* or *drenched*, literally *dripping much*. (**manantia** agrees with **haec** in line 7.)

    fraterno fletu: *with a brother's tears*. In Mediterranean countries, it has never been seen as a sign of weakness for men to express their grief in tears.

10   **ave atque vale!** *Hail and farewell!* These were the last words spoken in a Roman funeral ceremony.

Love and Devotion: Love's Partings

20 Ave atque Vale!

(Catullus 101)

About 57 BC, Catullus went to the province of Bithynia (now part of Turkey, lying at the south-west corner of the Black Sea) as a member of the governor's staff. On his way there, he visited the tomb of his brother who had died in Asia Minor some time before this and was buried near the ancient city of Troy.

multas per gentes et multa per aequora vectus
    advenio has miseras, frater, ad inferias
ut te postremo donarem munere mortis
    et mutam nequiquam alloquerer cinerem.
5 quandoquidem fortuna mihi tete abstulit ipsum,
    – heu miser indigne frater adempte mihi! –
nunc tamen interea haec, prisco quae more parentum
    tradita sunt tristi munere ad inferias,
accipe fraterno multum manantia fletu,
10   atque in perpetuum, frater, ave atque vale!

aequor (*n*), sea
postremus, last, final
alloquor (3), to address, speak to
quandoquidem, since
heu! alas!

indigne, undeservedly, cruelly
priscus, ancient
parens (*m*), ancestor
in perpetuum, for ever, for all time

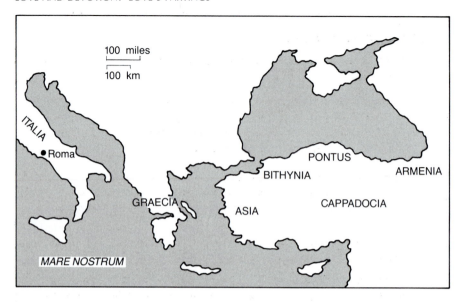

Asia Minor

Points for Discussion

1 What effect do you think Catullus is trying to produce in line 1? How does he achieve it?

2 Lines 5 and 6 both deal with the poet's sad loss, line 5 in a matter-of-fact way, line 6 as an emotional outburst. How in line 6 do the word order and the choice of words help to underline the depth of the poet's feelings? Quote the Latin words, as appropriate, to illustrate your answer.

3 The letter "m" appears frequently throughout the poem. What effect do you think Catullus is trying to produce by this sound? (See Alliteration and Assonance on page 259.) Is it the same effect as Tennyson produces in the following two lines?

> The moan of doves in immemorial elms,
> And murmuring of innumerable bees.

4 Comment on the mood of this poem as compared with that created by Catullus in "The Songbird Dies" (p. 43). What do we learn from this poem about Catullus' thoughts on what happens after death? Do you think he is merely going through a set ritual?

Virgil: See Notes on Authors on page 15.
Metre: Hexameter (See page 255.)

line

1 **ipse**: Orpheus.

   cava testudine: *on his hollow lyre.* In mythology, Mercury is credited with inventing the first lyre. He is supposed to have found a tortoise-shell (**testudo**) with the skin of the belly dried into thin strands across it. When he plucked these, they gave off different sounds. The earliest lyres were made by stretching strings across tortoise-shells.

2 **te . . . canebat**: *sang about you.*

   secum: This word emphasises his loneliness. In his grief, he deliberately kept away from other mortals all day long.

4 **Taenarias fauces**: *the narrow gorge at Taenarum.* This and **lucum** (line 5) are the direct objects of **ingressus** (line 6). At Taenarum (now Cape Matapan), on the southern tip of the Peloponnese, there was a cave reputed to be an entrance to the Underworld.

6 **manesque**: *the shades of the dead.* Note that the **–que** does not mean *and*; it is to be taken with **regemque** and **nesciaque**: *not just . . . but . . . and . . . .*

   regem tremendum: *the dreaded king*, i.e. Pluto (here called Dis).

7 **nescia mansuescere corda** : *hearts that knew not how to grow soft* (i.e. *yield*).

8 **at**: An important word in the story because it indicates that Orpheus' music was able to make an impact on the normally immovable powers of the Underworld.

   Erebi: Erebus was one of the names for the Underworld.

   de sedibus imis ibant: *came trooping from the lowest depths (of Hell).*

9 **simulacra luce carentum**: *the phantoms of those cut off from light* (i.e. *the dead*).

10 **quam multa**: *as many as* – introducing a simile. (For Simile, see page 260.)

12 **defuncta corpora vita**: *bodies finished with life.* Lines 12–14 give examples of the types of shades that throng round to hear Orpheus' music.

13 **magnanimum heroum**: *of great-hearted heroes.* **magnanimum** was the original genitive plural of Group 2 nouns. The **-orum** ending was introduced later by analogy with **-arum** of Group 1.

15 **quos** is the object of **alligat** and **coercet** (line 17); and **circum** is an adverb meaning *round about.*

   harundo: *the reeds.* Just as poets often use a plural noun instead of a singular, so here a singular noun is used for a plural. (See p. 262.)

16 **Cocyti**: The Cocytus was one of the rivers of the Underworld. Another, and possibly the best-known, was the River Styx, which is mentioned in line 17.

   tarda unda: *with its sluggish stream.* The scansion shows that the phrase is in the ablative case. (See An Introduction to Latin Metres on p. 254.)

21 Orpheus and Eurydice

(Virgil, *Georgics* IV, lines 464–506)

The minstrel Orpheus, grieving over the death of his wife Eurydice, dares to go down to the Underworld to recover her.

ipse cava solans aegrum testudine amorem
te, dulcis coniunx, te solo in litore secum,
te veniente die, te decedente canebat.
Taenarias etiam fauces, alta ostia Ditis,
5   et caligantem nigra formidine lucum
ingressus, manesque adiit regemque tremendum
nesciaque humanis precibus mansuescere corda.

Even the shades of the Underworld are moved by his songs.

at cantu commotae Erebi de sedibus imis
umbrae ibant tenues simulacraque luce carentum,
10   quam multa in foliis avium se milia condunt,
vesper ubi aut hibernus agit de montibus imber,
1998 matres atque viri, defunctaque corpora vita
magnanimum heroum, pueri innuptaeque puellae,
impositique rogis iuvenes ante ora parentum,
15   quos circum limus niger et deformis harundo
Cocyti tardaque palus inamabilis unda

solor (1), to console	**tenuis**, thin, insubstantial
aeger, troubled, sorrowful	**folium** (*n*), leaf
coniunx (*f*), wife	**condo** (3), to hide, conceal
solus, lonely	**hibernus**, wintry
decedo (3), to depart, end	**imber** (*m*), shower
ostium (*n*), mouth, entrance	**innuptus**, unwed
caligo (1), to be dark and gloomy	**impono** (3), to place upon
formido (*f*), terror, dread	**rogus** (*m*), funeral pyre
lucus (*m*), grove	**limus** (*m*), mud, slime
ingredior (3), to enter	**deformis**, unsightly, hideous
cantus (*m*), song, singing	**palus** (*f*), marsh
commoveo (2), to stir, startle	**inamabilis**, revolting, hateful
umbra (*f*), shade, spirit	

17 **novies interfusa**: *with its nine loops*, literally *flowing nine times in between* (*the Underworld and escape to the Upper World*). As it meandered backwards and forwards, the Styx presented nine separate obstacles which souls would have had to cross in order to escape to the land of the living.

18 **stupuere = stupuerunt**, *gaped*. The **-ere** form of the perfect indicative gave the poet a useful metrical alternative.

   intima Leti Tartara: *Tartarus, the innermost regions of Death*. Tartarus was, strictly speaking, that part of the Underworld in which the wicked were punished for their sins on earth, but here it is used loosely as a general name for the Underworld.

19 **caeruleos implexae crinibus angues**: *with dark snakes entwined in their hair*. The Furies (also called the Eumenides, *kindly ones*, to avoid offending them) were three avenging goddesses who inflicted punishments for crimes. Even the gods dreaded them.

20 **tenuit tria ora**: *held his three mouths still*. Cerberus was the three-headed dog which guarded the entrance to the Underworld.

21 **Ixionii vento rota constitit orbis**: *Ixion's wheel stood still as the wind stopped blowing*, literally *the wheel of Ixion's circle halted with the wind*. For attempting to seduce Juno, the queen of the gods, Ixion was committed to Tartarus where he was tied to a wheel which the wind kept constantly turning. When the wind dropped in response to the charm of Orpheus' music, the wheel also stopped.

23 **reddita**: *restored (to Orpheus)*.

25 **incautum amantem**: *the heedless lover*, i.e. his love made him forget Proserpina's warning.

26 **ignoscenda quidem**: *pardonable, indeed*.

   manes: here, not so much the dead spirits as *the powers of the Underworld*, i.e. Pluto and Proserpina.

27 **Eurydicen**: Greek accusative singular (see p. 262). Note the pathetic effect of the adjective **suam** – she was almost *his* again, but alas . . . . (Cf. **reddita** in line 23.)

   luce sub ipsa: *on the very threshold of daylight*.

28 **victus animi**: *weakened in his resolve*, literally *defeated in his mind*. (**animi** is locative case: see LL p. 20.)

29 **effusus labor**: Supply **est** – *his efforts were wasted*. Compare **rupta (sunt)** and **auditus (est)**.

30 **Averni**: Avernus is yet another name for the Underworld. Strictly speaking, Avernus was a lake (a few miles north of Naples) near which there was believed to be an entrance to the Underworld.

31 **illa**: *she*, i.e. Eurydice.

   quis is an adjective agreeing with **furor** (understood): *what madness*. It is strengthened in line 32 to **quis tantus furor**.

Cerberus, the three-headed dog

alligat et novies Styx interfusa coercet.
quin ipsae stupuere domus atque intima Leti
Tartara caeruleosque implexae crinibus angues
20 Eumenides, tenuitque inhians tria Cerberus ora,
atque Ixionii vento rota constitit orbis.

Proserpina, wife of Pluto, agreed to let him take
Eurydice back with him; but she made it a
condition that he must not look back at Eurydice
on the way up to earth.

iamque pedem referens casus evaserat omnes,
redditaque Eurydice superas veniebat ad auras
pone sequens (namque hanc dederat Proserpina legem),
25 cum subita incautum dementia cepit amantem,
ignoscenda quidem, scirent si ignoscere manes:
restitit, Eurydicenque suam iam luce sub ipsa –
immemor heu! – victusque animi respexit. ibi omnis
effusus labor atque immitis rupta tyranni
30 foedera, terque fragor stagnis auditus Averni.

Eurydice vanishes from his sight.

illa "quis et me" inquit "miseram et te perdidit, Orpheu,
quis tantus furor? en iterum crudelia retro

alligo (1), to hem in, imprison	**ignoscere** (3), to pardon, forgive
coerceo (2), to confine, surround	**resto** (1), **restiti**, to stop
quin, indeed, moreover	**immemor**, forgetful, heedless(ly)
inhio (1), to gape	**heu**, alas
casus, -us (*m*), misfortune, mishap	**respicio** (3), to look back
evado (3), to escape	**immitis**, ruthless
superus, (of the world) above	**tyrannus** (*m*), tyrant, ruler
aura (*f*), air	**foedus, -eris** (*n*), pact, agreement
pone, behind	**ter**, three times, thrice
namque, for	**fragor** (*m*), thunder-crash
lex, legis (*f*), condition	**stagnum** (*n*), pool
dementia (*f*), madness, mad folly	**en!** lo!
scio (4) (+ *infin.*), to know (how to)	**retro**, back, backwards

77

33 **natantia lumina**: *my swimming eyes*. This refers, not to tears, but to the effect on the eyes of swooning or death, when the eyesight goes out of focus.

34 **feror**: *I am being carried off.*

35 **non tua**: *no longer yours*. This echoes the **suam** in line 27.

36 **ceu**: *just like* – introduces a simile (see p. 260).

37 **fugit diversa**: *fled away.*

39 **portitor Orci**: *the ferryman of Orcus*, i.e. Charon, who for a fee carried the souls of the dead across the River Styx into the Underworld, here called Orcus.

40 **passus**: Supply **est** – *allowed.*

 obiectam paludem: *the barrier of the marsh*, literally *the marsh put in the way*. This refers to the marshy rivers which acted like a perimeter fence round the Underworld.

41 **quid faceret?** *what was he to do?* – a Deliberative Question (see LL p. 108). Compare **ferret** and **moveret**.

 rapta bis coniuge: *his wife having been twice snatched from him.*

42 **quo fletu**: *with what weeping*. (Cf. **qua voce**.)

43 **illa**: *she*, i.e. Eurydice.

 frigida: *chilled (by death).*

"Orpheus and Eurydice" by G.F.Watts

78

fata vocant, conditque natantia lumina somnus.
iamque vale: feror ingenti circumdata nocte
35   invalidasque tibi tendens, heu non tua, palmas."
dixit et ex oculis subito, ceu fumus in auras
commixtus tenues, fugit diversa, neque illum
prensantem nequiquam umbras et multa volentem
dicere praeterea vidit. nec portitor Orci
40   amplius obiectam passus transire paludem.
quid faceret? quo se rapta bis coniuge ferret?
quo fletu manes, qua numina voce moveret?
illa quidem Stygia nabat iam frigida cumba.

fatum (*n*), fate	**prenso** (1), to grasp, clutch at
ingens, vast	**nequiquam**, in vain
circumdatus, enveloped	**praeterea**, henceforth, after that
invalidus, weak, helpless	**nec amplius**, and no longer
tendo (3), to stretch out	**numen** (*n*), divine power, deity
palma (*f*), hand	**Stygius**, Stygian, of the Styx
fumus (*m*), smoke	**no** (1), to sail
commixtus, mixed, mingling	**cumba** (*f*), boat

Points for Discussion

1   What effect do you think Virgil is trying to create by using **te** four times in lines 2–3?

2   Why do you think Pluto is described as **tremendus** in line 6?

3   In lines 22–24, almost all the feet are dactyls, whereas in lines 29–30 there is a preponderance of spondees. In what way does the rhythm of the metre echo what is being said?

4   What reasons does Virgil give for Orpheus looking back (lines 22–28)? Suggest other reasons he might have had. Would *you* have looked back?

5   Neither **somnus** (line 33) nor **nocte** (line 34) is to be taken literally. To what do they really refer?

6   Study lines 31–43. Quote from the text the words which illustrate the helplessness of Eurydice in this situation.

7   Virgil twice uses the adjective **tenuis** in the passage above: **umbrae tenues** (line 9) and **in auras tenues** (lines 36–37). What do the nouns **umbrae** and **auras** have in common? How appropriate is the adjective in each example?

8   How appropriate do you think the simile of the birds is in line 10? What do the birds and the shades have in common? How appropriate is the simile of smoke in lines 36–37?

9   Do you feel greater pity for Orpheus or for Eurydice? Give reasons.

Virgil: See Notes on Authors on page 15.
Metre: Hexameter (See page 255.)

line

1   **flumina**: the rivers of the Underworld.

2   **terribili squalore**: For Ablative of Description, see LL page 15.

     cui mento: *on whose chin.* (For the Possessive use of the dative, see LL p. 11.)

3   **stant lumina flamma**: *his eyes are fixed in a fiery gaze*, literally *his eyes stand in fire.*

5   **velis ministrat**: *trims the sails*, literally *attends to the sails.*

6   **ferruginea**: *dark rust-coloured.* Scansion of the line tells us that it is ablative case.

7   **deo senectus**: *a god's old age.* (Cf. line 2 for the Possessive Dative.)

8   **effusa**: *pouring along*, i.e. the souls of the dead were surging on like a tide.

9   **defuncta corpora vita**: *bodies finished with life.*

10   **magnanimum heroum**: *of great-hearted heroes.* **magnanimum** was the original genitive plural of Group 2 nouns. The **-orum** ending was introduced later by analogy with **-arum** of Group 1.

12   **quam multa**: *as many as* – introducing a simile. (See page 260.)

13   **gurgite ab alto**: *from the deep ocean.*

14   **frigidus annus**: *winter*, literally *the cold (part of the) year.*

16   **transmittere cursum**: *to make the crossing.* The poet uses the infinitive to express an Indirect Command depending on **orantes**.

17   **ripae ulterioris amore**: *with a longing for the farther bank.* Before they crossed the Styx, the dead souls were in a kind of no-man's land – neither in the land of the living, nor in the land of the dead. The fate that befell anyone who had not received the proper funeral rites was to wander about on the banks of the Styx for a hundred years, waiting to be taken across.

22 Charon, Death's Ferryman

(Virgil, *Aeneid* VI. 298–316)

portitor has horrendus aquas et flumina servat
terribili squalore Charon, cui plurima mento
canities inculta iacet, stant lumina flamma,
sordidus ex umeris nodo dependet amictus.
5 ipse ratem conto subigit velisque ministrat
et ferruginea subvectat corpora cumba,
iam senior, sed cruda deo viridisque senectus.
huc omnis turba ad ripas effusa ruebat,
matres atque viri, defunctaque corpora vita
10 magnanimum heroum, pueri innuptaeque puellae,
impositique rogis iuvenes ante ora parentum:
quam multa in silvis autumni frigore primo
lapsa cadunt folia, aut ad terram gurgite ab alto
quam multae glomerantur aves, ubi frigidus annus
15 trans pontum fugat et terris immittit apricis.
stabant orantes primi transmittere cursum,
tendebantque manus ripae ulterioris amore.
navita sed tristis nunc hos nunc accipit illos,
ast alios longe summotos arcet harena.

portitor (*m*), ferryman
horrendus, dreaded
servo (1), guard, watch over
terribilis, frightening, appalling
squalor (*m*), filth
canities (*f*), grey hair
incultus, untrimmed, unkempt
sordidus, filthy
umerus (*m*), shoulder
nodus (*m*), knot
dependeo (2), to hang down
amictus (*m*), cloak
ratis (*f*), boat
contus (*m*), pole
subigo (3), to drive along, propel
subvecto (1), to carry, ferry
cumba (*f*), boat, skiff

senior, quite old
crudus, hardy, vigorous
viridis, green
senectus (*f*), old age
labor (3), **lapsus sum**, to glide, float down
folium (*n*), leaf
glomero (1), to gather
pontus (*m*), sea
apricus, sunny
tendo (3), to stretch
navita = nauta, boatman
tristis, grim
ast, but
summoveo (2), to move back
arceo (2), to keep away (from)
harena (*f*), sand, river-side

Mercury delivering a dead soul to Charon, from an early 4th century oil flask

Points for Discussion

1 Why do you think that Charon's old age is described as "green" (line 7)?

2 Identify the ways in which Virgil contrasts the power and strength of the aged Charon with the weakness of the dead souls. Why should this difference exist?

3 Although lines 9–11 of this passage and lines 12–14 of the "Orpheus and Eurydice" passage are identical, Virgil uses different similes to describe the crowds of dead souls. How appropriate are the similes used here? Which of the three similes do you think is most effective and why?

4 In what ways does Virgil build up the sinister atmosphere of the passage? Quote and translate any words or phrases which support your answer.

5 Identify the ways in which Virgil arouses sympathy for the dead souls, quoting where necessary from the passage.

23 Death of a Young Bride-to-be

(Pliny the Younger, *Letters* V. 16)

It is with very great sadness that I write to tell you that the younger daughter of our friend Fundanus has died. A more lively and lovable girl I have yet to meet, the sort of person who not only merits a longer life but almost deserves to live for ever. She was only thirteen, but already she displayed the wisdom that one associates with age and the poise that comes with maturity, without having lost any of her girlish sweetness and innocence. She was forever putting her arms round her father's neck. As for us, her father's friends, she would embrace us affectionately but modestly. She never failed to show warm appreciation to her nurses, teachers and tutors for what they had individually done for her. In her studies, she applied herself with intelligence and industry; in her play she showed restraint and good sense.

What composure, patience and amazing strength of character she displayed throughout her last illness! She did everything the doctors told her; it was she who constantly kept up the spirits of her sister and her father; and she kept herself going by sheer willpower, even when her bodily strength had failed her. And this made our sorrow over her loss even greater. What a truly sad and tragic death hers was! But even worse than her actual death was the timing of it. For she was already engaged to be married to a fine young man; the wedding-day had been chosen; we had all received our invitations. Suddenly, all that joy was changed into sorrow. I just can't put into words how deeply moved I was when I heard Fundanus giving instructions that the money he had set aside for clothes and pearls and jewels for the bride was now to be spent on incense, ointment and spices.

Point for Discussion

Do you think this is a genuine letter of grief? Give reasons for your answer.

Pliny: See Notes on Authors on page 13.

line

1   **C. Plinius Acilio Suo S.** : This is one of the normal ways of opening a letter. The person to whom it is addressed appears in the dative case (**Acilio Suo**, *to his friend Acilius*), and the letter "**S**" (or sometimes **S. D.**) stands for **salutem dicit**, *sends greetings to*. (Cf. the use of **vale!** *Keep well* or *Farewell* to close the letter.)

2   **nec tantum epistula dignam**: *and deserving more (publicity) than a letter*, literally *and deserving not only a letter*. (For **dignus** + ablative, see LL p. 16.)

    vir praetorius: *a man of praetorian rank*, i.e. he was an ex-praetor. Praetors were senior Roman officials whose main task was to administer the laws and the courts, in which they often acted as judges. It is interesting to note that Macedo reached this rank, although his father had originally been a slave.

4   **Formiana**: *at Formiae*, on the west coast of Italy, about 75 miles (120 km) south of Rome.

    alius ... alius ... alius ... : *one ... a second ... a third*.

5   **(eum) exanimem (esse)**: an Accusative and Infinitive depending on **putarent**.

6   **in fervens pavimentum**: *on to the hot tiled floor*. The *hot-room* (**caldarium**) was heated by an under-floor system.

    an viveret: *(to see) whether he was alive*.

8   **fidem peractae mortis implevit**: *he convinced them that they had succeeded in killing him*, literally *he filled (fulfilled) the belief in his completed death*.

11   **vivere se confitetur**: *he revealed he was alive*.

    tutum: *safe*. Note that this is neuter.

    magna pars: *the majority* or *most*.

12   **aegre focilatus**: *resuscitated with difficulty*.

    non sine ultionis solacio: *not without the consolation of vengeance*. Murder of a master by slaves was not very common but, when that did happen, it was normal practice to put to death all the slaves who happened to be in the house at the time of the murder.

14   **nec est quod quisquam possit esse securus**: *and there is no reason for anyone to feel secure*, literally *and there is not (a reason) that anyone is able to be free from anxiety*.

15   **non enim iudicio domini sed scelere perimuntur**: Note that **domini** is nominative case – *masters are not murdered (by slaves) for rational reasons* (**iudicio**) *but through sheer wickedness* (**scelere**).

17   **verum haec hactenus**: *but enough of this*.

    alioqui subiungerem: *otherwise, I would add it*.

Master and Slave

24 Death of a Cruel Master

(Pliny, *Letters* III. 14)

C. Plinius Acilio Suo S.

rem atrocem nec tantum epistula dignam Larcius Macedo, vir praetorius, a
servis suis passus est, superbus dominus et saevus.
    lavabatur in villa Formiana. repente eum servi circumsistunt. alius fauces
5   invadit, alius os verberat, alius pectus et ventrem contundit; et cum exanimem
putarent, abiciunt in fervens pavimentum, ut experirentur an viveret. ille sive
quia non sentiebat, sive quia se non sentire simulabat, immobilis et extentus
fidem peractae mortis implevit. tum demum quasi aestu solutus effertur;
excipiunt servi fideliores, concubinae cum ululatu et clamore concurrunt. ita et
10 vocibus excitatus et recreatus loci frigore sublatis oculis agitatoque corpore
vivere se (et iam tutum erat) confitetur. diffugiunt servi; quorum magna pars
comprehensa est, ceteri requiruntur. ipse paucis diebus aegre focilatus non sine
ultionis solacio decessit.
    vides quot periculis, quot contumeliis, quot ludibriis simus obnoxii; nec est
15 quod quisquam possit esse securus, quia sit remissus et mitis; non enim iudicio
domini sed scelere perimuntur.
    verum haec hactenus. quid praeterea novi? quid? nihil, alioqui

atrox, terrible, shocking	**quasi**, as if
tantum, only	**aestus** (*m*), heat
superbus, proud, overbearing	**solutus**, overcome
saevus, cruel, savage	**effero** (3), to carry out
lavor (1), to take a bath	**excipio** (3), to receive, take over
repente, suddenly	**concubina** (*f*), concubine, female slave
circumsisto (3), to surround	**ululatus** (*m*), howling, shrieking
fauces (*f. pl*), throat	**recreo** (1), to restore
invado (3), to attack, go for	**agito** (1), to move
verbero (1), to hit, strike	**diffugio** (3), to flee, scatter
venter (*m*), belly, stomach	**requiro** (3), to hunt, hunt down
contundo (3), to pound, thump	**decedo** (3), to die
exanimis, lifeless, dead	**contumelia** (*f*), insult, affront
abicio (3), to throw down	**ludibrium** (*n*), outrage
experior (4), to test, check	**obnoxius** (+ *dat*.), exposed (to)
sive ... sive ... ,whether ... or ...	**remissus**, lenient, easy-going
sentio (4), to be conscious	**mitis**, gentle, kindly
immobilis, motionless	**quid novi?** what news?
extentus, stretched out	**praeterea**, besides
tum demum, then and only then	

18 **dies feriatus**: *holiday*, on which there was no official business to be carried out.

contexi: *to be written*. **contexi** is present infinitive passive.

19 **quod opportune succurrit**: *(something) which has opportunely occurred to me.*

20 **in publico**: *in one of the public baths* – a favourite meeting-place for citizens of all ranks. (Cf. a modern social club.)

21 **eques Romanus**: *a Roman knight*. The **equites** were the businessmen of Rome.

eius refers to Macedo.

ut transitum daret: Lictors went ahead of senior magistrates, clearing the way for them. Macedo was using his slave like a lictor.

manu leviter admonitus: *when requested by a light tap of the hand.*

23 **palma percussit**: literally *struck with the palm*, i.e. *slapped*.

ut paene concideret: There is no way of knowing whether **concideret** is a compound of **cadere** or of **caedere**. If it is the former, the subject is Macedo – *that he almost fell to the ground*. If it is the latter, the subject is the Roman knight – *that he almost knocked him to the ground*.

illi: *for him*, i.e. for Macedo.

quasi per gradus quosdam: *by stages, as it were.*

24 **locus**: *scene.*

paus inf.

subiungerem; nam et charta superest et dies feriatus patitur plura contexi. addam quod opportune de eodem Macedone succurrit.

20   cum in publico lavaretur, notabilis atque etiam, ut exitus docuit, ominosa res accidit. eques Romanus a servo eius, ut transitum daret, manu leviter admonitus convertit se nec servum, a quo erat tactus, sed ipsum Macedonem tam graviter palma percussit ut paene concideret. ita balineum illi quasi per gradus quosdam primum contumeliae locus, deinde exitii fuit. vale!

ends on 'clever analysis.

charta (*f*), sheet (of paper)	**ominosus**, ominous
superesse, to be left over	**transitus** (*m*), passage, way
contexo (3), to compose, write	**converto** (3), to turn
notabilis, remarkable	**graviter**, heavily, violently
exitus (*m*), outcome	**balineum** (*n*), baths
doceo (2), to teach, show	**exitium** (*n*), death

Points for Discussion

1 What effect do you think Pliny is trying to create (*a*) by repeating the word **alius** in lines 4–5? (*b*) by repeating **quot** in line 14?

2 (*a*) Pliny frequently uses historic presents when relating an exciting part of his narrative. Three examples from this passage are: **circumsistunt** (line 4), **concurrunt** (line 9) and **diffugiunt** (line 11). Find three other examples in the passage.

   (*b*) Account for the imperfect tense as used in **lavabatur** (line 4), **sentiebat** (line 7) and **simulabat** (line 7).

   (*c*) Now consider lines 20–24. Why do you think he uses only past tenses in this paragraph?

3 In line 3, Macedo is described as **superbus et saevus**. Which two adjectives in line 15 are contrasted with these two words? Explain in your own words the point that Pliny is making in drawing this contrast.

4 When the slaves carried Macedo out of the baths (line 8), what explanation did they give for his condition? Why do you think they went to the bother of carrying him outside?

5 In your opinion, which of the two explanations given in lines 6–8 is the more likely? Give reasons for your answer. What do the words **et iam tutum erat** (line 11) tell us about Pliny's own thinking?

6 With hindsight, Pliny saw the incident described in the last paragraph as an omen (**ominosa res** – line 20), i. e. as a grim foreboding of what was to come. Consider both of the incidents which involved Macedo and identify the ominous links between them. *baths, slaves, beating*

7 "Pliny had mixed feelings about the murder of Macedo." Gather evidence from the passage to support this statement.

Phaedrus: See Notes on Authors on page 13.

Metre: Iambic Senarius (See page 258.)

line

2 **Aesopo**: Aesop was a Greek writer of fables (sixth century BC) who had himself originally been a slave. Many of his fables were turned into Latin verse by Phaedrus (first century AD).

 notus e vicinia: *known (to Aesop) because he lived near by.*

3 **quid tu confusus?**: Supply **es** – *why are you so distressed?* The speaker is Aesop.

 pater: *sir*, literally *father*, used as a term of respect.

4 **es dignus appellari**: *you deserve to be called.*

5 **apud te deponitur**: *is laid before you.*

8 **totis noctibus**: *all night long.* The plural is used because it happened repeatedly.

9 **sive est vocatus**: *or if he is invited out*, i.e. to dine at another's house.

11 **ullius essem culpae mihi si conscius**: *if I were aware of having done any wrong*, literally *if I were conscious within myself* (**mihi**) *of any fault.* (For Conditional Clauses, see LL p. 54.)

12 **ferrem**: *I would bear (it).*

13 **infelix saevum patior dominium**: *I have the bad luck to suffer harsh treatment from my master.* Note that the noun is **dominium** *(the power a master has)*, not **dominum**.

14 **et quas longum est promere**: *and (other reasons) which it would be tedious* (**longum est**) *to relate.*

15 **destinavi**: *I have decided.*

16 **inquit**: The subject is Aesop.

 cum mali nil feceris: *although you have done no wrong.* (For Partitive Genitive, see LL p. 9.)

17 **ut refers**: *according to what you say*, literally *as you relate.*

18 **quid si peccaris?**: *what if you do something wrong?* **peccaris = peccaveris**, literally *you will have done wrong.*

 te passurum (esse): an Accusative and Infinitive depending on **putas**.

25 Aesop and the Runaway Slave

(Perotti's Appendix to Phaedrus)

servus profugiens dominum naturae asperae
Aesopo occurrit notus e vicinia.
"quid tu confusus?" "dicam tibi clare, pater,
hoc namque es dignus appellari nomine,
5   tuto querela quia apud te deponitur.
plagae supersunt, desunt mihi cibaria.
subinde ad villam mittor sine viatico.
domi si cenat, totis persto noctibus;
sive est vocatus, iaceo ad lucem in semita.
10   emerui libertatem, canus servio.
ullius essem culpae mihi si conscius,
aequo animo ferrem. numquam sum factus satur,
et super infelix saevum patior dominium.
has propter causas et quas longum est promere
15   abire destinavi quo tulerint pedes."
"ergo" inquit "audi! cum mali nil feceris,
haec experiris, ut refers, incommoda;
quid si peccaris? quae te passurum putas?"
tali consilio est a fuga deterritus.

profugio (3), to flee, run away from
asper, harsh, cruel
clare, clearly
namque, for indeed
tuto, safely
querela (*f*), complaint
plaga (*f*), blow, beating
supersum, -esse, to abound, be in abundance
desum, -esse, to be lacking
cibaria (*n. pl*), food, rations
subinde, from time to time
viaticum (*n*), food for the journey
ceno (l), to dine

persto (1), to be kept standing
semita (*f*), path, street
emereo (2), to earn
canus, grey-haired
servio (4), to be a slave
aequo animo, patiently, calmly
satur, full (of food)
super (*adverb*), besides that
quo, where, wherever
ergo, well then
experior (4), to experience, suffer
incommodum (*n*), misfortune
deterreo (2), to deter

Points for Discussion

1 What complaints are made by the slave against his master?

2 For what reasons was the slave lying in the street (line 9)?

3 Translate and explain **canus servio** (line 10).

4 What advice did Aesop give to the runaway slave? Do you think it was good advice? What do you think you would have done in the slave's position? Explain why.

5 Can you think of modern examples of people trying to escape, even though they know the consequences of recapture?

6 The sub-heading of this poem is **non esse malo addendum malum**, literally *Bad should not be added to bad*. Which of the following English expressions, in your opinion, comes closest to the point of this story?

(a) Never trouble trouble till trouble troubles you.

(b) Sufficient unto the day is the evil thereof.

(c) Don't make matters worse.

(d) Two wrongs don't make a right.

Female slaves tending their mistress's hair

Pliny: See Notes on Authors on page 13.

line

1   **Paternus** was a literary friend of Pliny.

     S. : For this normal way of opening a letter, see passage 24.

2   **meorum**: *of my household slaves.*

3   **solacia**: Supply **sunt** (*there are*).

     unum: Supply **solacium**. Compare **alterum** in line 5.

     facilitas manumittendi: *my readiness to grant slaves their freedom*, literally *the willingness of freeing*. (For Gerund, see LL p. 60.) Many Romans saw the value to themselves of holding out to their slaves the prospect of freedom as a reward for good or long service. It was very likely that an ex-slave would continue to be loyal to his former master, partly through gratitude, but also because he would probably have to look to him to help his own advancement and that of his children. After being manumitted (literally *sent from the hand/control of the master*), the slave became a freedman with almost all the rights of a citizen. He could not stand for public office himself; but that was possible for his children, since they became free men with full civil rights.

4   **immaturos perdidisse**: *to have lost prematurely those (whom).*

5   **quod**: *the fact that*, explaining **alterum**.

     quasi testamenta: *a kind of will*. Most slaves received pocket-money, and some were even given wages; but any savings they made from these belonged in law to their master. Legally, therefore, slaves could not make wills; hence the reason why Pliny speaks of "quasi-wills" (i. e. wills in appearance only) and emphasises that he treated them *as legally binding documents* (**ut legitima**).

6   **quod visum (est)**: *as they choose*, literally *as has seemed fitting (to them).*

     pareo ut iussus: *I comply (with their wishes) as requested*, literally *I obey as ordered.*

7   **respublica quaedam et quasi civitas**: *what you might call the community where they exercise a kind of citizenship*, literally *a sort of commonwealth and as it were a (form of) citizenship*. Whereas free-born citizens relied on the laws and communal strength of the state to look after them and protect their rights, the conditions under which slaves lived depended entirely on what the master decided would happen within his household.

8   **domus** is the subject of this sentence.

10 **humanitate**: *compassion*. This noun encompasses the finer feelings that one associates with human beings, but not with animals. Compare the use of **hominis est** in line 13.

     ut hoc ipsum permitterem: This Indirect Command depends on **me induxit**.

     velim durior fieri: *I would wish to become harder (of heart).*

26 A Good Master

(Pliny, *Letters* VIII. 16)

C. PLINIUS PATERNO SUO S.

confecerunt me infirmitates meorum, mortes etiam, et quidem iuvenum.
solacia duo, nequaquam paria tanto dolori, solacia tamen: unum facilitas
manumittendi (videor enim non omnino immaturos perdidisse, quos iam liberos
5   perdidi), alterum quod permitto servis quoque quasi testamenta facere, eaque ut
legitima custodio. mandant rogantque quod visum; pareo ut iussus. dividunt,
donant, relinquunt, dumtaxat intra domum; nam servis respublica quaedam et
quasi civitas domus est.

sed, quamquam his solaciis adquiescam, debilitor et frangor eadem illa
10   humanitate, quae me ut hoc ipsum permitterem induxit. non ideo tamen velim

---

conficio (3), to overcome, distress
infirmitas (*f*), illness
solacium (*n*), consolation, comforting thought
nequaquam, by no means
permitto (3) (+ *dat.*), to allow, grant
custodio (4), to preserve, regard
dono (l), to bestow, make a gift

dumtaxat, at least, provided that
adquiesco (3), to be content, take comfort
debilito (l), to weaken, unnerve
frango (3), to unnerve, shatter
induco (3), to lead on, persuade
ideo, for that reason

11 **nec ignoro**: *nor am I unaware*, i. e. *I am well aware* – introducing the Accusative and Infinitive **alios ... vocare**.

    nihil amplius quam damnum: *no more than a (business) loss*.

12 **sibi videri**: *they regard themselves*, literally *they seem to themselves*. The infinitive **videri** forms a second Accusative and Infinitive with **alios** (understood).

    sapientes: Not so much *wise* as *philosophical*, i. e. able to remain unruffled in times of trouble.

    qui an ... sint: *whether they are ....* (For Linking Relative, see LL p. 26.) Pliny frequently uses **an** to introduce Indirect Questions.

13 **hominis est**: *it is the mark of a human being*. (For this use of the genitive, see LL p. 8.) The infinitives **adfici, sentire, resistere, admittere** and **egere** are all to be taken with this phrase.

    adfici: *to be affected* (present infinitive passive).

14 **resistere tamen**: *but not to give in (to these feelings)*. These words are to be taken closely with **solacia admittere**, providing a corrective to **adfici dolore** and **sentire**.

    non (hominis est) ... non egere: *it is not a human characteristic not to need comfort*. (For this use of the genitive, see LL p. 8.)

15 **plura**: *(I have written) more*.

16 **quaedam etiam dolendi voluptas**: *a certain pleasure even in grieving*. (For Gerund, see LL p. 60.)

    in sinu: *in the arms*, literally *in the bosom*.

durior fieri. nec ignoro alios eius modi casus nihil amplius vocare quam damnum, eoque sibi magnos homines et sapientes videri. qui an magni sapientesque sint, nescio; homines non sunt. hominis est enim adfici dolore, sentire, resistere tamen et solacia admittere, non solaciis non egere.

15   verum de his plura fortasse quam debui; sed pauciora quam volui. est enim quaedam etiam dolendi voluptas, praesertim si in amici sinu defleas, apud quem lacrimis tuis vel laus sit parata vel venia.   vale!

eius modi, of this kind
casus, -us (*m*), misfortune
eo, on that account, because of that
admitto (3), to allow, accept
egeo (2) (+ a*bl.*), to be in need (of), do
   without

verum, but
praesertim, especially
defleo (2), to weep
apud (+ *acc.*), in whom, in whose heart
vel ... vel, either ... or
venia (*f*), pardon, forgiveness

Points for Discussion

1 Put into your own words what Pliny is saying within the brackets in lines 4 – 5. Comment on what he says.

2 What limitation did Pliny put on the kinds of will which he allowed his slaves to make (lines 5–8)? How does he justify this? Do you think this was justifiable or not? Justify your answer.

3 What does Pliny mean by describing the death of a slave as "a business loss" (**damnum** in line 12)?

4 What justification might other masters have claimed for taking a harder line with their slaves? How do you think they might have reacted to Pliny's more humane attitude?

5 What do you think Pliny means by saying there is "a kind of pleasure" in grieving (line 16)? **voluptas** is quite a strong, positive word. From what aspects of grieving do *you* think pleasure might be derived?

6 Explain very briefly the meaning of the last two clauses of the letter (**praesertim ... venia**).

Seneca: See Notes on Authors on page 14.

line

1   **ex iis**: *from those (people)*.

2   **servi sunt**: Seneca pretends that someone interrupts and objects to what he is saying.

4   **si cogitaveris tantundem in utrosque licere fortunae**: *if you consider that we are both equally at the mercy of fate*, literally *if you think that fortune is allowed (to do) so much against both of us*.

5   **est ille**: *he (the master) eats.* (**est** is the present tense of **edere**. It is pronounced ēst, whereas the Latin for "he is" is pronounced ĕst.)

   plus quam capit: *more than he (can) hold*.

7   **quam**: *than (the effort with which)*. **egerere** (*to throw out, vomit*) and **ingerere** (*to throw in*) are both compounds of **gerere**. Compare our slang expressions "to throw up" and "to shovel in". Some Romans were so gluttonous that they sometimes deliberately induced vomiting so that they could eat more.

   movere: The infinitive depends on **licet**.

   ne in hoc quidem, ut loquantur: *not even to speak.* The **ut** clause explains **hoc**, literally *not even in this (circumstance), that they may speak*.

8   **fortuita**: *chance things*, explained by **tussis**, **sternumenta** and **singultus**.

11 **sic fit ut**: *and so the result is* (literally *it happens*) *that*.

13 **porrigere cervicem**: *to face execution*, literally *to stretch out the neck*. Note that **cervicem** is singular although **parati erant** is plural. The logic was that each of them had only one neck.

   in caput suum: *on their own head(s)*. Again, the singular is used where English would tend to use the plural.

14 **in tormentis tacebant**: *they kept silent when tortured.* When the magistrates suspected a Roman of some crime and wished to secure evidence against him, they would torture his slaves on the grounds that only under torture could slaves be trusted to tell the truth.

   eiusdem arrogantiae proverbium iactatur: *the same arrogant behaviour has brought about the old saying*, literally *the proverb about the same arrogance is tossed about*. On this depends the Accusative and Infinitive **totidem … servos**.

15 **non habemus illos hostes**: *we do not take them into our possession as enemies*, i. e. they (the slaves) are not our enemies when we buy them.

17 **quod**: *the fact that*. The clause which follows explains in more detail the words **crudelia** and **inhumana**.

27 How to Treat Slaves

(Seneca, *Moral Letters* 47)

libenter ex iis qui a te veniunt cognovi familiariter te cum servis tuis vivere: hoc prudentiam tuam, hoc eruditionem decet. "servi sunt." immo homines. "servi sunt." immo contubernales. "servi sunt." immo humiles amici. "servi sunt." immo conservi, si cogitaveris tantundem in utrosque licere fortunae.

5   itaque rideo istos qui turpe existimant cum servo suo cenare. est ille plus quam capit, et ingenti aviditate onerat distentum ventrem ut maiore opera omnia egerat quam ingessit. at infelicibus servis movere labra ne in hoc quidem, ut loquantur, licet; virga murmur omne compescitur, et ne fortuita quidem verberibus excepta sunt, tussis, sternumenta, singultus; nocte tota ieiuni

10   mutique perstant.

    sic fit ut isti de domino loquantur quibus coram domino loqui non licet. at illi quibus non tantum coram dominis sed cum ipsis erat sermo, parati erant pro domino porrigere cervicem, periculum imminens in caput suum avertere; in conviviis loquebantur, sed in tormentis tacebant. deinde eiusdem arrogantiae

15   proverbium iactatur, totidem hostes esse quot servos: non habemus illos hostes sed facimus.

    alia interim crudelia, inhumana praetereo, quod ne tamquam hominibus

familiariter, on friendly terms
prudentia (*f*), good sense
eruditio (*f*), education
decet (+ *acc.*), is in keeping with
immo, on the contrary, no
contubernalis (*m*), comrade, companion
humilis, humble
conservus (*m*), a fellow-slave
iste, that person
turpis, degrading
ceno (1), to dine
aviditas (*f*), greed
onero (l), to load
distentus, swollen, stuffed full
venter (*m*), belly
opera (*f*), effort, exertion
labrum (*n*), lip
virga (*f*), rod, stick
murmur (*n*), murmur, grumble under one's breath
compesco (3), to curb, repress

verber (*n*), blow
excipio (3), to except, exempt
tussis (*f*), cough
sternumentum (*n*), sneeze
singultus, -us (*m*), hiccup
ieiunus, fasting, not taking food
mutus, silent
persto (l), to continue standing
coram (+ *abl.*), in the presence of, in front of
tantum, only
paratus, ready, prepared
pro (+ *abl.*), on behalf of, in defence of
imminens, imminent, threatening
averto (3), to turn aside, divert
convivium (*n*), banquet, dinner-party
totidem ... quot ..., as many as
inhumanus, inhuman
praetereo, to pass over, say nothing about
tamquam, as if, as though

18   **abutimur**: *we maltreat* really applies only to **sed tamquam iumentis**. With **ne tamquam hominibus quidem** supply **utimur** (*we treat*) which also governs the ablative case.

    vis tu cogitare: *you should reflect*, literally *you want to think*, a colloquial way of issuing a command in Latin. There follow five Accusative and Infinitive clauses, all depending on **cogitare**.

    istum ortum: Supply **esse** (*that man . . . has sprung*).

22   **praecepti mei summa**: *the sum total of my advice.*

    sic . . . quemadmodum: *in the same way as.* (For Correlatives, see LL p. 64.)

    vivas: *you should live.* The present subjunctive expresses a command. (See LL p. 107.)

23   **velis**: *you would wish.*

    bona aetas est: *you are still young*, literally *your age is good.*

24   **nescis**?: *don't you know?*

    Hecuba, the Queen of Troy, was enslaved when the Greeks captured Troy. **King Croesus** lost his mighty empire in Asia Minor when he was defeated in battle by the Persians. **Diogenes'** fame as a philosopher was so great that Alexander the Great went to visit him. Such was Diogenes' arrogance that, when Alexander asked him if there was anything he could do for him, Diogenes asked him to stand aside so that he could enjoy the sunshine! However, while sailing across the Mediterranean, Diogenes was captured by pirates and sold as a slave.

27   **quid ergo**? *what, then, are you saying?*

29   **quemadmodum . . . sic . . .** : *just as . . . so . . . .* (For Correlatives, see LL p. 64.)

30   **empturus**: *when planning to buy* (future participle).

32   **animo**: *in spirit.*

33   **ostende quis non sit**: Supply **servus**.

    alius . . . , alius . . . , alius . . . : *one man . . . , another . . . , another . . . .*

quidem sed tamquam iumentis abutimur. vis tu cogitare istum quem servum tuum vocas ex isdem seminibus ortum eodemque frui caelo, aeque spirare,
20 aeque vivere, aeque mori! tam tu illum videre ingenuum potes quam ille te servum.

haec praecepti mei summa est: sic cum inferiore vivas quemadmodum tecum superiorem velis vivere. "at ego" inquis "nullum habeo dominum." bona aetas est: forsitan habebis. nescis qua aetate Hecuba servire coeperit, qua Croesus,
25 qua Diogenes? vive cum servo clementer, comiter quoque, et in sermonem illum admitte et in consilium et in convictum.

"quid ergo? omnes servos admovebo mensae meae?" non magis quam omnes liberos. non ministeriis illos aestimabo sed moribus: sibi quisque dat mores, ministeria casus assignat. quemadmodum stultus est qui equum
30 empturus non ipsum inspicit sed stratum eius et frenos, sic stultissimus est qui hominem aut ex veste aut ex condicione aestimat.

"servus est." sed fortasse liber animo. "servus est." hoc illi nocebit? ostende quis non sit: alius libidini servit, alius avaritiae, alius ambitioni, omnes spei, omnes timori.

iumentum (*n*), beast of burden
semen (*n*), seed
fruor (3) (+ *abl.*), to enjoy
aeque, equally
spiro (1), to breathe
tam ... quam ..., as much ... as ...
ingenuus, free-born
forsitan, perhaps
servio (4), to be a slave
clementer, gently
comiter, on good terms
consilium (*n*), consultation, decision-making
convictus (*m*), social life

admoveo (2), to move towards
ministerium (*n*), employment, task
aestimo (1), to judge
mores (*m. pl*), character
quisque, each
casus (*m*), fortune, luck
assigno (1), to assign, allot
quemadmodum, how
inspicio (3), to examine
stratum (*n*), saddle
freni (*m. pl*), reins
condicio (*f*), social status
libido (*f*), lust
avaritia (*f*), greed

Points for Discussion

1 In what sense does Seneca regard everyone as slaves (*a*) in his opening paragraph, and (*b*) in his final paragraph?

2 According to Seneca, what sort of heroic actions have been performed by slaves who have been well treated?

3 What well-known Christian precept (Matthew 7.12) corresponds to what Seneca says in lines 22–23?

4 Can you see any practical disadvantages that might have arisen for the Romans if Seneca's attitudes had prevailed? If you had lived in ancient Rome, how do you think you would have handled the master/slave relationship?

Cato and his wife

28 A Guide for Landowners

(M. Porcius Cato, *De Re Rustica* II)

If productivity is low and your bailiff claims he has worked himself to a standstill, but offers as excuses the fact that the slaves have been ill, or that the weather has been bad, or that slaves have run away, or that they have sometimes been commandeered for employment on public works schemes – well, when the bailiff has brought up these and many other excuses, get him back to the question of how he organises his work-programme and manages his workforce.

"You've had bad weather, have you? Well, lots of jobs could have been tackled on wet days, such as washing out wine-casks, mending leaky ones, house-cleaning, moving grain, cleaning out dung and setting up dung-hills, husking corn-seed, splicing ropes and making new ones! The slaves should also be making patchwork caps and smocks for themselves. When they weren't working on the crops, they could have been clearing old ditches, building roads, clearing scrub, digging the garden, clearing the pasture of thistles, tying up twigs in bundles, rooting out thorns, grinding corn and generally tidying-up. Illness among the slaves should also have provided you with an opportunity to cut down on their food rations."

The landowner should check his stock to see if he can put any up for sale. He should sell his oil if it is fetching a good price, and get what he can for his surplus wine and grain. He should sell off old oxen, any sheep not of top quality, old carts, old farm implements, any slaves that are old or sickly; in fact, anything surplus to requirements! The landowner's motto should be "Rake in!" not "Pay out!"

Points for Discussion

1 How does Cato's attitude towards the treatment of slaves differ from the principles advocated by Pliny in "A Good Master" and Seneca in "How to Treat Slaves"? Quote evidence from the three passages to support your answer.

2 Which of these three masters would you have preferred to serve (a) as bailiff (**vilicus**), (b) as an ordinary slave? Give reasons for your answer.

Martial: See Notes on Authors on page 12.
Metre: Elegiac Couplet (See page 257.)

line

1   **Frontŏ and Flaccilla**: It is likely that these were Martial's father and mother. They are already dead, and Martial asks them to look after the little girl's spirit when it reaches the darkness and horrors of the Underworld.

2   **oscula ... deliciasque meas**: *my sweetheart* (literally *kisses*) *and darling*. These words are in apposition to **hanc puellam**.

3   **parvula Erotion**: *poor little Erotion*. The diminutive form of **parva** is used to arouse our sympathy. In English, we use diminutive endings to express smallness (e.g. duck, duckling) and tenderness (e.g. dear, darling). Latin does this also with nouns and adjectives, e.g. **puella** (*girl*) and **puellula** (*a little girl*), **anus** (*an old woman*) and **anicula** (*a poor old woman*), **miser** (*wretched*) and **misellus** (*wretched little*).

  ne horrescat: *so that (she) may not tremble at* – a Purpose Clause.

  umbras: The main meaning is *shadows*, but it also probably hints at the *shades* or *ghosts* of the dead.

4   **Tartarei canis**: *of the dog of Tartarus*. This was the three-headed dog, Cerberus, which stood guard at the entrance to Tartarus (i.e. the Underworld).

5   **impletura fuit**: *she would have completed*.

  sextae frigora brumae: *her sixth winter with all its chills*, literally *the chills of a sixth winter*.

6   **vixisset totidem ni minus illa dies**: *if she had lived just six days more*, literally *if she had not lived the same number of days less*, i.e. the same number as her years. **totidem** means *just as many*.

7   **ludat**: *may she play*. The present subjunctive is used to express a wish (see LL p. 107). Compare **garriat**, *may she chatter* in line 8.

  inter tam veteres patronos: *among such old protectors* – another reference to Martial's parents, who had no doubt kept a kindly watch over her during their lifetime. When a slave was set free in Roman times, his former master became his "patron". Perhaps Martial is suggesting that Erotion has been set free by death, and her relationship with her former masters is now rather different.

9   **non rigidus**: *softly*, literally *not hard*.

  tegat: For this use of the present subjunctive compare **ludat** (line 7) and **garriat** (line 8).

10   **Terra**: *O Earth* – Martial appeals directly to the earth that lies upon her body.

  nec illi gravis fueris: *and don't be heavy upon her*. (Here, **nec** = **et ne**.) **ne** or **nec** with the perfect subjunctive (**fueris**) is a common way of expressing a negative command (see LL p. 108).

  non fuit (gravis) illa tibi: This clause balances the previous clause.

29 Poor Little Erotion

(Martial, *Epigrams* V. 34)

Erotion was a little slave girl who had belonged to Martial or to Martial's father. She had died just before her sixth birthday, and she was buried on Martial's little estate at Nomentum, 15 miles (24km) north-east of Rome.

> hanc tibi, Fronto pater, genetrix Flaccilla, puellam
>   oscula commendo deliciasque meas,
> parvula ne nigras horrescat Erotion umbras
>   oraque Tartarei prodigiosa canis.
> 5 impletura fuit sextae modo frigora brumae,
>   vixisset totidem ni minus illa dies.
> inter tam veteres ludat lasciva patronos
>   et nomen blaeso garriat ore meum.
> mollia non rigidus caespes tegat ossa; nec illi,
> 10   Terra, gravis fueris; non fuit illa tibi.

genetrix (*f*), mother
commendo (1), to entrust
prodigiosus, monstrous
ni = nisi
lascivus, playful, mischievous

blaesus, lisping
mollis, soft, tender
caespes (*m*), turf
tego (3), to cover

Points for Discussion

1 What impression have you formed of Erotion? From the poem, quote and translate Latin words/phrases to support your answer.

2 Translate the last four words of the poem, and explain in your own words the point Martial is making.

3 How does Martial arouse sympathy for the little girl? Quote and translate the relevant words and phrases.

4 Suggest an alternative title for the poem.

Ovid: See Notes on Authors on page 12.
Metre: Hexameter (See page 255.)

line

1 **Creten longumque exsilium**: *his long exile in Crete*, literally *Crete and his long exile*.
(For Hendiadys, see page 259, and for the Greek accusative ending in **-n**, see page 262.)

2 **loci natalis amore**: *by longing for his birthplace*, i.e. he wanted to return to Athens.

3 **licet obstruat**: *although he (Minos) blocks*. In an argument, **licet** (literally *it is allowed*)
is used with the present subjunctive to make an admission – *granted that...* (see
LL p. 109); the speaker (here, Daedalus) then proceeds to counter the argument by
making another suggestion (here introduced by **at certe**, *yet at least*).

5 **omnia**: *everything (else)*.

possideat: Supply **licet** – *although he controls* (see LL p. 109).

aëra: *the air*, or *the sky*. (For this Greek accusative ending, see page 262.)

6 **dixit et**: *he finished speaking and ...* It must be remembered that, in ancient times,
stories such as this would be recited. Certain stock expressions were used to indicate
when one of the characters in the story began to speak (e.g. **inquit** or **ait**) or stopped
speaking (e.g. **dixit** or **dixerat**).

ignotas animum dimittit in artes: *he devised completely new techniques*, literally *he
directed his mind to unknown skills*.

8 **a minima coeptas**: *starting at the smallest*. The feathers were laid out according to size
to produce the tapering shape of the wing.

longam breviore sequente: *the shorter (feathers) lying behind the long(er) ones*.

9 **medias**: Supply **pennas,** *(the feathers) at the middle*. Compare **imas,** *(the feathers) at
the bottom*. The quills were stuck together with wax, and the thread attached further up
the feathers held the wing together.

10 **ita compositas**: Again, understand **pennas** – *when they were arranged in this way*.

11 **ut veras imitetur aves**: *to resemble the wings of real birds*, literally *to imitate true birds*
(Purpose Clause).

12 **sua se tractare pericla**: *that he was handling things that were to bring danger to
himself*, literally *that he was handling his own dangers*. The Accusative and Infinitive
depends on **ignarus**. The contracted form **pericla** is common in poetry.

13 **ore renidenti**: *with a happy smile on his face*, literally *his face shining with joy*.

modo ... modo ...: *at one time ..., at another ....*

quas: This clause refers to **plumas** in line 14.

Myth and Legend

30 Daedalus and Icarus

(Ovid, *Metamorphoses* VIII. 183–235, omitting 191–2)

Daedalus was a skilled craftsman who had been forced to flee from Athens after killing his nephew in a fit of jealousy. Along with his son Icarus, he sought refuge in Crete, which at that time was ruled by King Minos. While there, he designed and built for Minos a maze, the famous labyrinth, which housed the Minotaur – a terrifying monster which was half-man and half-bull.

After the completion of the labyrinth, Minos refused to allow Daedalus and his son to leave Crete. Since Minos controlled the sea with his fleet, it was impossible to escape by sea. Daedalus therefore had to use his ingenuity to devise another means of escape.

Plan of escape

TWINE

WAX

```
     Daedalus interea Creten longumque perosus
     exsilium, tactusque loci natalis amore,
     clausus erat pelago. "terras licet" inquit "et undas
     obstruat, at caelum certe patet; ibimus illac:
 5   omnia possideat, non possidet aëra Minos."
     dixit, et ignotas animum dimittit in artes
     naturamque novat;  nam ponit in ordine pennas
     a minima coeptas, longam breviore sequente.
     tum lino medias et ceris alligat imas,
10   atque ita compositas parvo curvamine flectit
     ut veras imitetur aves.  puer Icarus una
     stabat et, ignarus sua se tractare pericla,
     ore renidenti modo quas vaga moverat aura
     captabat plumas, flavam modo pollice ceram
```

perosus, detesting
exsilium (n), exile
tactus, touched, moved
pelagus, -i (n), sea
pateo (2), to lie open
illac, by that route
novo (1), to change
in ordine, in sequence, one
   after the other
penna (f), feather
linum (n), thread, twine

cera (f), wax, (pl) bits of wax
alligo (1), to bind
parvus, slight, gentle
curvamen (n), curve
flecto (3), to bend
una, together, beside
vagus, wandering
aura (f), breeze
flavus, yellow, golden
pollex, -icis (m), thumb

15   **mollibat = molliebat**.

16   **manus ultima**: *the finishing touches*, literally the final hand

17   **opifex**: *the craftsman*, i.e. Daedalus.

18   **mota in aura**: *in the air which was moved (by the flapping of the wings)*.

19   **instruit et natum**: *he equipped his son also (with wings)*.

    -que links **instruit et natum** and **ait**.

    medio ut limite curras: *to fly on a middle course* – an Indirect Command depending on **moneo** (line 20).

20   **ne** introduces two Purpose clauses, i.e. **ne unda gravet pennas** and (**ne**) **ignis adurat**.

    demissior: *too low*. Compare **celsior**, *too high*.

21   **ignis**: *the heat (of the sun)*.

22   **nec** goes closely with **Boöten** (balanced by **aut Helicen**); and **te** is the object of **iubeo** (line 23). Daedalus warns his son not to steer his course using the constellations as sailors do, but to follow where he (Daedalus) goes.

    Boöten ... Helicen ... Orionis: These are the great constellations. Boötes was "the Bear-keeper" (sometimes called Arcturus), Helice was "the Great Bear" and Orion was "the Hunter". For the accusative ending in **–n**, compare line 1.

24   **me duce**: *with me as your guide*, literally *me being leader*. (For this type of Ablative Absolute, see LL p. 30.) Icarus was to be guided by his father, not the stars.

    carpe viam!: *make your way!*

    praecepta volandi: *instructions for flying*. (For the Gerund, see LL p. 60.)

26   **inter opus monitusque**: *as he worked and gave his warnings*, literally *amid the work and warnings*.

    maduere = maduerunt: *became wet*. (Cf. **tremuere = tremuerunt** in line 27.)

    seniles (*belonging to an old man*) and **patriae** (*belonging to a father*) both refer to Daedalus.

28   **non iterum repetenda**: *never again to be repeated*. The phrase agrees with **oscula**.

    suo agrees with **nato** (line 27).

29   **velut ales**: *just like a bird*; **ales** is the antecedent of **quae** in the next line.

    comiti timet: *feared for his companion*.

    ab alto is to be taken with **nido** in line 30.

30   **in aëra**: *into the air*. (Cf. line 5.)

31   **hortatur**: *he (Daedalus) urged*.

    damnosas erudit artes: *he taught (him) skills that would bring about his death*.

32   **alas**: Take with both **suas** and **nati**.

15 mollibat, lusuque suo mirabile patris
    impediebat opus. postquam manus ultima coepto
    imposita est, geminas opifex libravit in alas
    ipse suum corpus, motaque pependit in aura.

Final instructions

    instruit et natum, "medio"que "ut limite curras,
20 Icare," ait "moneo ne, si demissior ibis,
    unda gravet pennas, si celsior, ignis adurat.
    inter utrumque vola! nec te spectare Boöten
    aut Helicen iubeo strictumque Orionis ensem:
    me duce carpe viam!" pariter praecepta volandi
25 tradit et ignotas umeris accommodat alas.
    inter opus monitusque genae maduere seniles,
    et patriae tremuere manus. dedit oscula nato
    non iterum repetenda suo, pennisque levatus
    ante volat comitique timet, velut ales, ab alto
30 quae teneram prolem produxit in aëra nido,
    hortaturque sequi, damnosasque erudit artes,
    et movet ipse suas et nati respicit alas.

mollio (4), to soften
lusus, -us (*m*), play
mirabilis, wonderful
coeptum (*n*), task, undertaking
impono (3), to put, apply
geminus, twin, two
libro (1), to balance, poise, swing
ala (*f*), wing
pendeo (2), **pependi**, to hang, hover
ait, he says, said
gravo (1), to weigh down
aduro (3), to burn, scorch
volo (1), to fly
stringo (3), to draw (a sword)
ensis (*m*), sword

pariter, at the same time
umerus (*m*), shoulder
accommodo (1), to fit on, attach
monitus, -us (*m*), warning
gena (*f*), cheek
tremo (3), to tremble
osculum (*n*), kiss
levatus, supported, raised up
ante, in front
tener, tender
proles (*f*), offspring, fledgling
produco (3), to lead forth
nidus (*m*), nest
respicio (3), to look back at

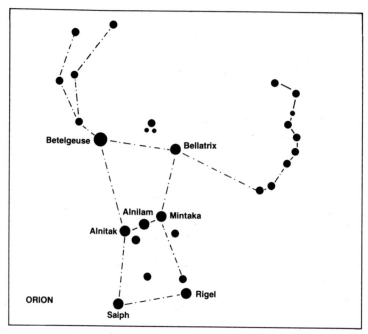

The Constellation Orion

33 **hos**: *them*, referring to Daedalus and Icarus. This is the object of **vidit et obstipuit** (line 35).

aliquis dum captat pisces: *someone while fishing.*

tremula harundine: *with quivering rod.*

34 **innixus**: *leaning on.* The ablatives **baculo** and **stiva** both depend on **innixus**.

35 **quique aethera carpere possent**: *and, since they were able to fly through the air.* (For Causal **qui**, see LL p. 103.) Note that **-que** links **credidit** to **vidit et obstipuit**.

36 **esse deos**: Supply **eos** as the antecedent of **qui** (line 35).

Iunonia laeva parte Samos: *Samos, sacred to Juno, (was) on the left side.* Samos was the birthplace of Juno and one of her most famous temples was situated there. There follows a list of four more islands in the Aegean Sea past which Ovid says Daedalus and Icarus flew. The naming of places was a convention used by poets to lend local colour, regardless of its geographical accuracy (see map). Samos, Delos, Paros, Lebinthos and Calymne (lines 37–38) are all Greek nominatives.

38 **dextra**: *on the right side.*

fecunda melle: *rich in honey*; **fecunda** is nominative case agreeing with **Calymne**.

40 **caeli cupidine tactus**: *tempted by the lure of the open sky*, literally *moved by longing for the sky.*

41 **altius**: *too high.*

It all goes wrong

hos aliquis tremula dum captat harundine pisces
aut pastor baculo stivave innixus arator
35 vidit et obstipuit, quique aethera carpere possent
credidit esse deos. et iam Iunonia laeva
parte Samos (fuerant Delosque Parosque relictae),
dextra Lebinthos erat fecundaque melle Calymne,
cum puer audaci coepit gaudere volatu
40 deseruitque ducem, caelique cupidine tactus
altius egit iter. rapidi vicinia solis

pastor (*m*), shepherd
baculum (*n*), stick, crook
stiva (*f*), plough-handle
-ve, or
arator (*m*), ploughman
obstipesco (3), **-stipui**, to be amazed

mel, mellis (*n*), honey
gaudeo (2) (+ *abl.*), to enjoy, delight in
volatus, -us (*m*), flight
iter agere, to steer a course
vicinia (*f*), nearness
rapidus, fierce, scorching

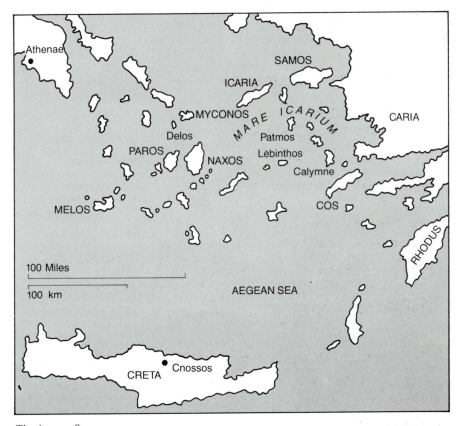

The Aegean Sea

42 **pennarum vincula**: *which bound the feathers together*, literally *the bonds of the feathers*. The phrase is in apposition to **ceras**.

43 **nudos lacertos**: This does not mean *bare arms*, but *arms that were now bare* (because the wings had fallen away). The position of **nudos** is very emphatic.

44 **remigio carens**: *lacking the driving-power (of his wings)*, literally *lacking the oarage (of his wings)*. He was propelled by his wings as a boat is by its oars.

   non ullas percipit auras: *he couldn't get any purchase on the air*, literally *he could not catch any air*.

45 **ora excipiuntur aqua**: *his mouth was engulfed by the water*. (For Poetic Plural, see page 262.)

   caerulea (*dark blue*): Only scansion here shows that **caerulea** is ablative agreeing with **aqua** (line 46), and *not* nominative agreeing with **ora** (though *blue lips* would have made sense since the boy had drowned). (See Introduction to Latin Metres on p. 253.)

   patrium clamantia nomen: *shouting "Father!"*, literally *the name of father*. The participle **clamantia** is nominative agreeing with **ora**.

46 **traxit**: *derived*. The Icarian Sea is part of the Aegean Sea, which lies in the eastern Mediterranean off the coast of modern Turkey, between the islands of Cos and Samos.

48 **qua regione**: *where*, literally *in what area*.

49 **dicebat**: Note how, after using the perfect tense (**dixit**) in lines 47–48, Ovid changes here to the imperfect tense – *he kept shouting "Icarus!"*. Then he switches back to the perfect tense (**aspexit**) to indicate that *he (suddenly) noticed* the feathers floating on the water.

50 **corpus sepulcro condidit**: Ovid does not say how Daedalus recovered the body from the sea.

51 **tellus a nomine dicta sepulti**: *the island (Icaria) was called after (Icarus) who was buried there*, literally *the land was called from the name of the buried person*.

Daedalus and Icarus, an antique bas-relief, Villa Albani, Rome

mollit odoratas, pennarum vincula, ceras:
tabuerant cerae; nudos quatit ille lacertos
remigioque carens non ullas percipit auras,
45 oraque caerulea patrium clamantia nomen
excipiuntur aqua, quae nomen traxit ab illo.
at pater infelix, nec iam pater, "Icare," dixit,
"Icare," dixit "ubi es? qua te regione requiram?
Icare" dicebat: pennas aspexit in undis,
50 devovitque suas artes, corpusque sepulcro
condidit, et tellus a nomine dicta sepulti.

odoratus, sweet-smelling, fragrant
tabesco (3), **tabui**, to melt
quatio (3), to shake, flap
requiro (3), to look for
aspicio (3), **-exi, -ectum**, to catch sight of,
  notice

devoveo (2), to curse
sepulcrum (*n*), tomb
condo (3), to bury
tellus (*f*), land

Points for Discussion

1 Suggest two interpretations of the words **naturam novat** (line 7).

2 Study the bas-relief illustration along with lines 6–16. Do you think the artist has been successful in illustrating this passage? Give reasons for your answer.

3 Ovid mentions three eye-witnesses of the flight of these first "airmen". What do you think he aims to achieve by this, and why does he choose people engaged in the particular activities mentioned in lines 33–35?

4 What explanation did the three witnesses give of the strange sight they saw in the sky (lines 35–36)? What sorts of explanation do you think we might give if we experienced some equally abnormal phenomenon today, such as a ghost or UFO? In what ways are our reactions likely to be similar to, or different from, those of people in ancient times?

5 Study the map of the Aegean Sea and trace the route Daedalus and Icarus are supposed to have taken (lines 36–38). How accurate do you think Ovid's description is?

6 What prompted Icarus to steer *too high a course* (**altius egit iter**, line 41)?

7 Explain the apparent contradiction in line 47: **pater . . . nec iam pater**.

8 "The value of this passage lies, not so much in the tale itself, as in the poet's shrewd understanding of human nature." Can you find evidence to support this claim in Ovid's portrayal of (*a*) Icarus and (*b*) Daedalus?

Ovid: See Notes on Authors on page 12.
Metre: Hexameter (See page 255.)

line

1   **dixerat**: *he finished speaking.* In ancient times, poetry was usually recited to an audience, not read silently from a book. So that the audience might know when someone had finished speaking, poets used certain words such as **dixerat**, which acted as "markers".

3   **nec tu meus esse negari dignus es**: *you deserve to be recognised as my son*, literally *and you are worthy not to be denied to be mine.*

4   **veros edidit ortus**: *told you the truth about your birth*, literally *gave out true origins.* (See page 262 for Poetic Plural.)

5   **quoque minus dubites**: a Purpose clause introduced by **quo** because it contains a comparative adverb (**minus**) – *to set your mind at rest*, literally *and so that you may have less doubt.*

       quodvis munus: *whatever gift you like.*

       ut illud feras: another Purpose clause – *so that you may take it away.* Apollo seems to have assumed that Phaëthon would choose a gift which he could actually carry away with him.

6   **testis adesto!** *be a witness!*

7   **dis iuranda palus**: *O pool that the gods must swear by*, literally *"O pool (which) must be sworn by the gods."* (For Dative of Agent used with Gerundives, see LL p. 62.) **palus** is vocative case, and the words are addressed to the River Styx which flowed round the Underworld. The most solemn oath that the gods and goddesses could take was to swear by the River Styx. If any of them broke the oath, they were deprived of ambrosia and nectar (the food and drink of the gods) for one year, and for the following nine years they had to keep apart from the other deities.

       incognita: *unknown*, used because Apollo's rays never penetrated the darkness of the Underworld.

       nostris: *my.* (See page 262 for Poetic Plural.)

8   **vix bene**: Here, **bene** merely emphasises **vix** – *only just* or *little more than*; and, to add even more emphasis, no conjunction (such as "when") links it to the next clause.

       rogat: The Historic Present is used to tell the story more vividly. Throughout the passage, Ovid frequently alternates between past tenses and the Historic Present.

       ille indicates the change of subject and refers to Phaëthon.

9   **in diem**: *for a day.*

       ius et moderamen: *permission to drive*, literally *the right and control.* (See page 259 for Hendiadys.)

10   **paenituit iurasse patrem**: *the father regretted having bound himself by his oath*, literally *to have sworn the oath made the father sorry* (**iurasse = iuravisse**). The abruptness of the sentence emphasises the sudden realisation of his mistake.

31 Phaëthon

(Ovid, *Metamorphoses* II, lines 40–332 – abridged)

Phaëthon was the son of Clymene and the Sun-god, Phoebus Apollo. Phaëthon was a vain and boastful youth and, one day, when one of his friends challenged his claim to be Apollo's son, he decided to ask his mother for proof. She suggested that he go to Apollo and ask him in person. So the boy travelled far into the East until he came to the splendid palace of the Sun and asked Apollo if he really was his father. Apollo welcomed Phaëthon and, to clear away any doubts Phaëthon had about his parentage, offered to give him any gift he cared to request.

A foolhardy request

dixerat. at genitor circum caput omne micantes
deposuit radios, propiusque accedere iussit,
amplexuque dato, "nec tu meus esse negari
dignus es, et Clymene veros" ait "edidit ortus.
5   quoque minus dubites, quodvis pete munus, ut illud
me tribuente feras. promissis testis adesto,
dis iuranda palus, oculis incognita nostris!"
vix bene desierat, currus rogat ille paternos
inque diem alipedum ius et moderamen equorum.
10 paenituit iurasse patrem. qui terque quaterque

The sun-god driving his chariot – detail on a drinking bowl in the British Museum

genitor (*m*), father	**promissum** (*n*), promise
mico (1), to gleam, shine	**incognitus**, unknown
radius (*m*), ray	**desino** (3), **-sii**, to cease
propius, nearer	**currus, -us** (*m*), chariot
accedo (3), to come to, approach	**paternus**, belonging to a father
amplexus (*m*), embrace	**alipes, -pedis**, winged
ait, he said	**ter**, three times
tribuo (3), to grant, give	**quater**, four times

113

11 **temeraria vox mea facta tua (voce) est**: *your request has shown how rash my promise was*, literally *my words* (**vox**) *have been made rash by your* (*words*).

12 **utinam liceret**: *would that it were possible* (literally *permitted*). (For the imperfect subjunctive used in Wishes, see LL p. 108.) Breaking promises was not only morally unacceptable but liable to bring retribution upon the culprit. **dare** here means *to fulfil* or *keep* a promise.

13 **solum hoc tibi negarem**: *this is the only thing I would (want to) deny you*.

15 **magna petis munera**: *it is a big favour you are asking*, literally *you are asking for big gifts*. With **munera** goes not only the adjective **magna** but also the relative clause beginning with **et quae** (*and one which*). Translate **et quae non conveniant** as *and quite unsuited*, literally *and such as does not suit*. (For Generic Subjunctive, see LL p. 103; for Poetic Plural, see page 262.)

Phaëthon is pronounced in Latin as three syllables (Pha-e-thon), and the "Ph" is not pronounced like an "f", but as a "p" with a breath after it, as in "cup-hook". Similarly, "-th-" is pronounced as a "t" with a breath after it, as in "coat-hanger."

17 **(id) quod optas**: *what you ask*.

18 **finierat**: Compare line 1 for this way of marking the end of direct speech.

ille again indicates the change of subject. (Compare line 8.)

19 **cupidine currus**: *with a desire to drive the chariot*, literally *with longing for the chariot*.

Note how the double use of alliteration (**propositum premit** and **cupidine currus**) tends to emphasise how persistent the boy was. (See page 259 for Alliteration.)

20 **qua licuit cunctatus**: *having delayed as much as he could*.

21 **Vulcania munera** (*the gift of Vulcan*) is used in apposition to **altos currus**. Vulcan was the craftsman of the gods, and it was he who had made the chariot of the Sun.

22 **ille**: Compare lines 8 and 18.

23 **super**: *on high*, indicating his position above the horses and perhaps also suggesting the pride and elation he felt in being the driver of such a chariot.

datas: *which had been handed over to him*.

24 **invito**: *reluctant*. His father feared what might happen.

25 **Pȳrŏïs, Eōūs, Aëthon** and **Phlegon** were the names of the four horses which pulled the Sun-god's chariot.

27 **repagula**: *the barriers*, referring to the stall or enclosure in which they were kept when they had completed their journey across the sky.

concutiens illustre caput "temeraria" dixit
"vox mea facta tua est. utinam promissa liceret
non dare! confiteor, solum hoc tibi, nate, negarem.
dissuadere licet. non est tua tuta voluntas.
15 magna petis, Phaëthon, et quae nec viribus istis
munera conveniant nec tam puerilibus annis.
sors tua mortalis. non est mortale quod optas."
finierat monitus. dictis tamen ille repugnat,
propositumque premit flagratque cupidine currus.
20 ergo qua licuit genitor cunctatus ad altos
deducit iuvenem, Vulcania munera, currus.

The horses break free

occupat ille levem iuvenali corpore currum
statque super manibusque datas contingere habenas
gaudet et invito grates agit inde parenti.
25 interea volucres Pyroïs et Eous et Aëthon,
Solis equi, quartusque Phlegon hinnitibus auras
flammiferis implent pedibusque repagula pulsant.

concutio (3), to shake
illustris, bright, shining
confiteor (2), to confess
natus (*m*), son
dissuadeo (2), to dissuade,
  advise against
voluntas (*f*), wish, request
nec...nec..., neither...nor...
iste, that (of yours)
convenio (4) (+ *dat.*), to suit
puerilis, boyish, youthful
sors (*f*), lot, fate, destiny
finio (4), to finish, end
monitus, -us (*m*), warning
dictum (*n*), word
repugno (1) (+ *dat.*), to rebel
  against, reject

propositum (*n*), proposal
premo (3), to press for, urge
flagro (1), to burn, to be on fire
ergo, therefore
deduco (3), to escort, accompany
occupo (1), to jump into
iuvenalis, youthful
contingo (3), to handle
habenae (*f. pl*), reins
grates agere (+ *dat.*), to thank
inde, then
volucer, swift-flying, winged
hinnitus (*m*), neighing, whinnying
aura (*f*), breeze, air
flammifer, flame-bearing, fiery
impleo (2), to fill
pulso (1), to beat, kick against

28 **quae**: *them*, referring to **repagula** in the previous sentence.

Tethys was a sea-goddess who was the mother of Clymene; she was therefore the grandmother of Phaëthon. Why the involvement of a sea-goddess? Because the sun appeared to set in the sea at the end of the day and emerge from it at dawn; and it was the duty of Tethys, as wife of Oceanus, to dispatch and receive the horses daily.

29 **facta est immensi copia caeli**: *the opportunity (to drive through) the vast heavens was offered him*, i.e. *the vast expanse of heaven lay open before him*.

30 **corripuere** (= **corripuerunt**) **viam**: *they (the horses) surged forward*, literally *they seized the way*. Note how the sound of this line, which contains five dactyls, depicts the galloping of the horses, whereas the opening spondees of the next line suggest how they buffeted aside the momentary resistance of the clouds.

per aëra: *through the air*. (See page 262 for Greek accusatives.) Note that **aëra** has three syllables: a-er-a.

32 **ortos isdem de partibus Euros**: *the East winds which had risen in the same place (as the Sun's chariot)*.

33 **nec quod cognoscere possent**: *and not such as (they) could recognise*. From the weight pressing down on the yoke, the horses sensed there was something different. Gods and goddesses were thought to be larger and heavier than human beings, and Phaëthon was a light-weight youth. (For Generic Subjunctive, see LL p. 103.)

35 **utque**: *and just as*. **ut** introduces a simile in which the chariot is likened to unladen ships being tossed about on the sea. (For Simile, see p. 260.)

iusto sine pondere: *when they are not fully laden*, literally *without their normal weight*. The ships are designed to carry a full cargo, not to go empty.

36 **nimia levitate**: *because they are too light*, literally *from* (i.e. as a result of) *their too great lightness*.

37 **sic** balances **ut** in line 35 and marks the return to the description of how the chariot is faring.

onere adsueto vacuus: *without its normal load*, literally *empty of its accustomed load*.

dat in aëra saltus: *leapt into the air*, literally *gave leaps into the air*. The subject of **dat** is **currus** (line 38). For the Greek accusative form **aëra**, compare line 30.

38 **inani**: Supply **currui**.

39 **quod**: a Linking Relative, referring to what is said in the previous sentence. (For Linking **qui**, see LL p. 26.)

sensere = **senserunt**: *they realised*. (Cf. **intremuere** in line 45.)

tritum spatium: *the well-worn track*, i.e. their normal course.

40 **quo prius ordine**: *in their usual course*. **quo prius** (with **currebant** understood) is a relative clause describing **ordine** – literally *in the course in which they previously (ran)*.

quae postquam Tethys, fatorum ignara nepotis,
reppulit et facta est immensi copia caeli,
30   corripuere viam pedibusque per aëra motis
obstantes scindunt nebulas pennisque levati
praetereunt ortos isdem de partibus Euros.
sed leve pondus erat nec quod cognoscere possent
Solis equi, solitaque iugum gravitate carebat;
35   utque labant curvae iusto sine pondere naves
perque mare instabiles nimia levitate feruntur,
sic onere adsueto vacuus dat in aëra saltus
succutiturque alte similisque est currus inani.
quod simulac sensere, ruunt tritumque relinquunt
40   quadriiugi spatium nec quo prius ordine currunt.

fata (*n.pl*)), fate, destiny
nepos, -otis (*m*), grandson
repello (3), to pull back, pull aside
copia (*f*), opportunity
obsto (l) (*+ dat.*), to stand in the
    way of, obstruct
scindo (3), to cut
nebula (*f*), cloud
penna (*f*), wing
levo (l), to raise, support
praetereo, to outstrip, speed past
pondus (*n*), weight
solitus, usual

iugum (*n*), yoke
gravitas (*f*), weight
careo (2) (*+ abl.*), to lack
labo (l), to toss about
curvus, curved
instabilis, unsteady
vacuus (*+ abl.*), empty of, free from
succutio (4), to fling aloft,
    toss up
alte, high, high up
inanis, empty
simulac, as soon as
quadriiugi (*m.pl*), four-horse team

41 **qua**, meaning *how* in line 41 and *where* in line 42, introduces two Indirect Questions depending on **nec scit**. The first of these (**qua flectat**) is a Deliberative Question (see LL p. 38): *how he is to control* or *how to handle.*

42 **nec, si sciat, imperet illis**: *and he could not have controlled them even if he had known.* Ovid continues the use of vivid present tenses in this Conditional sentence as if the action were actually happening at that moment. (See LL p. 54.)

44 **penitus penitusque**: *far, far down below.* The repetition of **penitus** and the alliterative use of the "p" sound (**Phaëthon, penitus, palluit**) produce an effect of heightening panic and gasping for breath. See line 15 for the pronunciation of Phaëthon.

46 **suntque oculis tenebrae per tantum lumen obortae**: *and he was dazzled by the strong light*, literally *and darkness came over* (**sunt obortae**) *his eyes because of the so strong light.*

47 **mallet numquam tetigisse**: *he wished he had never touched*, literally *he would have preferred never to have touched.*

48 **cognosse (= cognovisse) genus piget**: *he was sorry he had found out who his father was*, literally *it grieved (him) to have discovered his parentage.* (For Impersonal Verbs, see LL p. 58.)

   valuisse rogando: *having got his own way*, literally *to have prevailed by asking.* (For Gerund, see LL p. 60.)

49 **Meropis dici**: *to be called (the son) of Merops.* Merops was the husband of Clymene and, until shortly before this incident, had been thought by Phaëthon to be his father.

   ita fertur, ut: *was carried along just like . . . .* As in line 35, **ut** introduces a simile.

50 **pinus cui victa remisit frena suus rector**: *a ship whose rudder its helmsman has let go when it is taken over (by the force of the wind).* Normally, **frenum** is used of the "bridle" of a horse; here, the plural (**frena**) applies to the ropes which steer the rudder. The wind wins the battle of strength with the helmsman to control these ropes. Note that **pinus** is also the antecedent of **quam** in line 51.

52 **quid faciat?**: *what was he (Phaëthon) to do?* (Compare line 41 for Deliberative Question.)

   multum caeli: *much of the sky.* Supply **est** with **relictum**.

53 **animo metitur utrumque**: *mentally he measured both*, i.e. the part of the course he had already covered and what still lay before him.

54 **quos**: The antecedent of this Relative clause is **occasus**, *the West*, (literally *the settings* (*of the Sun*) (line 55), i.e. where the sun sets.

   illi fatum non est: *it was not his destiny.*

56 **quid agat**: *what to do* – an Indirect Deliberative Question depending on **ignarus**, *not knowing.* (Compare lines 41 and 52.)

58 **in vario caelo**: *in the ever-changing sky.*

59 **simulacra ferarum**: *images of beasts*, referring to the names given to the constellations such as the Bear, the Bull, the Lion and the Scorpion.

Panic sets in

ipse pavet nec qua commissas flectat habenas
nec scit qua sit iter, nec, si sciat, imperet illis.
ut vero summo despexit ab aethere terras
infelix Phaëthon penitus penitusque patentes,
45   palluit et subito genua intremuere timore,
suntque oculis tenebrae per tantum lumen obortae.
et iam mallet equos numquam tetigisse paternos,
iam cognosse genus piget et valuisse rogando.
iam Meropis dici cupiens ita fertur, ut acta
50   praecipiti pinus borea, cui victa remisit
frena suus rector, quam dis votisque reliquit.
quid faciat? multum caeli post terga relictum,
ante oculos plus est: animo metitur utrumque;
et modo, quos illi fatum contingere non est,
55   prospicit occasus, interdum respicit ortus.
quidque agat ignarus stupet et nec frena remittit
nec retinere valet nec nomina novit equorum.
sparsa quoque in vario passim miracula caelo
vastarumque videt trepidus simulacra ferarum.

paveo (2), to be afraid
committo (3), to entrust
despicio (3), to look down at
aether (*m*), heaven
pateo (2), to lie open, be revealed
palleo (2), to turn pale
subitus, sudden
genu (*n*), knee
intremo (3), to tremble, shake
praeceps, -cipitis, rushing, headlong
pinus (*f*), pine tree, ship (made of pine)
boreas (*m*), North Wind
votum (*n*), prayer
modo, sometimes

contingo (3), to touch, reach
prospicio (3), to look ahead
occasus, -us (*m*), the west
interdum, sometimes
respicio (3), to look back
ortus, -us (*m*), the East
stupeo (2), to be dazed, be stunned
valeo (2), to be able
novi (*perf.*), I know
sparsus, scattered
passim, everywhere, on all sides
miraculum (*n*), marvel
vastus, huge
trepidus, fearful

60 **mentis inops**: *totally at a loss about what to do*, literally *destitute of mind*.

61 **quae**: Linking Relative referring to **lora** in line 60. (See LL p. 26.)

summum tetigere iacentia tergum: *touched the hide of* (**summum** = *the surface of*) *their backs and lay (loosely) there.* Note again the perfect form ending in **-ere** used instead of **-erunt**.

62 **nullo inhibente**: an Ablative Absolute – *since no one was holding (them) back.*

63 **quaque impetus egit, hac sine lege ruunt**: *and rushed out of control* (**sine lege**) *wherever their momentum took them.* **qua** (*where*) and **hac** (*there*) are Correlatives (see LL pp. 63–4).

64 **alto sub aethere**: *under the vault of heaven.*

fixis stellis: According to ancient theories of the universe, the earth was surrounded by a series of spheres. The highest of these was heaven, and beneath this was a sphere in which the constellations were set . The Moon (**Luna**) was in the sphere nearest to the earth (see line 68), and the Sun was between that and the stars.

65 **per avia**: *through pathless regions.*

67 **spatio terrae propiore**: *along a track nearer to the earth.*

68 **suis**: *than her own (horses).* See the note on line 64. Diana, the sister of Apollo, was goddess of the Moon.

70 **ut quaeque altissima, tellus**: *all the highest parts of the earth*, literally *the earth, according as each (part is) highest.*

71 **fissa agit rimas**: *it split and opened up cracks.*

72 **arbor**: *trees* – a singular with plural meaning – quite common in poetry. (See page 262.)

74 **parva queror**: *these are minor things (happenings) which I bemoan*, i.e. minor when compared with what he is about to describe.

79 **auras ore trahit**: *he gulped in air.*

Global catastrophe

60   mentis inops gelida formidine lora remisit;
    quae postquam summum tetigere iacentia tergum,
    exspatiantur equi nulloque inhibente per auras
    ignotae regionis eunt, quaque impetus egit,
    hac sine lege ruunt altoque sub aethere fixis
65   incursant stellis rapiuntque per avia currum.
    et modo summa petunt, modo per declive viasque
    praecipites spatio terrae propiore feruntur,
    inferiusque suis fraternos currere Luna
    admiratur equos, ambustaque nubila fumant.
70   corripitur flammis, ut quaeque altissima, tellus
    fissaque agit rimas et sucis aret ademptis;
    pabula canescunt, cum frondibus uritur arbor,
    materiamque suo praebet seges arida damno.
    parva queror: magnae pereunt cum moenibus urbes,
75   cumque suis totas populis incendia gentes
    in cinerem vertunt; silvae cum montibus ardent.

No escape for Phaëthon

    tum vero Phaëthon cunctis e partibus orbem
    aspicit accensum nec tantos sustinet aestus;
    ferventesque auras velut e fornace profunda
80   ore trahit, currusque suos candescere sentit;

gelidus, cold, chill
formido (*f*), fear
lora (*n.pl*), reins
exspatior (1), to wander from the course
fixus, set, placed
incurso (1) (+ *dat.*), to rush among
stella, -ae (*f*), constellation
rapio (3), to carry along violently
modo ... modo ..., now ..., now ...
declive (*n*), slope
inferius, lower
fraternus, belonging to a brother
admiror (1), to be amazed at
ambustus, scorched
nubila (*n.pl*), clouds
fumo (1), to smoke, steam
corripio (3), to seize
quaeque, *feminine of* **quisque**
tellus (*f*), the earth
fissus, split, cracked

sucus (*m*), juice, moisture
areo (2), to be dry
adimo (3), to take away
pabulum (*n*), grass, crop
canesco (3), to grow white
frons, -ndis (*f*), leaf
uro (3), to burn
materia (*f*), fuel
seges (*f*), crop
damnum (*n*), destruction
pars (*f*), part, side
orbis (*m*), world
aspicio (3), to behold, look at
accendo (3), to set on fire
sustineo (2), to endure, stand
aestus, -us (*m*), heat
ferveo (2), to be hot, boil
velut, as if, just like
fornax (*f*), furnace
profundus, deep
candesco (3), to begin to glow

*Jupiter holding a thunderbolt
in his left hand, with the eagle
which was sacred to him.*

83   **quo eat** and **ubi sit** are Indirect Questions depending on **nescit** (line 84).

85   **credunt:** *they (i.e. people) believe.*

      in corpora summa: *into the surface of their bodies*, i.e. their skins. (Cf. line 61.)

86   **Aethiopum populos traxisse:** *that the tribes of Ethiopians acquired* – an Accusative and Infinitive depending on **credunt**.

89   **ipsum** refers to Apollo.

91   **interitura:** Supply **esse**. Together with **omnia**, these words form an Accusative and Infinitive depending on **testatus**.

      summam arcem: *the highest point.*

      arduus: *towering above all* or *drawing himself up to his full height.*

93   **vibrata fulmina iactat:** *he brandished and hurled his thunderbolts.*

94   **quas:** The antecedent is **nubes**.

et neque iam cineres eiectatamque favillam
ferre potest, calidoque involvitur undique fumo;
quoque eat, aut ubi sit, picea caligine tectus
nescit, et arbitrio volucrum raptatur equorum.
85 sanguine tunc credunt in corpora summa vocato
Aethiopum populos nigrum traxisse colorem.
tum facta est Libye raptis umoribus aestu
arida.

Jupiter intervenes

at pater omnipotens, superos testatus et ipsum,
90 qui dederat currus, nisi opem ferat, omnia fato
interitura gravi, summam petit arduus arcem,
unde solet nubes latis inducere terris,
unde movet tonitrus vibrataque fulmina iactat.
sed neque quas posset terris inducere, nubes

eiecto (1), to throw out
favilla (*f*), ash
calidus, warm
involvo (3), to wrap, envelop
fumus (*m*), smoke
piceus, pitch-black
caligo (*f*), darkness
tectus, covered
arbitrium (*n*), will, whim
rapto (1), to sweep along
tunc, then
color (*m*), colour

Libye (*f*), Libya
umor (*m*), moisture
aridus, dry, parched
omnipotens, all-powerful
superi (*m.pl*), the gods
testor (l), to call to witness
opem ferre, to bring help
intereo, -ire, to be destroyed, perish
induco (3), to spread over
tonitrus, -us (*m*), thunder
neque...nec..., neither...nor...

95 **quos demitteret**: *which he could send down*. (For the relative used in Purpose clauses, see LL p. 44.)

96 **libratum**: *balanced*, just as one would balance a spear or javelin when preparing to throw it.

dextra ab aure: *beside his right ear*.

97 **pariter**: *at one and the same time*.

anima rotisque expulit: *parted him from his life and his chariot*. This is an example of the figure of speech called Zeugma, in which two different types of expression are incongruously linked by the same verb to produce a comic effect. For example, "She went home in a flood of tears and a taxi", "She broke the valuable vase and her mother's heart" or "He took his hat and his leave."

100 **abruptaque lora relinquunt**: *bursting free from the reins, they left them far behind*. **lora** is the direct object of **relinquunt**.

101 **illic ... illic ... in hac parte**: literally *there... there ... in this place*. What is needed is an expression which indicates that the debris flew in all directions, e.g. *in one place ... in another place ... in yet another place*.

temone revulsus axis: *the axle which had been torn from the pole*. The axle was fixed to the chariot. The wheels were attached to the ends of the axle, and the pole (**temo**) which passed between the horses, went into a socket in the middle of it.

105 **longo per aëra tractu fertur**: *was swept across the sky trailing (fire) far behind him*, literally *was carried across the sky in a long course*.

106 **ut** introduces a simile. (Cf. lines 35 and 49.)

107 **potuit cecidisse videri**: *gave the impression of having fallen*, literally *was able to seem to have fallen*.

108 **quem** refers to Phaëthon. (For Linking Relative, see LL p. 26.)

procul a patria diverso orbe: *far from his homeland in a remote region*. Eridanus was a Greek name for the River Po, in northern Italy, whereas Apollo's palace was in the East.

109 **fumantia ora**: *smoke-blackened face*. (**ora** is a Poetic Plural – see page 262.)

110 **Naïdes Hesperiae**: *the water-nymphs of the western land*, i.e. of Italy.

trifida fumantia flamma: *still smouldering from the three-forked flame (of the thunderbolt)*.

111 **corpora**: For Poetic Plural, see page 262.

112 **hic situs est**: *here lies*, a common opening to epitaphs on Roman tombs.

113 **si**: The use of **tamen** in the main clause indicates that **si** means *even if* or *even although*.

magnis excidit ausis: *he failed in a great enterprise*, literally *he fell out of a great deed of daring*.

95 tunc habuit, nec quos caelo demitteret, imbres.
   intonat et dextra libratum fulmen ab aure
   misit in aurigam pariterque animaque rotisque
   expulit, et saevis compescuit ignibus ignes.
   consternantur equi et saltu in contraria facto,
100 colla iugo eripiunt abruptaque lora relinquunt.
   illic frena iacent, illic temone revulsus
   axis, in hac radii fractarum parte rotarum,
   sparsaque sunt late laceri vestigia currus.
   at Phaëthon, rutilos flamma populante capillos,
105 volvitur in praeceps longoque per aëra tractu
   fertur, ut interdum de caelo stella sereno,
   etsi non cecidit, potuit cecidisse videri.
   quem procul a patria diverso maximus orbe
   excipit Eridanus, fumantiaque abluit ora.

Mourning for Phaëthon

110 Naïdes Hesperiae trifida fumantia flamma
   corpora dant tumulo, signant quoque carmine saxum:
   "hic situs est Phaëthon, currus auriga paterni;
   quem si non tenuit, magnis tamen excidit ausis."

imber (*m*), rain
intono (1), to thunder
auris (*f*), ear
auriga (*m*), charioteer
rota (*f*), wheel
compesco (3), to quench, curb,
   hold in check
consterno (1), to terrify
saltus (*m*), leap
in contraria, in opposite directions
collum (*n*), neck
eripio (3), to wrench from
frenum (*n*), bridle, bit
radius (*m*), spoke
fractus, broken

spargo (3), to scatter
late, widely
lacer, mangled, shattered
vestigia (*n.pl*), traces, remains
rutilus, red
populor (1), to ravage, destroy
capilli (*m.pl*), hair
volvo (3), to roll, tumble
in praeceps, headlong
serenus, clear
excipio (3), to receive
abluo (3), to wash
tumulus (*m*), mound, grave
signo (1), to mark
teneo (2), to hold, control

114 **luctu aegro**: *sick with grief*, literally *with sick grief*. The adjective **aeger** has been transferred from Apollo to his grief. (For Transferred Epithet, see page 261.)

116 **isse = ivisse**, *went by*.

The lines of *Metamorphoses* II which make up this selection are: 40–56, 103–106, 150–170, 178–194, 200–216, 227–238 and 304–332.

Points for Discussion

1 Explain in your own words what Apollo is saying in line 17.

2 Study lines 27, 31 and 62 and state, in each case, what effects you think Ovid is trying to produce by the sound and the rhythm of the words.

3 Discuss the significance of the words **iam Meropis dici cupiens** in line 49. What lesson had Phaëthon learned? Compare this reaction with his earlier feelings.

4 Why do you think the crops turned white (line 72)? What made Phaëthon's chariot glow (line 80)?

5 Explain in your own words the meaning of line 73.

6 How do lines 90–98 support or contradict the concept of **pater omnipotens** in line 89? What do you think is Ovid's attitude towards the Olympian gods? Using lines 90–98, give reasons for your answer.

7 Explain in your own words what happened in lines 96–98. Why do you think Jupiter resorted to such desperate measures?

8 In lines 114–117, what was the significance of Apollo's action, and what the result? Explain the meaning of the last six words.

9 "Myths largely represent man's early attempts to explain natural phenomena." Give two examples from the passage to illustrate this statement.

10 In line 7, Apollo swore an oath "by the Styx" – the most powerful oath a god could swear.

(a) Give examples of different occasions on which a solemn oath is taken today. How are these oaths sworn?

(b) Do you think there is any difference between an oath and a promise?

(c) Do you think there are circumstances in which a solemn oath can legitimately be broken? Justify your answer.

(d) What would you have done if you had been Apollo?

nam pater obductos, luctu miserabilis aegro,
115 condiderat vultus: et si modo credimus, unum
isse diem sine sole ferunt. incendia lumen
praebebant, aliquisque malo fuit usus in illo.

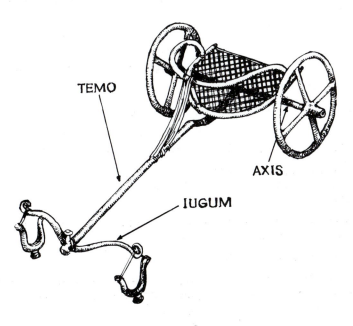

obduco (3), to veil, cover
luctus (*m*), grief
miserabilis, pitiable, to be pitied
aeger, sorrowful
condo (3), to hide, cover

si modo, if only, provided
ferunt, they say
aliquis, some
malum (*n*), evil, disaster
usus (*m*), usefulness, benefit

Gellius: See Notes on Authors on page 11.

line

1   **cantator fidibus**: *a minstrel*, someone who sang to his own lyre-accompaniment.

    is loco et oppido ... Lesbius fuit: Though Arion's actual birthplace was the town of Methymna, the whole island of Lesbos claimed him as its own.

2   **eum Arionem**: *this Arion*.

4   **visere**: The infinitive expresses Purpose.

    aures omnium mentesque: The genitive (**omnium**) is associated with both nouns. The pleasing sound of his songs made everyone feel completely relaxed.

6   **navitas**: *sailors*. The more usual form would be **nautas**.

    ut notiores: literally *as being more familiar*, i.e. on the grounds that they were the kind of people with whom he was more familiar. **notus** (like **nobilis** in line 1) is derived from the verb **noscere** (3), **novi, notum**, *to get to know*.

9   **de necando Arione** : *about killing Arion*. (For this use of the Gerundive, see LL p. 61.)

    tum ... ibi: *then and there*, i.e. *immediately*.

10   **pernicie intellecta**: *realising they were going to kill him*.

    vitam modo sibi: Take with **ut parcerent**.

11   **navitas... commiseritum est**: *The sailors showed pity*. The verb is used impersonally (cf. **me miseret**), and the object of their pity is in the genitive case (**precum harum**). (For Impersonal Verbs, see LL p. 58.)

    ei necem adferre: *to murder him*, literally *to bring death to him*.

14   **ibi**: *thereupon* – again used with a time sense as in line 9.

    id unum is explained by the **ut** clause which follows.

15   **induere ... indumenta**: *to put on his garments*. Both the verb and its object come from the same family of words. For this use of Cognate Accusative, compare the English expressions "fight the good fight" and "sing a song", and the Latin phrases **cursum currere** and **pugnam pugnare**.

    sua: This refers to *his special* costume, i.e. the one he wore as a minstrel.

16   **prolubium audiendi**: *a longing to hear*. (For Gerund, see LL p. 60.)

    tamen: The use of this word presupposes an "although" clause. Translate **feros et immanes navitas** *although the sailors were fierce and cruel*.

17   **subit**: *came over (them)*, i.e. took possession of them.

    quod: *what*. It stands for **id quod**.

    de more ornatus: *dressed up in his usual costume*, i.e. in the clothes he would normally wear for a performance.

    in summae puppis foro: *on the open deck at the highest point of the stern*.

32 Arion and the Dolphin

The minstrel Arion is believed to have lived on the island of Lesbos during the reign of the tyrant Periander (625–585 BC). The two versions of the story which follow were written for quite different purposes.

(*a*) **Aulus Gellius**, *Noctes Atticae XVI. 19*

Conspiracy

vetus et nobilis Arion cantator fidibus fuit. is loco et oppido Methymnaeus, terra atque insula omni Lesbius fuit. eum Arionem rex Corinthi Periander amicum habuit artis gratia. is inde a rege proficiscitur, terras inclutas Siciliam atque Italiam visere. ubi eo venit, aures omnium mentesque in utriusque terrae
5   urbibus demulsit. is tum postea, grandi pecunia et re bona multa copiosus, Corinthum instituit redire. navem igitur et navitas, ut notiores amicioresque sibi, Corinthios delegit.

     sed ei Corinthii, homine accepto navique in altum provecta, praedae pecuniaeque cupidi ceperunt consilium de necando Arione. tum ille ibi,
10 pernicie intellecta, pecuniam ceteraque sua dedit, vitam modo sibi ut parcerent oravit. navitas precum eius harum commiseritum est illactenus ut ei necem adferre per vim suis manibus temperarent; sed imperaverunt ut iam statim coram desiliret praeceps in mare.

Escape

homo ibi territus, spe omni vitae perdita, id unum postea oravit ut, priusquam
15 mortem obpeteret, induere permitterent sua sibi omnia indumenta et fides capere et canere carmen. feros et immanes navitas prolubium tamen audiendi subit; quod oraverat, impetrat. atque ibi mox de more ornatus stansque in

vetus, old, of olden times	**altum** (*n*), the open sea
nobilis, famous, well-known	**provehor** (3), to sail out
fides (*f.pl*), lyre	**illactenus ut**, to the extent that
Corinthus (*f*), Corinth	**per vim**, violently
gratia (+ *gen.*), because of	**tempero** (1) (+ *infin.*), to refrain (from)
inclutus, famous	**coram**, before their eyes
viso (3), to visit, see	**desilio** (4), to leap down
auris (*f*), ear	**praeceps**, headlong
demulceo (2), to soothe	**priusquam**, before
grandis, large, great	**mortem obpetere**, to meet (his) death
res bona (*f*), possessions	**induo** (3), to put on
copiosus, well-supplied	**permitto** (3), to allow
instituo (3), to decide	**impetro** (1), to gain (a request)
Corinthius, from Corinth, Corinthian	

18   **ad postrema cantus**: *at the end of the song.*

19   **sicut stabat canebatque**: *just as (he had been when) he was standing and singing.*

20   **haudquaquam dubitantes quin ...**: *being in no doubt at all that he ...* (For Doubting clauses, see LL p. 105.)

     perisset = periisset. (Cf. **audissent** in line 28.)

     cursum tenuerunt: *they continued on the voyage,* literally *they held the course.*

22   **fluitanti sese homini subdidit**: *(The dolphin) positioned itself under the man as he floated (on the surface).*

23   **Taenarum** was a promontory on the south coast of Greece, now called Cape Matapan.

25   **talem ... qualis fuerat**: *(dressed) exactly as he had been (when ...).* (For Correlatives, see LL p. 63.)

26   **sese obtulit**: *he presented himself.* **talem** agrees with **sese**; **inopinanti** agrees with **Periandro regi**.

27   **custodiri**: *to be guarded* (present infinitive passive).

28   **dissimulanter**: *pretending not to know.* The verb **simulare** means *to pretend to be what is not the case;* **dissimulare**, *to pretend not to be what is the case.*

35   **quod**: *the fact that.* The clause which follows explains **argumentum**.

Woman holding a cithara

summae puppis foro, carmen voce sublatissima cantavit. ad postrema cantus cum fidibus ornatuque omni, sicut stabat canebatque, iecit sese procul in 20 profundum. navitae, haudquaquam dubitantes quin perisset, cursum quem facere coeperant tenuerunt. sed novum et mirum facinus contigit. delphinus repente inter undas adnavit fluitantique sese homini subdidit, et dorso super fluctus edito vectavit incolumique eum corpore et ornatu Taenarum in terram Laconicam devexit.

Villains exposed

25 tum Arion prorsus ex eo loco Corinthum petivit; talemque Periandro regi, qualis delphino vectus fuerat, inopinanti sese obtulit eique rem, sicut acciderat, narravit. rex istaec parum credidit; Arionem, quasi falleret, custodiri iussit; navitas inquisitos, ablegato Arione, dissimulanter interrogavit ecquid audissent in his locis unde venissent super Arione. ei dixerunt hominem, cum inde irent, 30 in terra Italia fuisse eumque illic florere, atque in gratia pecuniaque magna opulentum fortunatumque esse.

tum inter haec eorum verba Arion cum fidibus et indumentis, cum quibus se in salum eiaculaverat, exstitit; navitae stupefacti convictique ire infitias non quierunt.

35 eam fabulam dicunt Lesbii et Corinthii, atque est fabulae argumentum, quod simulacra duo aenea ad Taenarum visuntur, delphinus vehens et homo insidens.

sublatus, loud
ornatus, -**us** (*m*), finery
sese = se
profundum (*n*), the sea, the deep
facinus (*n*), a happening
contingit, it happens, occurs
delphinus (*m*), dolphin
repente, suddenly
adno (1), to swim up
dorsum (*n*), back
edo (3), to raise
vecto (1), to carry
Laconicus, Spartan
deveho (3), to bring (to land)
prorsus, immediately
inopinans, not expecting
istaec, those events
parum, too little, scarcely
quasi, as if
fallo (3), to tell lies

inquiro (3), to seek out
ablego (1), to keep out of the way
interrogo (1), to ask, question
ecquid, if . . . anything
super (+ *abl.*), about
illic, there
floreo (2), to prosper, do well
gratia (*f*), popularity
opulentus, rich, thriving
salum (*n*), the sea
eiaculo (1), to hurl, throw out
exsto (1), to appear
stupefactus, astounded
convinco (3), to prove guilty
ire infitias, to deny
queo, quire, quii, to be able
argumentum (*n*), proof
simulacrum (*n*), statue
aeneus, made of bronze
insideo (2), to sit on

Ovid: See Notes on Authors on page 12.
Metre: Elegiac Couplet (See page 257.)

line

1   **quod** and **quae** are interrogatives meaning *which?* or *what?*

     novit: *knows.* **novi** is the perfect tense of **nosco** (3), *to get to know.*

     Ariona: This is the Greek accusative form (see page 262). It is the object of both verbs in this line.

2   **tenebat**: *held back.* Lines 2 –10 describe the power of Arion's music over nature. For example, even rivers stopped flowing as if spellbound by Arion's singing. Shakespeare *(Henry VIII*, Act III, i, 3) gives a similar description of the effect of Orpheus' music:
       Orpheus with his lute made trees,
       And the mountain tops that freeze,
       Bow themselves when he did sing.

3   **agnam**: object of **sequens**.

4   **restitit**: *stopped in its tracks.*

5   **cubuere = cubuerunt**. Both forms of the 3rd person plural of the perfect tense are quite common. Poets found it useful to have the two forms because of their different patterns of long and short syllables. (See Introduction to Latin Metres on p. 254.)
     For the sentiments expressed in lines 5 – 6, compare the Old Testament (Isaiah XI. 6 – 7): "Wolves and sheep will live together in peace, and leopards will lie down with young goats; calves and lion cubs will feed together, and little children will take care of them. Cows and bears will eat together, and their calves and cubs will lie down in peace." (*Good News Bible*)

7   **Palladis alite**: *the bird of Pallas*, i.e. the owl, which was the symbol of wisdom and so the emblem of the goddess of wisdom, called Pallas Athene by the Greeks, and Minerva by the Romans. Athene disliked the crow because of its constant chattering and reputation for tale-telling.

8   **iuncta fuit**: *associated with*, literally *was united with.*

9   **Cynthia**: Another name for Diana, the goddess of hunting. She and her brother Apollo, the god of music, had been born on Mount Cynthus on the island of Delos.

     fertur: *is said*; take it with **obstipuisse**.

     tuis: Supply **modis** (*by your melodies*) to balance the phrase **fraternis modis** in the next line. Arion's playing seemed to her as excellent as Apollo's.

     vocalis: literally *giving voice*, but it may be translated as *minstrel* in this context.

     For variety and poetic effect, the poet addresses Arion, instead of telling the story as a narrative. He does this again in line 15, where he calls Arion **infelix**. Similarly, he speaks directly to the helmsman in line 19 and to Apollo in line 24.

(b) **Ovid**, *Fasti II. 83–118*

Ovid's version of this story comes from the *Fasti* (meaning "calendar" or "almanac"), six books of poetry in which he used the framework of the Roman year to describe stories and legends associated with various important dates, the rising and setting of constellations, and the religious festivals which marked the rhythm of the months.

    The Arion story, as the final two lines of the following extract indicate, celebrates Jupiter's decision to honour the dolphin for his rescue of Arion by turning it into a constellation – still called "Delphinus" today. It is to be found near the bright star Altair in the Aquila group, and its setting is in early February.

> quod mare non novit, quae nescit Ariona tellus?
>> carmine currentes ille tenebat aquas.
> saepe sequens agnam lupus est a voce retentus,
>> saepe avidum fugiens restitit agna lupum:
> 5 saepe canes leporesque umbra cubuere sub una,
>> et stetit in saxo proximo cerva leae:
> et sine lite loquax cum Palladis alite cornix
>> sedit, et accipitri iuncta columba fuit.
> Cynthia saepe tuis fertur, vocalis Arion,
> 10   tamquam fraternis obstipuisse modis.

tellus (*f*), land	**loquax**, talkative, chattering
agna (*f*), lamb	**cornix** (*f*), crow
avidus, greedy	**accipiter** (*m*), hawk
lepus, -oris (*m*), hare	**columba** (*f*), dove
umbra (*f*), shade	**tamquam**, as if
cubo (1), to lie down	**fraternus**, belonging to a brother
cerva (*f*), deer, hind	**obstipesco** (3), to be amazed
lea (*f*), lioness	
lis, litis (*f*), strife, quarrelling	

12 **lyricis sonis**: *with the sounds of his lyre.*

Ausonis ora: *the Ausonian coast*, i.e. Italy, so called after the Ausones, one of the old tribes of Italy. Roman poets often use these roundabout equivalents for proper names, either to fit the metre or to avoid repetition.

13 **domum**: i.e. back to Methymna in Lesbos.

14 **ita**: *in this way*, i.e. by boat.

quaesitas arte: *earned by his skill.*

16 **nave tua**: Ablative of Comparison (see LL p. 16), to be taken with **tutius**, which agrees with **aequor**.

17 **constitit**: *took his stand.* The helmsman seems to have been the ringleader. Supply the same verb with **turba** (line 18).

18 Scansion of the line reveals that **conscia** and **turba** are nominative because the final **-a** is short, while **armata** is ablative singular feminine because the final **-a** is long. (See Introduction to Latin Metres on p. 254.)

19 **quid tibi**: Supply **est**. Translate *What business have you (with...)?*

rege: imperative of **regere** (*to control, steer*).

20 **haec arma**: There is a play on the word **arma**, which has two meanings – the implements of a craftsman or the arms of a soldier. The implements normally handled by a sailor would be the ship's tackle, not a sword.

sunt digitis tenenda tuis: *should be held by your fingers* (i.e. in your hands). **tenenda** is Gerundive (see LL p. 61).

21 **ille**: This pronoun is often used to mark a change of subject. Here it refers to Arion.

22 **liceat**: Supply **mihi** with this present subjunctive which expresses a Command (see LL p. 107). Translate *allow me*, literally *let permission be given to me.*

Scansion reveals that **sumpta** and **lyra** are both ablative since the final **-a** is long, whereas the final **-a** of **pauca** is short.

pauca referre: *to perform a few songs.*

24 **quae possit crines, Phoebe, decere tuos**: *which could well adorn your locks, Phoebus.* The garland was splendid enough for the head of Apollo (often referred to as Phoebus, "brightly shining", an allusion to his other role as god of the sun).

25 **Tyrio murice**: *with Tyrian purple.* This favourite dye of the Romans was made from the murex, a shellfish found off the coast of Phoenicia. The crimson colour was rendered even more striking by a double-dyeing process (**bis tinctam**). The ancient city of Tyre, on the coast of modern Lebanon, was a famous centre of the industry.

pallam: a long flowing robe worn by musicians.

26 By scanning the line, we discover that both **icta** and **chorda** are nominative because the final **-a** in both words is short.

suos sonos: suos is emphatic – *its well-known sounds.* Only Arion could produce such sounds on the lyre.

nomen Arionium Siculas impleverat urbes,
   captaque erat lyricis Ausonis ora sonis.
inde domum repetens puppem conscendit Arion,
   atque ita quaesitas arte ferebat opes.
15 forsitan, infelix, ventos undasque timebas;
   at tibi nave tua tutius aequor erat.
namque gubernator destricto constitit ense
   ceteraque armata conscia turba manu.
quid tibi cum gladio? dubiam rege, navita, puppem!
20   non haec sunt digitis arma tenenda tuis.
ille, metu vacuus, "mortem non deprecor" inquit,
   "sed liceat sumpta pauca referre lyra."
dant veniam, ridentque moram: capit ille coronam,
   quae possit crines, Phoebe, decere tuos.
25 induerat Tyrio bis tinctam murice pallam:
   reddidit icta suos pollice chorda sonos,

Based on a painting on a 5th-century Greek wine-jar (amphora)

Siculus, Sicilian
impleo (2), to fill
repeto (3), to seek again
puppis (*f*), stern, ship
conscendo (3), to board (a ship)
forsitan, perhaps
aequor (*n*), sea
namque, for
gubernator (*m*), helmsman
destringo (3), to draw (a sword)
ensis (*m*), sword

conscius, conspiring, guilty
turba (*f*), band, crew
dubius, wavering, unsteady
vacuus (+ *abl.*), empty (of),
   free (from)
deprecor (1), to pray against
venia (*f*), permission, leave
induo (3), to put on
ico (3), to strike
pollex (*m*), thumb
chorda (*f*), string

27–8 *In a mournful song* (**flebilibus numeris**) *such as* (**veluti**) *a swan* (**olor**) *sings when its snow-white temples have been pierced* (**canentia tempora traiectus**) *by a cruel arrow* (**dura penna**). There was an old belief that swans sang sweetly just before they died. (For Simile, see p. 260.)

29 **ornatus**: *dressed in all the finery of a minstrel.*

30 Again, scansion helps to identify the cases of **impulsa** and **aqua** (long -a) and **caerula** (short **-a**). Translate **impulsa aqua** as *by the water that was dashed against it* (by Arion diving in).

31 **fide maius**: *beyond belief* or *incredibly*, literally *greater than belief.*

   delphina (*dolphin*) is a Greek accusative (see p. 262) to be taken with **se subposuisse** to form an Accusative and Infinitive depending on **memorant** (*they say*).

32 **se oneri subposuisse novo**: *supported its strange burden,* literally *placed itself under its new load.*

33 **pretiumque vehendi cantat**: *and sang as payment* (to the dolphin) *for carrying him.* (For Gerund, see LL p. 60.)

35 **astris**: *among the stars.*

36 **stellas novem**: As a reward, Jupiter gave orders for the dolphin to become a constellation in the heavens. The constellation Delphinus actually consists of a little group of not very bright stars (see diagram).

flebilibus numeris veluti canentia dura
   traiectus penna tempora cantat olor.
protinus in medias ornatus desilit undas,
30   spargitur impulsa caerula puppis aqua.
inde (fide maius) tergo delphina recurvo
   se memorant oneri subposuisse novo.
ille sedens citharamque tenet pretiumque vehendi
   cantat et aequoreas carmine mulcet aquas.
35 di pia facta vident: astris delphina recepit
   Iuppiter et stellas iussit habere novem.

numeri (*m.pl*), notes
caneo (2), to be white
tempus (*n*), temple (of head)
traicio (3), to pierce
protinus, at once
spargo (3), to splash

caerulus, dark blue
recurvus, curved
cithara (*f*), lyre
aequoreus, of the sea
mulceo (2), to soothe, charm
pius, dutiful, good
stella (*f*), star

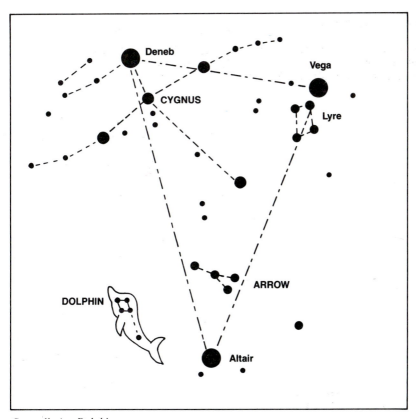

Constellation Delphinus

137

Points for Discussion

(a) Gellius' version

1   In addition to the noun **mare** (line 13), Gellius uses three other words for "sea" (lines 8, 20 and 33). What are these words? What do they mean literally? What are the English variants for "sea" which translate these words most closely? What effect does the use of such words have on the telling of the story? (Compare the use of **undas** and **fluctus** in lines 22 and 23.)

2   **aures omnium mentesque demulsit** (line 4): It would seem as if **mentesque** was added almost as an afterthought. What would have been lost if it had been omitted?
    Gellius is fond of using two nouns in this way. Find similar examples of two nouns linked together (lines 1–2, 5, 6, 8–9, 19, 23, 30, 32) and discuss the effect of using the pair of words instead of only one of them.

3   Gellius is also fond of using two adjectives to describe the same noun, e.g. **vetus et nobilis** (line 1). Find other examples in lines 6, 16, 21, and 31. In each example, do you think the second word adds anything, or is it simply a stylistic fad?

4   What effect is produced by keeping the following phrases to the end of the sentence: **artis gratia** (line 3), **praeceps in mare** (line 13), **procul in profundum** (line 19)?

5   Why do you think Arion went to Sicily and Italy?

6   **stansque in summae puppis foro** (line 17): Why do you think Arion stood here? Give at least two possible reasons.

7   Collect other examples throughout history of animals helping men.

(*b*) **Ovid's version**

1 Note how, in line 3, Ovid emphasises the power of Arion's music by placing side by side the words **agnam lupus** – normally arch-enemies. Show how he uses the same technique in the next four lines.

2 Sometimes Ovid splits up phrases to fit his metre; sometimes he does this to produce a deliberate effect. What effect do you feel is produced by keeping the following to the end of the line: **aquas** (line 2), **sub una** (line 5), **tuis** (line 20)?

3 Ovid uses four different words for "sea" (lines 1, 15, 16 and 30). Discuss these as in question (*a*) 1 above. Are there any close English equivalents?

4 Why is the adjective **dubiam** applied to **puppem** in line 19?

5 **rident moram** (line 23): Why do you think the sailors laughed?

6 Strictly speaking, lines 27–28 have nothing to do with the Arion story. At what particular effect is Ovid aiming in these lines? Does he succeed?

7 Why do you think the dolphin's load is described as **novo** (line 32)?

8 Discuss the value of various techniques used by Ovid in telling the story, e.g. asking a question (line 1), changing from narrative to addressing individuals (e.g. lines 9, 19, 24), using direct speech (lines 21–22).

9 Study An Introduction to Latin Metres on page 253. Scan the following couplets: 21–22 and 29–30 (where there are no elisions), 5–6 and 17–18 (where an elision occurs), and 7–8 (where the initial **i-** of **iuncta** is a consonant).

(*c*) **Comparison of the two versions**

1 Gellius tells the story in great detail, whereas Ovid relies on his readers' existing knowledge and concentrates only on certain episodes. List the points of information given by Gellius which are omitted by Ovid. On what sorts of things does Ovid concentrate? Whose technique do you prefer – Gellius' or Ovid's? Explain why.

2 Discuss the different ways in which Gellius (first paragraph) and Ovid (lines 1–12) build up a picture of Arion's reputation. Which do you feel is the more effective?

3 Do you think Ovid should have simply used the nouns **ulula** (*owl*) and **Italia** instead of the phrases **cum Palladis alite** (line 7) and **Ausonis ora** (line 12)? What are the advantages and disadvantages of doing what Ovid did? Would there be any place for such uses in Gellius?

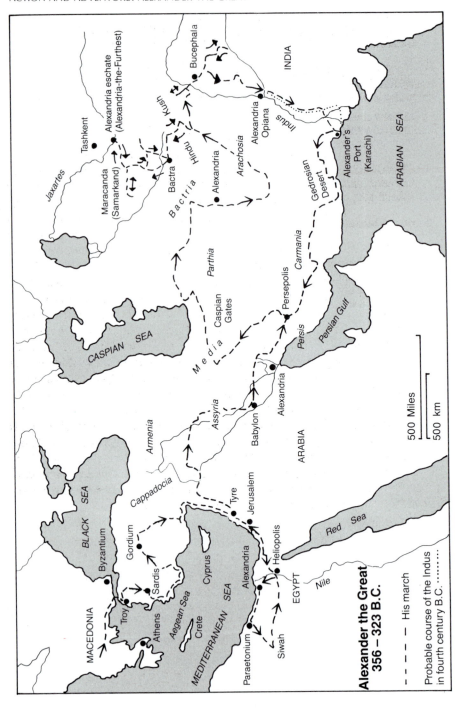

Alexander the Great
356 – 323 B.C.

– – – – His march

Probable course of the Indus
in fourth century B.C. ....

Action and Adventure: Alexander the Great

Alexander (356–323 BC) was the son of King Philip II of Macedonia, a powerful monarch who dominated most of Greece. His first task, after succeeding his father at the age of twenty, was to deal with attempts by Greek states to free themselves from the domination of Macedonia. Having put down these revolts, he then turned his attention to the mighty empire of Persia which was ruled at that time by King Darius. He crossed the Hellespont with his army in 334 BC and, for the next eleven years, he won victory after victory until his empire extended from Greece and Egypt in the West to the boundaries of India in the East. Only a brilliant general and inspired leader could have achieved so much.

Nothing should detract from his great military achievements; but, although his exploits were legendary, he had some human failings. He could be magnanimous and generous with his praise and friendship, but he could also be resentful towards anyone who stole the limelight from him. He tended to be particularly moody during bouts of heavy drinking. He even killed a lifelong friend who dared to criticise him for executing one of his own generals accused of conspiring against him and for belittling the achievements of his father, King Philip. It is likely that his excessive feasting and drinking affected his health so much that, when he contracted fever, he was unable to shake it off and died at the age of only thirty-two.

The following stories, which illustrate the heroic and romantic side of his character, are drawn from three different authors. Quintus Curtius and Aulus Gellius were Roman writers, while Ekkehardus Uraugiensis was a German monk who lived towards the end of the eleventh century. For details of Gellius, see page 11. Curtius is thought to have lived about AD 50, but nothing is really known about him apart from the fact that he wrote a history of Alexander the Great.

Hammon was an Egyptian god worshipped in the form of a ram. The Greeks and Romans identified him with their king of the gods, Zeus and Jupiter respectively.

line

2   **transeuntibus**: *for those crossing.* The present participle is used here almost as the equivalent of a noun (see LL p. 28).

     Compare **ingredientes** in line 3.

4   **induens se figuram**: *adopting the guise.*

6   **caballis**: *horses.* In Classical times, this word was used disparagingly of an inferior type of horse, a "nag". This colloquial word came into French as **cheval** and into Italian as **cavallo**, from which our word "cavalry" is derived.

     stadii: A stade was a Greek measure equal to about 185 metres (202 yards).

7   **abiens itaque Alexander**: *and so Alexander went away and....* This phrase really belongs to the **cum** clause, since **Persae** (not Alexander) is the subject of the main verb **mirati sunt**.

     civitatis: *of the capital city.*

8   **mirati sunt in figura . . .**: *marvelled at the nature . . . .* In Medieval Latin, the meanings of prepositions are much less precise than they are in Classical Latin.

11   **Mithram**: Mithras was the sun-god of the Persians. From the second half of the first century AD, the cult of Mithras (which was confined to men) spread through the Roman empire. Many Romans found the mystic rites surrounding the worship of such eastern gods as Mithras more exciting than the worship of their traditional gods. The worship of Mithras was particularly common in the Roman army, and temples of Mithras have been excavated in London and on Hadrian's wall.

13   **quia**: *that.* In Medieval Latin, **quod** and **quia** frequently introduce Indirect Statements where Classical Latin would have Accusative and Infinitive . When used in this sense, there will be a "speaking" or "thinking" type of word to introduce the clause.

Reconstruction of Roman Temple of Mithras

33 A Daring Exploit on his Own

(Ekkehardus Uraugiensis 578 A–579 B)

Having invaded the territory of King Darius of Persia, Alexander was keen to fight a pitched battle against him as soon as possible. The Egyptian god Hammon appeared to him in a dream, wearing a linen cloak and Macedonian tunic, and urged him to go to Darius disguised as a messenger and wearing clothes similar to the god's. Hammon promised to protect him. Alexander regarded the dream as a good omen and, along with one of his officers, set off with three horses towards Darius' camp. Alexander rode one horse, the officer the second, while the third was riderless.

Alexander crosses the River Stragas

pergentes igitur ambo venerunt ad fluvium qui dicitur Stragan. hic fluvius prae
nimio frigore congelatur noctu, praebetque iter tota nocte transeuntibus. mane,
cum incaluerit sol, dissolvitur et perfundissimus efficitur et ingredientes
absorbet. veniens itaque Alexander invenit eum congelatum, induensque se
5   figuram quam viderat in somno, dimisit ibi principem illum cum duobus
caballis, et ipse cum suo transivit. erat autem fluvius in latitudine stadii unius.

Alexander meets Darius

abiens itaque Alexander, cum venisset ad portam civitatis Darii, videntes eum
Persae mirati sunt in figura vultus eius, aestimantes illum esse deum.
interrogatus autem ab eis quis esset, respondit se apocrisiarium esse regis
10   Alexandri. et duxerunt eum ad Darium. qui videns eum adoravit ut deum,
cogitans illum esse Mithram deum descendentem de caelis. interrogavit ergo
eum "quis es tu?"
        cui ille: "apocrisiarius sum regis Alexandri, missus nuntiare tibi quia moram
facit in campo exspectans te. unde, si tibi placet, constitue diem proeliandi."
15   cui Darius: "forsitan tu es Alexander, qui cum tanta loqueris audacia. non

pergo (3), to go, proceed	**latitudo** (*f*), breadth
ambo, both	**Persa, -ae** (*m*), Persian
fluvius (*m*), river	**aestimo** (1), to judge, consider
prae (+ *abl*.), on account of	**interrogo** (1), to ask
nimius, excessive, intense	**apocrisiarius** (*m*), representative
congelo (1), to freeze	**adoro** (1), to address, worship
noctu, at night	**ut**, as
incalesco (3), **-ui**, to grow warm	**ergo**, therefore
dissolvo (3), to melt	**unde**, therefore
perfundus, very deep	**si tibi placet**, (if you) please
efficio (3), to make	**constituo** (3), to decide, fix
ingredior (3), to go in, enter	**proelio** (1), to fight a battle
absorbeo (2), to swallow up, drown	**forsitan**, perhaps
princeps (*m*), officer	

line

16 **scias pro certo**: *you may be sure.* (For the present subjunctive used to express a Command, see LL p. 107.)

17 **quia** here has its normal Classical meaning *because.*

et: *also.* (Cf. line 22.)

19 **per dexteram**: *by the right hand.* (For Medieval use of prepositions, compare line 8.)

20 **pro signo tenuit in corde suo**: *in his own mind regarded as a sign.* In ancient times, the heart (**cor**) was thought to be the seat not only of the emotions but also of the intellect. Compare the English expression "to take to heart".

hoc quod: *the fact that.*

24 **eo quod**: *because of the fact that.*

25 **vasculum**: *a small vessel* or *cup.* This expression corresponds to the Scots saying "Guid gear gangs in sma' bouk", meaning "Don't use size as a measure of a person's worth."

27 **exigere censum**: *to demand tribute.* Successive kings of Persia looked upon themselves as overlords of Greece and often sent messengers to the various states of Greece demanding that they acknowledge the Persian king's sovereignty over them and pay tribute (i.e. taxes) to him.

32 **de illo**: *about him*, i.e. about Alexander himself.

39 **antequam exiret**: *before it could get out.* (For **antequam** + the subjunctive, see LL p. 51.)

tulit eum fluvius: *the river carried it (the horse) away.*

40 **iunctus principi**: *rejoining* (literally *joining*) *the officer.* This is the officer referred to in line 5 of the text.

enim loqueris sicut nuntius, sed sicut ipse Alexander. scias tamen pro certo quia audacia tua nullo modo conturbat me. sed manduca hodie mecum quia et Alexander sedit ad cenam cum missis meis." et extendens manum, apprehendit eum per dexteram, introduxitque in palatium suum.

20   Alexander vero pro signo tenuit in corde suo hoc, quod induxit eum per dexteram, quasi iam teneret palatium inimici sui; ingressusque triclinium, in quo erat convivium praeparatum, sedit cum rege, sederunt et principes Darii facie ad faciem. Persae itaque sedentes in convivio despexerunt vultum Alexandri, eo quod esset parvus, nescientes qualis virtus et qualis audacia erat
25   in vasculo tali.

Alexander recognised

unus autem ex principibus militiae, cui nomen Anepolis, quondam missus ad Philippum exigere ab eo censum, vidit tunc Alexandrum; sedensque nunc in convivio cum eo facie ad faciem, intuitus est faciem eius, coepit cogitare in corde suo "nonne iste est Alexander?" intellegens enim vocem et signa illius,
30   accessit ad Darium et dixit: "domine, iste missus quem vides ipse est Alexander."

cognoscens autem Alexander quia loquebantur de illo et de cognitione eius, exiliit de sede sua, tollensque faculam de manu cuiusdam Persae tenentis eam ante mensam, percussit eum et ascendens equum abiit. Persae vero
35   insequebantur eum armati cum omni velocitate, sed ipse ferens in manu faculam ardentem, tenuit iter rectum. insequentes autem cadebant in foveas; erat enim obscura nox.

Alexander itaque veniens ad fluvium Stragan transiit. statimque dissolutus est fluvius, mortuusque est caballus eius antequam exiret, et tulit eum fluvius.
40   Alexander vero exiliit in ripam, iunctusque principi quem reliquerat, reversus est ad suos.

sicut, as, like	**intueor** (2), to look at
manduco (1), to dine	**iste**, that (man)
missus (*m*), messenger	**intellego** (3), to recognise
extendo (3), to stretch out	**signum** (*n*), sign, mannerism
apprehendo (3), to seize, take	**accedo** (3), to go to, approach
introduco (3), to lead inside	**cognosco** (3), to realise
palatium (*n*), palace	**cognitio** (*f*), identity
vero, truly, now	**exilio** (4), to leap out
quasi, as if	**tollo** (3), to grab
triclinium (*n*), dining-room	**facula** (*f*), small torch
convivium (*n*), feast	**percutio** (3), to strike
facies (*f*), face	**insequor** (3), to pursue
despicio (3), to despise	**velocitas** (*f*), speed
militia (*f*), army, soldiers	**rectus**, straight
quondam, formerly	**fovea** (*f*), pit, hole
tunc, then, on that occasion	

line

42   **eminentiorem**: *higher* (than the soldiers he was addressing).

43   **multitudo nostra non aequatur**: *our numbers are not equal to* – a subtle way of admitting that the Macedonians were greatly outnumbered.

44   **non conturbet nos multitudo illorum**: *do not let their (superiority in) numbers trouble us.* (For present subjunctive used to express a Command, see LL p. 107.)

48   **Stragan**: For this Greek accusative ending, see p. 262.

      habebat: The subject is **Darius**.

      currus falcatos: *scythed chariots.* In the chariots used by the Persians, the scythes extended about a metre from the axles, and there were other scythes beneath the axles pointing to the ground. The chariots charged into the midst of the enemy with a view to trampling them down or cutting them to pieces. There were drawbacks: if the drivers were killed, the horses would be out of control and might just as easily charge through the Persian troops.

51   **super**: *against him.* (For Medieval use of prepositions, compare lines 8 and 19.)

53   **cecidere = ceciderunt**: *had fallen.*

57   **qui**: The antecedent of this Relative clause is **eos** in line 58.

59   **super faciem suam**: *on his face.* (For Medieval use of prepositions, compare lines 8, 19 and 51.)

60   **ex alto pectore**: *from the depths of his breast.*

61   **humiliatus**: Supply **est** – *has been brought down to earth*, i.e. *humbled*.

62   **subiugavitque**: Normally, **-que** at the end of a word would be translated by *and* in front of that word. Here, **-que** links **subiugavit** to what follows: *subdued and . . . .*

      in puncto articuli unius diei: *in a fraction of a second*, literally *in a small part of a moment of a single day.*

63   **usque deorsum**: *down as far as they can go.*

Preparations for battle

congregataque omni militia sua, ascendit in locum eminentiorem et confortavit milites suos, dicens: "multitudo nostra non aequatur multitudini Persarum, sed non conturbet nos multitudo illorum, etiamsi centumpliciter augerentur, quia
45 non praevalet multitudo muscarum parvitati vesparum." qui audientes haec laudaverunt eum.

Darius itaque movit exercitum suum valde magnum, transiitque fluvium Stragan ut pugnaret cum exercitu Alexandri. habebat autem currus falcatos. cum autem venisset uterque exercitus in campum, ascendit Alexander equum
50 cui nomen Bucephalus, et stetit in medio ante omnes Persas. videntes autem eum Persae timuerunt ire super eum quia divinitas quaedam cooperiebat eum.

Victory

mixtis autem utrisque partibus, pugnabant acriter multique cadebant; sed ex parte Darii plurimi. videns itaque Darius quia multi cecidere de suis, fugam iniit. fugerunt et Persae, multitudo vero curruum falcatorum fugientes
55 occidebant suos, iacebantque sicut messis in campo. veniens autem Darius ad fluvium, et inveniens eum adhuc congelatum, transiit. sed sequenti multitudine ingrediente, dissoluta est glacies, et plurimi mortui sunt. qui vero ingredi non poterant, eos insequentes Macedones occidebant.

fugit autem Darius, et ingressus palatium suum, prostravit se super faciem
60 suam in terram, ex altoque pectore dura trahens suspiria, dixit: "heu me! quanta tribulatio apprehendit Persidem quia humiliatus Darius, qui subiugavitque in potentiam suam redegit multas gentes! in puncto articuli unius diei evenit quod humiles exaltentur super nubes, et sublimes humilientur usque deorsum."

congrego (1), to assemble	**messis** (*f*), harvested crops
etiamsi, even if	**adhuc**, still
centumpliciter, one hundred times	**glacies** (*f*), ice
augeo (2), to increase	**prosterno** (3), **-stravi**, to throw down on
praevaleo (2) (+ *dat.*), to be superior	the ground
musca (*f*), fly	**durus**, hoarse
parvitas (*f*), smallness, small number	**suspirium** (*n*), sigh
vespa (*f*), wasp	**heu!** alas!
valde, very	**tribulatio** (*f*), catastrophe
divinitas (*f*), divine aura	**Persis, -idis** (*f*), Persia
cooperio (4), to surround	**evenit**, it has happened
misceo (2), to mix, clash	**humilis**, humble, lowly
pars (*f*), side	**exalto** (1), to raise, elevate
fugam inire, to flee	**sublimis**, high and mighty

Medieval Forms

In Passage 33, certain Medieval forms have been printed with Classical spelling. (The numbers in brackets represent the lines in which they occur.) For more detailed information on Medieval Latin, see LL pages 132–137.

CLASSICAL FORM	MEDIEVAL FORM
prae (1)	**pre**
praebet (2)	**prebet**
aestimantes (8)	**estimantes**
praevalet (45)	**prevalet**
caelis (11)	**coelis**
proeliandi (14)	**praeliandi**
cenam (18)	**coenam**
nuntiare (13)	**nunciare**
nuntius (16)	**nuncius**
Philippum (27)	**Phylippum**
Bucephalus (50)	**Bucefalus**
centumpliciter (44)	**centupliciter**
Persidem (61)	**Persidam**

Points for Discussion

1 Why do you think Alexander and the officer took three horses with them, and why did the officer remain behind with two of them (lines 5–6)?

2 Do you think Darius really thought Alexander was a god (line 10)? Collect evidence from the rest of the passage to support your answer.

3 On what did the Persians base their contempt (lines 23–25)? What was the counter-argument used by the author, Ekkehardus?

4 The present participle is used in Classical Latin to describe an action which is taking place at the same time as that of the main verb, whereas in English, as in Medieval Latin, it is used also to describe an action which takes place before that of the main verb. From the following list (taken from lines 27–38) identify those which conform to Classical usage and those which do not: **sedens, intellegens, cognoscens, tollens, tenentis, ascendens, ferens, ardentem, insequentes, veniens.**

5 What happened to Alexander's pursuers, and why (line 36)?

6 How good an analogy is Alexander's comparison of flies and wasps with the armies of Darius and Alexander (lines 44–45)? Can you suggest a better analogy?

7 Why do you think Darius crossed the river instead of waiting for Alexander to cross (lines 47–48)? How vital to the story is his decision?

8 Comment on the position of the word **suos** in the sentence (line 55).

9 Discuss the effectiveness of the simile used in line 55.

10 What happened to the fleeing Persians (lines 54–58)?

11 Explain in your own words what Darius says in lines 60–64.

12 What do you think Alexander was hoping to achieve by going to Darius' camp?

Curtius: See Notes on Authors on page 11.

line

2   **Midas** was the son of Gordius. On one occasion, he entertained the god Bacchus so well that Bacchus offered in return anything he wished. Midas asked that everything he touched should turn to gold, but his pleasure was short-lived as he discovered that even his food and drink turned to gold.

3   **in semetipsos implicatis**: *tangled up with one another*. The pronoun **semetipsos** is a strong form of **se + ipsos**.

4   **editam esse oraculo sortem**: *that it had been predicted by the oracle*, literally *that the prophecy had been given out by the oracle*.

    (eum) Asiae potiturum (esse) qui: *that the man who ... would gain control of Asia*. This is an Accusative and Infinitive clause depending on **editam esse sortem**.

5   **sortis eius explendae**: *to fulfil* (literally *of fulfilling*) *that prophecy*. (For this use of the Gerundive, see LL p. 61.)

6   **illa ... haec ...** : *the former ... the latter ...* , since "that" refers to something farther away, and "this" to something nearer.

    exspectatione suspensa: *keyed up* (literally *hanging*) *with expectation*. **suspensa** is nominative agreeing with **illa**.

7   **sollicita ex temeraria fiducia**: *anxious because of the rash (over-)confidence*.

8   **nihil interest**: *it doesn't matter at all*. (See LL p. 58.)

Points for Discussion

1   What is meant if it is said that someone has the "Midas touch"?

2   Which words tell us that Curtius was not convinced that Alexander had fulfilled the terms of the oracle?

3   What does this story tell us about Alexander's character? Using the evidence of the last three lines of the passage, discuss how (*a*) an admirer and (*b*) a critic might have described the event.

4   In what respect is the modern expression "cutting through red-tape" similar to "cutting the Gordian knot"?

34 The Gordian Knot

(Quintus Curtius III. 1)

In the course of his march through Phrygia, which lies in the western interior of modern Turkey, Alexander came to the city of Gordium, which was named after Gordius. According to legend, when Phrygia was being torn by serious internal strife, the people were told by an oracle that their troubles would end if they appointed as their king the first man to ride into their midst. At that point, Gordius, a poor peasant, arrived riding in a wagon. After he was made king, he dedicated the wagon to Zeus (Jupiter). Its pole was fixed to the yoke (**iugum**) by a very complicated knot (**nodus**). According to an oracle, whoever succeeded in untying that knot would rule the whole of Asia. Up to the time of Alexander's arrival in Gordium, no one had succeeded in untying the knot. When told of the prophecy, Alexander adopted an unconventional method of undoing it.

Alexander, urbe in dicionem suam redacta, Iovis templum intrat. vehiculum, quo Gordium Midae patrem vectum esse constat, aspexit. notabile erat iugum, adstrictum compluribus nodis in semetipsos implicatis et celantibus nexus.

5　incolis deinde affirmantibus editam esse oraculo sortem, Asiae potiturum qui inexplicabile vinculum solvisset, cupido incessit animo sortis eius explendae. circa regem erat et Phrygum turba et Macedonum, illa exspectatione suspensa, haec sollicita ex temeraria regis fiducia.

ille, nequiquam diu luctatus cum latentibus nodis, "nihil" inquit "interest quomodo solvantur"; gladioque ruptis omnibus loris, oraculi sortem vel elusit
10　vel implevit.

in dicionem redigere, to bring under one's sway	**incedo** (3), to enter
vehiculum (*n*), wagon	**circa** (+ *acc.*), around
constat, it is commonly believed	**Phryges** (*m.pl*), Phrygians
aspicio (3), to look at	**Macedones** (*m.pl*), Macedonians
notabilis, noteworthy, remarkable	**nequiquam**, in vain
adstringo (3), to bind	**luctor** (1), to struggle
nexus, -us (*m*), fastening	**latens**, hidden, concealed
affirmo (1), to declare	**lorum** (*n*), a thong
inexplicabilis, unable to be loosened	**oraculum** (*n*), oracle
vinculum (*n*), bond, knot	**vel...vel...**, either...or...
cupido (*f*), desire	**eludo** (3), to mock, foil
	impleo (2), to fill, fulfil

Curtius: See Notes on Authors on page 11.

line

1   **secutos**: *who had followed.*

     fidus admodum: *very loyal.*

2   **puero comes ... datus**: *having been appointed as a companion to (Alexander when he was) a boy.*

3   **potione medicata**: *by giving him medicine to drink,* literally *with a medicated drink.*

5   **nulli placebat**: *pleased no one.* **nulli** is dative singular of **nullus**, used as the dative of **nemo**.

     ipsum: Supply **regem**.

6   **in eo positam esse si ... potuisset**: The **si** clause explains the words **in eo**; literally *was placed on the fact if he could.* Translate *depended on his being able.*

7   **id ipsum** is the object of **aegre ferens**: *being annoyed by the very fact (that).* The reason for his irritation is explained in the **quod** clause.

8   **sumpturus**: *due to take* (future participle).

10   **inter haec**: A variation of **interea** (**inter + ea**).

     purpuratorum: The **purpurati** were senior officials at the king's court, so called because they were dressed in purple.

11   **mille talentis**: The talent was the most valuable of the Greek coins. It is impossible to give an exact modern equivalent; but 1000 talents then would represent hundreds of thousands of pounds today.

     mille ... esse corruptum: Supply **eum** with **esse corruptum**. This Accusative and Infinitive requires no introductory word of speaking, since **denuntiabat** has already introduced an Indirect Command, and the indirect speech continues under its influence. In English, we might insert something like "he said".

13   **quidquid ... pensabat**: *in his inner thoughts he weighed up the situation according as fear or hope tipped the balance one way or the other,* literally *he weighed up in secret calculation whatever either fear or hope had cast into either side (of the scales).* The image is of Alexander putting into the opposite pans of a set of scales the arguments for and against trusting the doctor.

15   **perseverem**: *should I stick to my decision?* The present subjunctive indicates that this is a Deliberative Question, i.e. he is putting the question to himself as he deliberates on what to do. Compare **damnem** and **patiar**. (For Deliberative Subjunctive, see LL p. 107.)

     damnem medici fidem: There appears to be a confusion of two ideas here. We would expect either *condemn the doctor for his disloyalty* or *distrust the doctor's loyalty*, not *condemn the loyalty of the doctor.* The two ideas seem to have been fused together. Translate *am I to doubt my doctor's loyalty?*

16   **satius est**: *it would be better.*

     nostro: *my own.*

35 A Difficult Decision

(Quintus Curtius III.6)

Alexander falls ill

erat inter nobiles medicos ex Macedonia regem secutos Philippus, fidus
admodum regi. puero comes et custos salutis datus, non ut regem modo sed
etiam ut alumnum eximia caritate diligebat. is vim morbi potione medicata se
levaturum esse promisit.

5   nulli promissum eius placebat praeter ipsum. omnia quippe facilius quam
moram perpeti poterat; arma et acies in oculis erant, et victoriam in eo positam
esse arbitrabatur, si tantum ante signa stare potuisset, id ipsum quod post diem
tertium medicamentum sumpturus esset (ita enim medicus praedixerat) aegre
ferens.

A letter arrives

10   inter haec a Parmenione, fidissimo purpuratorum, litteras accipit, quibus ei
denuntiabat ne salutem suam Philippo committeret: mille talentis a Dario et spe
nuptiarum sororis eius esse corruptum.

     ingentem animo sollicitudinem litterae incusserant et, quidquid in utramque
partem aut metus aut spes subiecerat secreta aestimatione pensabat:

15   "bibere perseverem? damnem medici fidem? in tabernaculo ergo me
opprimi patiar? at satius est alieno me mori scelere quam metu nostro!"

nobilis, distinguished	**tantum**, only
salus, -utis (*f*), health, well-being	**medicamentum** (*n*), medication
non modo ... sed etiam ..., not only ... but also ...	**praedico** (3), to instruct
ut, as	**litterae** (*f.pl*), a letter
alumnus (*m*), foster-child	**denuntio** (1), to tell
eximius, very great, exceptional	**committo** (3), to entrust
caritas (*f*), affection	**nuptiae** (*f.pl*), marriage
vim (*acc.*), severity	**corrumpo** (3), to corrupt, bribe
levo (1), to relieve	**sollicitudo** (*f*), anxiety
promissum (*n*), promise	**incutio** (3)(+ *dat.*), to strike (into)
praeter (+ *acc.*), more than	**quidquid**, whatever
quippe, for, for in fact	**tabernaculum** (*n*), tent
perpetior (3), to endure	**ergo**, therefore, then
	patior (3), to allow, let

17 **in diversa**: *in different directions*.

   nulli: See line 5.

23 **legentis**: *of the reader*. (For the present participle used as a noun, see LL p. 28.)

   ratus ... posse: *thinking he might be able*.

25 **perlecta**: **perlegere** is a compound of **legere**.

   proiectis is to be taken with both **amiculo** and **litteris**.

26 **semper quidem ... ore trahi tuo**: *to be sure* (**quidem**), *my own life* (**spiritus meus**) *has always depended* (**pependit**) *on you* (**ex te**), *but in the present circumstances* (**nunc**) *I really think* (**vere arbitror**) *that (my own breath) is drawn* (**trahi**) *through your own sacred and revered mouth*. (Supply **spiritum meum** with **trahi** to form an Accusative and Infinitive depending on **arbitror**.) In other words, his own life depends on whether Alexander survives or not. The noun **spiritus** is thus used in two senses – *the breath he breathes* and *his life*, which depends on that breath.

28 **quod mihi obiectum est**: *which has been brought against me*. The verb **obicere** (*to throw in one's teeth*) contains the notion of malice.

   diluet: *will remove*. The basic meaning of **diluere** is *to loosen*. In line 20, the medicine was *dissolved*; here, the basis of the accusation is *washed away*.

   servatus a me: *if you are saved by me*, i.e. if you survive.

29 **dederis**: *you will have given* (future perfect).

   oro quaesoque: *I beg and beseech you,* a very strong *please*.

   patere: The imperative of **patior**.

   concipi is present infinitive passive.

31 **moleste seduli**: *officious*, literally *diligent in a troublesome manner*.

32 **haec vox**: *these words*.

33 **hac epistola accepta**: Since this Ablative Absolute is followed by **tamen**, it should be translated by an "although" clause.

diu animo in diversa versato, nulli quid scriptum esset enuntiat; epistolamque, sigillo anuli sui impresso, pulvino cui incubabat subicit.

A decision is reached

inter has cogitationes biduo absumpto, illuxit a medico destinatus dies; et ille
20 cum poculo, in quo medicamentum diluerat, intravit. quo viso, Alexander, levato corpore in cubili, epistolam a Parmenione missam sinistra tenens, accipit poculum et haurit interritus. tum epistolam legere Philippum iubet, nec a vultu legentis movit oculos, ratus aliquas conscientiae notas in ipso ore posse deprehendere.
25 ille, epistola perlecta, plus indignationis quam pavoris ostendit; proiectisque amiculo et litteris ante lectum "rex," inquit "semper quidem spiritus meus ex te pependit, sed nunc vere arbitror sacro et venerabili ore trahi tuo. crimen parricidii, quod mihi obiectum est, tua salus diluet. servatus a me, vitam mihi dederis. oro quaesoque, omisso metu, patere medicamentum concipi venis!
30 laxa paulisper animum quem intempestiva sollicitudine amici, sane fideles sed moleste seduli, turbant."
non securum modo haec vox sed etiam laetum regem ac plenum bonae spei fecit. itaque "Philippe," inquit "hac epistola accepta, tamen quod dilueras bibi." haec elocutus, dextram Philippo offert.

versor (1), to turn	**nota** (*f*), sign
sigillum (*n*), seal	**deprehendo** (3), to detect
anulus (*m*), ring	**pavor** (*m*), fear
imprimo (3), to stamp	**proicio** (3), to throw forward
pulvinus (*m*), pillow	**amiculum** (*n*), cloak
incubo (1), to lie	**lectus** (*m*), couch
subicio (3), to put under	**pendeo** (2), **pependi**, to hang, depend on
cogitatio (*f*), thought	**vere**, truly
biduum (*n*), (a period of) two days	**venerabilis**, revered, respected
absumo (3), to use up, consume	**parricidium** (*n*), murder
illucesco (3), to dawn	**obicio** (3) (+ *dat.*), to cast up (to)
destino (1), to appoint, choose	**omitto** (3), to let go, lay aside
poculum (*n*), cup	**concipio** (3), to take in, absorb
diluo (3), to dissolve, mix	**vena** (*f*), vein
levo (1), to raise	**laxo** (1), to relax
cubile (*n*), bed, couch	**paulisper**, for a short time
sinistra (*f*), left hand	**intempestivus**, untimely, ill-timed
haurio (4), to drink up	**sane**, doubtless
interritus, unafraid, showing no fear	**turbo** (1), to stir up
aliqui, some	**securus**, free from anxiety
conscientia (*f*), guilty conscience	**offero**, to offer, hold out

Points for Discussion

1 In line 5, Curtius uses the word **omnia**. While it is possible to translate this as *everything*, what word in this context would English more naturally use?

2 When using subordinate clauses of Indirect Speech, Curtius tends to place the verb of speaking after the clause. Find three examples of this in lines 1–18.

3 In line 6, does **in oculis** mean that he actually *saw* arms and battle? Give an idiomatic translation for **in oculis** which retains the basic idea of "eye" and "seeing".

4 Identify and discuss the tenses of the following participles: **ferens** (9), **versato** (17), **impresso** (18) and **tenens** (21).

5 Explain in your own words what Alexander meant when he said **in tabernaculo ergo me opprimi patiar?** (lines 15–16).

6 Why do you think Alexander sealed the letter and did not tell anyone of its contents (lines 17–18)?

7 Why do you think Alexander drank the medicine before he handed the letter to the doctor (line 22)?

8 If the doctor had poisoned him, what could Alexander have done to eliminate the effects of the drug once he had swallowed it?

9 How much choice do you think Alexander had in the matter?

10 If you had been faced with Alexander's predicament, what would you have done?

11 What does this passage tell us about Alexander's character?

Alexander riding Bucephalus – from the Alexander Sarcophagus found in Sidon

Curtius: See Notes on Authors on page 11.

line

1   **unus**: *alone*.

    tanti mali patiens: *able to endure such a disaster*. There had been a terrific storm.

    circumire: Latin authors occasionally use a Historic Infinitive instead of a verb in the indicative when they wish to describe something in a vivid and exciting way. (Compare **contrahere, allevare, ostendere** and **hortari**.) Translate all of these as if they were past tenses of the indicative. (For Historic Infinitive, see LL p. 32.)

    allevare prostratos: *he lifted up those who had collapsed on the ground*.

2   **ut proxima quaeque suffugia occuparent**: Although **quaeque** (*each*) agrees with **suffugia**, English would take "each" with the verb "urge" – *(he urged) each of them* (i.e. the soldiers) *to make for the nearest place of refuge*.

3   **saluti fuit**: *was a means of safety*, i.e. *contributed to their safety*. (For Predicative Dative, see LL p. 13.)

    quam quod: *than the fact that*.

4   **multiplicato labore**: *although his toil was (greatly) increased*.

    quis = quibus (referring to **malis**).

6   **efficacior ... invenit**: *was more effective in finding*, literally *more effective(ly) found*. Compare the English proverb "Necessity is the mother of invention."

8   **commovit**: *restored movement*, literally *moved*.

10   **male sustentans**: The use of **tamen** shows that this phrase means *although supporting with difficulty*.

11   **tum maxime**: *at that very moment*.

14   **ille** refers to the soldier.

16   **ecquid intellegis?** *Do you have any idea at all?*

    quanto meliore sorte ... vivatis: *how much better off you are living ...*, literally *with how much better fortune you live*.

17   **capital foret**: *would have been a capital offence*.

36 An Inspiration to his Troops

(Quintus Curtius VIII. 4)

rex unus tanti mali patiens circumire milites, contrahere dispersos, allevare prostratos, ostendere procul evolutum ex tuguriis fumum, hortarique ut proxima quaeque suffugia occuparent. nec ulla res magis saluti fuit quam quod, multiplicato labore, sufficientem malis (quis ipsi cesserant) regem deserere
5 erubescebant.

ceterum efficacior in adversis necessitas quam ratio frigoris remedium invenit. dolabris enim silvas sternere aggressi, acervos struesque accenderunt. hic calor stupentia membra commovit paulatimque spiritus, quem continuerat rigor, meare libere coepit.
10 forte Macedo gregarius miles, seque et arma male sustentans, tamen in castra pervenerat. quo viso rex, quamquam ipse tum maxime admoto igne refovebat artus, ex sella sua exsiluit torpentemque militem et vix compotem mentis, demptis armis, in sua sede iussit considere.

ille diu nec ubi requiesceret nec a quo esset exceptus agnovit. tandem,
15 recepto calore vitali, ut regiam sedem regemque vidit, territus surgit. quem intuens Alexander "ecquid intellegis, miles," inquit "quanto meliore sorte quam Persae sub rege vivatis? illis enim in sella regis consedisse capital foret, tibi saluti fuit."

contraho (3), to bring together	**paulatim**, gradually
dispersus, scattered	**spiritus** (*m*), breathing, circulation
evolvo (3), to roll forth, curl up from	**contineo** (2), to check
tugurium (*n*), hut	**rigor** (*m*), stiffness
fumus (*m*), smoke	**meo** (1), to flow
sufficio (3) (+ *dat.*), to cope (with)	**libere**, freely
malum (*n*), misfortune	**gregarius**, common, ordinary
cedo (3), to yield, give in	**admoveo** (2), to move towards
erubesco (3), to feel ashamed (to)	**refoveo** (2), to bring warmth back
ceterum, but	**artus** (*m*), limb
in adversis, in adversity	**sella** (*f*), seat
ratio (*f*), reason(ing), thinking	**exsilio** (4), to leap out
remedium (*n*), cure	**torpeo** (2), to be stiff
dolabra (*f*), axe	**compos mentis**, conscious
sterno (3), to lay low, cut down	**demo** (3), to take off
aggredior (3), to set about, begin	**consido** (3), to sit down
acervus (*m*), heap	**requiesco** (3), to rest
strues (*f*), heap, pile	**excipio** (3), to receive, welcome
accendo (3), to set fire to	**agnosco** (3), to recognise
calor (*m*), heat	**vitalis**, life-giving, vital
stupeo (2), to be numb	**regius**, royal
membrum (*n*), limb	**intueor** (2), to look at

Caesar: See Notes on Authors on page 8.

line

2   **daturos**: Supply **sese** and **esse** to form an Accusative and Infinitive depending on **polliciti sunt**. Similarly, add **esse** to **sese facturos**.

    quae imperasset: *what (Caesar) had ordered*. **imperasset** is a contracted form of **imperavisset**.

3   **Commius Atrebas**: *Commius the Atrebatian*. After conquering the Atrebates, who lived in the northern part of Gaul, Caesar had made Commius their king. Thinking Commius had influence with the British chiefs, Caesar had sent him into Britain before the main invasion to try to persuade the Britons to accept the protection of Rome.

4   **praemissum**: Supply **esse** to form an Accusative and Infinitive depending on **demonstraveram**.

    illi: *they* (the Britons).

5   **oratoris modo**: *acting as an envoy*, literally *in the manner of a spokesman*.

6   **tum**: *now (having been defeated)*.

7   **in petenda pace**: *in asking for peace*. (For this use of the Gerundive, see LL p. 61.)

    eius rei culpam: *the blame for that action*, i.e. the arrest and treatment of Commius.

8   **ut ignosceretur**: *to be forgiven*, an Indirect Command depending on **petiverunt**. (For verbs used impersonally, see LL p. 57.)

10   **ignoscere imprudentiae**: Supply **se** to form an Accusative and Infinitive depending on **dixit**. **imprudentiae** is dative depending on **ignoscere**.

Action and Adventure: Julius Caesar

37 End of First Invasion of Britain

(Caesar, *Bellum Gallicum* IV. 27– 36)

By 55 BC, Caesar had not only overcome the tribes of Gaul but had also crossed the Rhine in a display of force against the Germans. Being confident of his hold over Gaul, he then decided to invade Britain, ostensibly to cut off the military help which the Britons had been sending to their fellow Gauls on the continent. He also hoped to harness the economic potential which Britain offered mainly in the form of hides, slaves, woollen cloaks, pearls and hunting dogs. At this stage, he had no intention of conquering the island, as can be seen from the nature of the forces he took with him and from the fact that he had made no plans to establish supply-lines between the continent and Britain. The landing was made against stiff resistance from the Britons; but, despite the difficulties they faced in keeping formation as they waded ashore, the Romans put the enemy to flight.

Peace conditions imposed

hostes proelio superati, simulatque se ex fuga receperunt, statim ad Caesarem legatos de pace miserunt. obsides daturos quaeque imperasset sese facturos polliciti sunt. una cum his legatis Commius Atrebas venit, quem supra demonstraveram a Caesare in Britanniam praemissum. hunc illi e navi
5 egressum, cum ad eos oratoris modo Caesaris mandata deferret, comprehenderant atque in vincula coniecerant: tum proelio facto remiserunt. in petenda pace eius rei culpam in multitudinem coniecerunt et propter imprudentiam ut ignosceretur petiverunt. Caesar questus quod, cum ultro in continentem legatis missis pacem ab se petissent, bellum sine causa intulissent,
10 ignoscere imprudentiae dixit obsidesque imperavit. quorum illi partem statim dederunt, partem ex longinquioribus locis accersitam paucis diebus sese daturos

se recipere, to recover, withdraw
sese = se
una cum, along with
praemitto (3), to send ahead
mandatum (*n*), instruction, message
defero, to report, pass on
vinculum (*n*), chain
multitudo (*f*), large number, the masses, the common people

imprudentia (*f*), foolishness, lack of foresight
queror (3), **questus sum**, to complain
ultro, of one's own accord, voluntarily
continens (*f*), mainland, the Continent
bellum inferre, to make war
longinquus, distant
accerso (3), to summon

14 **his rebus**: *on these terms*. Caesar had agreed to make peace with the Britons on condition that they accepted the overlordship of Rome, dispersed their troops and handed over hostages.

post diem quartum quam: *three days after*. Latin authors frequently split the conjunction **postquam** in this way (see LL p. 52). For the Roman method of calculating time, see "inclusive reckoning" in LL p. 67.

est ventum: *they arrived*, literally *there was an arrival*. (For verbs used impersonally to emphasise the action rather than the people who performed the action, see LL p. 57.)

15 **ex superiore portu**: *from the more northerly port*, literally *from the port higher up (than the one from which he himself had sailed)*.

16 **quae cum**: *when these (ships)*. (For Linking Relative, see LL p. 26.)

18 **ad inferiorem partem**: Compare the use of **superiore** in line 16. This would be down-channel, in a south-westerly direction.

19 **magno sui cum periculo**: *with great danger to themselves*. **sui** is the genitive of the pronoun **se**. (For the genitive used to link two nouns or pronouns, see LL p. 7.)

20 **quae**: a Linking Relative (see LL p. 26.)

21 **adversa nocte**: *in a night of foul weather*.

in altum provectae: *having sailed out into the open sea*.

22 **luna plena**: This information helps to fix the date of Caesar's landing. The full moon was on the night of 30/31 August 55 BC.

qui dies ... efficere consuevit: *the day (of the month) which usually brings*, literally *which day is accustomed to produce*.

in Oceano: *in the Ocean*, i.e. the Atlantic.

23 **incognitum**: It is unlikely that this information was *unknown* to Caesar. At least some of the crews were Gauls, and they must have known about the tides. They may have decided not to tell Caesar; or it may have been so obvious to them that they did not think it worth mentioning; or Caesar may have decided to ignore the information because he was in a hurry to complete the reconnaissance before the end of the fighting season. Even if the intelligence was passed on, the changing tides would have been *beyond the experience* of the Roman soldiers, since their experience was confined to the Mediterranean, in which there are virtually no tides.

24 **quibus exercitum transportandum curaverat**: *which he had used to transport the army*, literally *in which he had arranged the transporting of the army*. (For this use of the Gerundive, see LL p. 61.)

26 **facultas aut administrandi aut auxiliandi**: *an opportunity to organise help for them*, literally *an opportunity of organising or helping*. (For the Gerund, see LL p. 60.)

28 **ad navigandum inutiles**: *useless for sailing*. (For Gerund, see LL p. 60.)

dixerunt. interea suos remigrare in agros iusserunt, principesque undique convenire et se civitatesque suas Caesari commendare coeperunt.

A storm upsets Caesar's plans

15 his rebus pace confirmata, post diem quartum quam est in Britanniam ventum, naves XVIII (de quibus supra demonstratum est), quae equites sustulerant, ex superiore portu leni vento solverunt. quae cum appropinquarent Britanniae et ex castris viderentur, tanta tempestas subito coorta est ut nulla earum cursum tenere posset, sed aliae eodem unde erant profectae referrentur, aliae ad inferiorem partem insulae (quae est propius solis occasum) magno sui cum 20 periculo deicerentur. quae tamen, ancoris iactis, cum fluctibus complerentur, necessario adversa nocte in altum provectae, continentem petierunt.

Some ships destroyed

eadem nocte accidit ut esset luna plena, qui dies maritimos aestus in Oceano efficere consuevit; nostrisque id erat incognitum. ita uno tempore et naves longas, quibus Caesar exercitum transportandum curaverat quasque in aridum 25 subduxerat, aestus complebat; et onerarias, quae ad ancoras erant deligatae, tempestas adflictabat; neque ulla nostris facultas aut administrandi aut auxiliandi dabatur. compluribus navibus fractis, reliquae cum essent (funibus, ancoris reliquisque armamentis amissis) ad navigandum inutiles, magna

remigro (1), to go back again
commendo (1), to entrust
confirmo (1), to establish
tollo (3), **sustuli, sublatum**, to take on board, pick up
lenis, light, gentle
solvo (3), to set sail, weigh anchor
coorior (4), to arise, blow up
eodem, to the same place
refero, to carry back
propius, nearer
solis occasus, the west
deicio (3), to drive down, sweep down

ancoram iacere, to drop anchor
necessario, of necessity, unavoidably
maritimus, of the sea
aestus, -us (*m*), tide
incognitus, unknown
navis longa (*f*), warship
aridus, dry
subduco (3), to draw up, beach
navis oneraria (*f*), transport-ship
ad ancoram deligatus, riding at anchor
adflicto (1), to batter, damage
funis (*m*), rope, cable
armamenta (*n. pl*), (ship's) tackle, gear

29 **id quod necesse erat accidere**: *as was bound to happen*, literally *that which was necessary to happen.*

31 **omnibus constabat**: *it was generally assumed.*

hiemare oportere: *that (the army) should spend the winter.* (For the impersonal verb **oportet**, see LL p. 58.)

32 **in hiemem**: *for the winter.*

33 **ad ea quae iusserat Caesar facienda**: *to do what Caesar had ordered.* (For this use of the Gerundive to express Purpose, see LL p. 61.)

36 **hoc etiam angustiora ... quod**: *all the smaller because*, literally *for this reason even smaller ... because.* The **quod** clause explains **hoc**.

37 **optimum factu esse duxerunt ... prohibere**: *they thought the best thing to do was to cut off ...* In the Accusative and Infinitive clause, the subject of **esse** is **prohibere** – literally *they thought that to cut off ... was the best thing to do.*

39 **belli inferendi causa**: *to make war (upon them)*, literally *for the sake of bringing war (upon them).* (See LL p. 61.)

41 **suos ex agris deducere**: *to bring their men back from the fields.* The Britons had laid down their arms and dispersed to their farms as ordered by Caesar.

43 **ex eventu navium**: *from what had happened to the ships*, literally *from the fate (outcome) of the ships.*

44 **ex eo quod**: *from the fact that.*

fore id quod accidit: *that things would turn out as they did*, literally *that that (**id**) would be which did happen.* The future infinitive (**fore**) and the accusative (**id**) form an Accusative and Infinitive depending on **suspicabatur**.

45 **ad omnes casus**: *to meet any eventuality*, literally *(for) all happenings.*

46 **quae**: The antecedent of this Relative Clause is **earum** (line 47); and, as often happens when clauses are inverted in this way, **naves** has been attracted into the same case as **quae**. The straightforward word order would have been **earum navium quae**.

47 **ad reliquas reficiendas**: See LL p. 61 for this use of **ad** + the Gerundive to express Purpose or Intention.

et quae = et ea quae.

ad eas res: For this use of **ad**, compare lines 28, 30 and 45.

48 **cum a militibus administraretur**: literally *as it was carried out by the soldiers.* Impersonal passive expressions like this are usually best translated actively in English: *as the soldiers carried out (the task).* (See LL p. 57.)

49 **reliquis ut navigari commode posset effecit**: literally *he brought it about* (**effecit**) *that sailing* (**navigari**) *was reasonably* (**commode**) *possible* (**posset**) *for the rest* (**reliquis**). Again, an active translation is the most natural way to deal with such impersonal expressions: *he was able to make the rest reasonably seaworthy.*

30 (id quod necesse erat accidere) totius exercitus perturbatio facta est. neque enim naves erant aliae quibus reportari possent, et omnia deerant quae ad reficiendas eas usui sunt, et (quod omnibus constabat hiemare in Gallia oportere) frumentum in his locis in hiemem provisum non erat.

British chiefs take advantage of the confusion

quibus rebus cognitis, principes Britanniae (qui post proelium factum ad ea quae iusserat Caesar facienda convenerant) inter se collocuti, cum equites et naves et
35 frumentum Romanis deesse intellegerent et paucitatem militum ex castrorum exiguitate cognoscerent (quae hoc erant etiam angustiora quod sine impedimentis Caesar legiones transportaverat), optimum factu esse duxerunt, rebellione facta, frumento commeatuque nostros prohibere et rem in hiemem producere, quod, eis superatis aut reditu interclusis, neminem postea belli
40 inferendi causa in Britanniam transiturum confidebant. itaque rursus coniuratione facta, paulatim ex castris discedere ac suos clam ex agris deducere coeperunt.

Remedial action by Caesar

at Caesar, etsi nondum eorum consilia cognoverat, tamen, et ex eventu navium suarum et ex eo quod obsides dare intermiserant, fore id quod accidit
45 suspicabatur. itaque ad omnes casus subsidia comparabat; nam et frumentum ex agris cotidie in castra conferebat et, quae gravissime adflictae erant naves, earum materia atque aere ad reliquas reficiendas utebatur, et quae ad eas res erant usui, ex continenti comportari iubebat. itaque cum summo studio a militibus administraretur, XII navibus amissis, reliquis ut navigari commode
50 posset effecit.

perturbatio (*f*), confusion, panic
deesse (+ *dat.*), to be lacking (to)
reficio (3), to repair
usui esse, to be of use
provideo (2), to arrange for, provide
princeps (*m*), chieftain
colloquor (3), to converse, confer, discuss
paucitas (*f*), small numbers, numerical weakness
exiguitas (*f*), smallness
impedimenta (*n. pl*), baggage
rebellio (*f*), renewal of hostilities
commeatus, -us (*m*), supplies, provisions
rem producere, to prolong the operation

intercludo (3), to cut off (from)
confido (3), to be confident
coniuratio (*f*), conspiracy
paulatim, little by little, a few at a time
clam, secretly
intermitto (3) (+ *infinitive*), to stop (doing something)
suspicor (1), to suspect
subsidia (*n. pl*), resources, the means
confero, to collect, gather
adfligo (3), to damage, wreck
materia (*f*), timber
aes, aeris (*n*), bronze, metal
comporto (1), to bring together, collect

51 **ex consuetudine**: *as usual*. The position of this phrase between **legione** and **una** indicates that it was normal practice to use one legion for foraging.

frumentatum: *to gather corn*. (For the Supine used to express Purpose, see LL p. 45.)

53 **hominum** refers to the local population.

54 **maiorem quam consuetudo ferret**: *greater than usual*, literally *greater than custom would suggest*.

55 **quam in partem**: Caesar often repeats the antecedent (**parte** = *direction*) in this way in the Relative Clause. English would not attempt to translate the noun **pars** twice.

56 **id quod erat**: *what was actually happening*. This is amplified in the Accusative and Infinitive which follows (**aliquid ... consilii**).

aliquid novi initum (esse) consilii: *that some new plan had been adopted*. (For the Partitive Genitive, see LL p. 9.)

59 **paulo longius**: *a short distance*, literally *a little farther*.

suos ... premi atque ... sustinere: Accusative and Infinitive clauses depending on **animadvertit** (line 60). (**premi** is present infinitive passive.) Compare **tela conici**.

60 **conferta legione**: *since the legion was crowded together*. The attack was so sudden that the soldiers, who had scattered to collect the corn, did not have time to group themselves in regular formation.

62 **dispersos**: *(them) while they were scattered*. This participle is the direct object of **adorti**. (Cf. **occupatos**, *fully-engaged*.)

63 **adorti**: *having attacked* – referring to the Britons, who are the subject of **perturbaverant** (line 64).

64 **incertis ordinibus**: *before they could form up*, literally *in uncertain ranks*.

essedis: The Romans themselves never used chariots in battle, and the only previous reference to their fighting against chariots was when the Gauls used them to rout the Roman cavalry in 295 BC during the Samnite Wars. It appears that, by Caesar's time, the Gauls had stopped using chariots, possibly because they had imported a new breed of horse big and strong enough to carry an armed soldier. Only the Britons continued to use war-chariots, pulled by a pair of small horses. There was a popular belief that British chariots, like those used by the Persians against Alexander (see page 146), had scythes protruding from the wheel-hubs – a belief which has continued to be promoted by the statue of Boudicca on Westminster Bridge. However, although excavations of the graves of warrior-chiefs have produced ample archaeological evidence of the use of chariots, there is *so far* no evidence of the use of scythed-chariots by the Britons.

68 **aurigae**: According to the historian Tacitus, who wrote an account of Agricola's later campaign in Britain, these *drivers* were of nobler birth than the fighters, who were only their retainers.

69 **illi** refers to the fighters who have leapt from the chariots.

71 **tantum efficiunt**: *they become so expert*, literally *they achieve so much*.

166

Ambushed in the fields

dum ea geruntur, legione ex consuetudine una frumentatum missa (quae appellabatur septima), neque ulla ad id tempus belli suspicione interposita, cum pars hominum in agris remaneret, pars etiam in castra ventitaret, ei qui pro portis castrorum in statione erant Caesari renuntiaverunt pulverem maiorem
55   quam consuetudo ferret in ea parte videri, quam in partem legio iter fecisset. Caesar, id quod erat suspicatus, aliquid novi a barbaris initum consilii, cohortes quae in stationibus erant secum in eam partem proficisci, duas ex reliquis in stationem succedere, reliquas armari et confestim sese subsequi iussit. cum paulo longius a castris processisset, suos ab hostibus premi atque aegre sustinere
60   et, conferta legione, ex omnibus partibus tela conici animadvertit. nam quod (omni ex reliquis partibus demesso frumento) una pars erat reliqua, suspicati hostes huc nostros esse venturos, noctu in silvis deliterant. tum dispersos, depositis armis, in metendo occupatos subito adorti, paucis interfectis, reliquos incertis ordinibus perturbaverant; simul equitatu atque essedis circumdederant.

Chariot-fighting

65   genus hoc est ex essedis pugnae: primo per omnes partes perequitant et tela coniciunt, atque ipso terrore equorum et strepitu rotarum ordines plerumque perturbant. et, cum se inter equitum turmas insinuaverunt, ex essedis desiliunt et pedibus proeliantur. aurigae interim paulatim ex proelio excedunt atque ita currus collocant ut, si illi a multitudine hostium premantur, expeditum ad suos
70   receptum habeant. ita mobilitatem equitum, stabilitatem peditum in proeliis praestant; ac tantum usu cotidiano et exercitatione efficiunt ut in declivi ac

suspicio (*f*), suspicion
interpono (3), to intervene, appear
remaneo (2), to remain
ventito (1), to keep coming and going
statio (*f*), guard-duty
pulvis, **-eris** (*m*), dust, cloud of dust
consilium inire, to form a plan
cohors (*f*), cohort
succedo (3), to take the place
armo (1), to arm
confestim, immediately, hurriedly
subsequor (3), to follow closely
sustineo (2), to hold out, hold back, control
animadverto (3), to see, observe
demeto (3), to cut down, reap
noctu, during the night
delitesco (3), **-ui**, to lie in wait, hide
dispersus, scattered
meto (3), to reap, harvest
essedum (*n*), chariot

circumdo (1), to surround
perequito (1), to ride through, drive about
strepitus, **-us** (*m*), noise, din
rota (*f*), wheel
plerumque, generally
turma (*f*), squadron
se insinuare, to penetrate , work one's way
    through
desilio (4), to leap down
proelior (1), to fight
excedo (3), to retire
currus, **-us** (*m*), chariot
expeditus, easy, ready, quick
receptus (*m*), retreat
mobilitas (*f*), mobility, speed
stabilitas (*f*), stability, steadiness
praesto (1), to display, show, combine
cotidianus, daily
usus, **-us** (*m*), practice
exercitatio (*f*), training
declivis, sloping

72 **incitatos**: *at full gallop.*

73 **temonem**: The **temo** was the *pole* to which the horses were harnessed by means of the yoke (**iugum**). See illustration on page 127.

74 **consuerint**: *it is their practice.* The perfect subjunctive has the force of a present tense here – literally *they have become accustomed.* This verb governs the six preceding infinitives.

75 **quibus rebus**: *by these tactics,* explained later by **novitate pugnae**. Both phrases depend on **perturbatis**.

   tempore opportunissimo: *in the very nick of time.*

77 **ad lacessendum (proelium)**: *for provoking a battle.* For this use of **ad** to express Purpose, compare lines 28, 30, 33, 45 and 47.

78 **arbitratus**: Although this is a perfect participle, English would more naturally use the present participle *thinking.*

79 **dum haec geruntur**: *meanwhile,* literally *while these things were happening.*

80 **qui**: The antecedent is **reliqui** (*the remaining Britons*). For the inversion of Relative Clauses, compare line 46.

81 **quae continerent**: *which were severe enough to keep.* The subjunctive of this verb and of **prohiberent** (line 82) shows that these storms were of a special type. (See Generic clauses in LL p. 103.)

83 **quanta**: This adjective introduces an Indirect Question depending on **demonstraverunt** (line 85). It agrees with **facultas** in line 84 – *what an excellent opportunity.*

   praedae faciendae atque sui liberandi: These genitives depend on **facultas** – *of getting booty and freeing themselves.* (For this use of the Gerundive, see LL p. 61.)

87 **etsi idem ... fore videbat**: *although he saw that the same thing would happen.*

   idem quod: *the same thing as.*

   ut effugerent: *namely, that they would escape,* explaining what had happened on previous days.

88 **celeritate**: *thanks to their speed.*

   tamen: *nevertheless* is inserted to remind the reader that the long explanation which has gone before all depends on **etsi** (line 87).

91 **quos**: *them.* (For Linking Relative, see LL p. 26.)

   tanto spatio ... quantum: *as far as.* (For Correlatives, see LL p. 63.)

92 **secuti** and **potuerunt**: The subject of both these words is the Romans; but, in an English translation, the idea contained in the phrase **cursu et viribus efficere** (literally *to achieve by running and strength*) would more naturally provide a subject for the second clause – *(as far as) their speed and strength allowed.*

93 **aedificiis**: *farm-houses.* By and large, the Britons did not live in towns.

praecipiti loco incitatos equos sustinere et brevi moderari ac flectere et per temonem percurrere et in iugo insistere et inde se in currus citissime recipere consuerint.

A lull in the fighting

75   quibus rebus perturbatis nostris novitate pugnae tempore opportunissimo Caesar auxilium tulit. namque eius adventu hostes constiterunt, nostri se ex timore receperunt. quo facto, ad lacessendum et ad committendum proelium alienum esse tempus arbitratus, suo se loco continuit et, brevi tempore intermisso, in castra legiones reduxit. dum haec geruntur, nostris omnibus
80   occupatis, qui erant in agris reliqui discesserunt. secutae sunt continuos complures dies tempestates, quae et nostros in castris continerent et hostem a pugna prohiberent. interim barbari nuntios in omnes partes dimiserunt paucitatemque nostrorum militum suis praedicaverunt; et quanta praedae faciendae atque in perpetuum sui liberandi facultas daretur, si Romanos castris
85   expulissent, demonstraverunt. his rebus celeriter magna multitudine peditatus equitatusque coacta, ad castra venerunt.

The enemy routed

Caesar, etsi idem quod superioribus diebus acciderat fore videbat – ut, si essent hostes pulsi, celeritate periculum effugerent – tamen nactus equites circiter XXX quos Commius Atrebas (de quo ante dictum est) secum transportaverat,
90   legiones in acie pro castris constituit. commisso proelio, diutius nostrorum militum impetum hostes ferre non potuerunt ac terga verterunt. quos tanto spatio secuti, quantum cursu et viribus efficere potuerunt, complures ex eis occiderunt. deinde, omnibus longe lateque aedificiis incensis, se in castra receperunt.

praeceps, -cipitis, steep
brevi, in a moment, in an instant
moderor (1), to check
flecto (3), to turn
percurro (3), to run along
iugum (*n*), yoke
insisto (3), to stand upon
cito, quickly
novitas (*f*), newness, novelty
namque, for
adventus, -us (*m*), arrival, approach
consisto (3), to halt, stop in one's tracks

proelium committere, to join battle
alienus, inappropriate
contineo (2), to confine
se continere, to remain
intermitto (3), to let pass, intervene
continuus, continuous, non-stop
praedico (1), to proclaim, report
in perpetuum, for ever
demonstro (1), to point out
peditatus, -us (*m*), infantry
cogo (3), to gather, collect
superior, previous
nanciscor (3), **nactus sum**, to obtain

94 **his**: *from them*, dative governed by **imperaverat**.

96 **adduci**: *to be taken* (present infinitive passive).

propinqua die aequinocti: *as the day of the equinox* (23 September) *was close at hand*.

hiemi navigationem subiciendam (esse): *that the crossing should be exposed to wintry weather*.

99 **eosdem quos reliqui portus**: *the same harbours as the rest (of the soldiers)*.

100 **paulo infra**: *a little farther south.* (See note on line 15.)

Points for Discussion

1 What do you think Caesar hoped to achieve by demanding hostages (line 2)? What motives do people have in taking hostages today? In your opinion, can hostage-taking ever be justified?

2 Why do you think the fighter ran along the pole of the chariot (line 73)?

3 Why do you think Caesar uses the present tense throughout lines 65–74?

4 Summarise the tactics the British chiefs intended to use (lines 38–42) and the arguments they used to stir up support for their revolt (lines 82–85).

5 The Britons seem to have had considerable skill in the use of war-chariots. Why do you think they did not use this to greater advantage in the battle mentioned in lines 87–93?

6 Why do you think Caesar burned the farm-houses (line 93)?

7 (a) The Romans regarded the ancient Britons as treacherous. Justify this Roman point of view using the above passage.

(b) How might the Britons have defended their actions?

8 Summarise the difficulties faced and overcome by Caesar and his men as described in the above passage.

9 The noun **pars** is used frequently in the above passage – lines 10, 19, 53, 55 (twice), 57, 60, 61(twice), 82. Suggest the various translations which could be used for each of these occurrences.

10 What qualities of Caesar as a general and as a leader are revealed in this passage? List those of his actions which would attract praise, and those for which he might have been criticised. Basing your views on this passage only, how do you think he emerges from this episode?

11 Caesar nearly always refers to himself in the third person (i.e. as "Caesar") when describing his military campaigns. Can you suggest why he did this?

Peace and return to Gaul

eodem die legati ab hostibus missi ad Caesarem de pace venerunt. his Caesar
95   numerum obsidum quem antea imperaverat duplicavit, eosque in continentem
adduci iussit, quod propinqua die aequinocti infirmis navibus hiemi
navigationem subiciendam non existimabat. ipse idoneam tempestatem
nactus, paulo post mediam noctem naves solvit, quae omnes incolumes ad
continentem venerunt; sed ex eis onerariae duae eosdem quos reliqui portus
100   capere non potuerunt et paulo infra delatae sunt.

duplico (1), to double	**navem solvere**, to set sail
tempestas (*f*), storm, weather	**portum capere**, to reach harbour
infirmus, damaged	**defero**, to carry down
paulo post, a short time after	

Roman silver coin minted around 48 BC, showing British chariot with its driver and armed warrior

Caesar: see Notes on Authors on page 8.

line

1   **studio pugnandi**: *in enthusiasm for fighting*. (For the use of the ablative, see LL p. 15; and for the Gerund, see LL p. 60.)

    ab duce: *by their general*, referring to the actions of Sabinus.

3   **quotiens quaeque cohors procurrerat**: *whenever each cohort (in turn) charged*. (For the pluperfect used to express actions which happened repeatedly, see LL p. 89.) When they were caught in the ambush, the Romans had formed themselves in a circle (**orbis**, mentioned in line 8) so that they could protect themselves on all sides. Every so often, in order to disrupt the enemy attack, a unit would make a charge from the circle and inflict as many casualties as possible before returning to the main group.

    ab ea parte: *in that area*.

4   **pronuntiari iubet**: *ordered the instruction to be given*. Four Indirect Commands (**ut ... coniciant neu ... accedant et ... cedant ... insequantur**) depend on **pronuntiari**, which is a present infinitive passive. Coming in between the third and fourth Indirect Command is an Accusative and Infinitive (**nihil eis noceri posse**) which also depends on **pronuntiari** (see note on line 6).

5   **quam in partem**: *wherever*.

6   **levitate armorum**: *because they were lightly-armed*, literally *by reason of the lightness of their arms*.

    nihil eis noceri posse: *(for) no harm could come to them*. See note on **pronuntiari iubet** (line 4) for the appearance of this Accusative and Infinitive among the Indirect Command clauses. (For the impersonal use (**nihil eis noceri**), see LL p. 57.)

7   **se recipientes** refers to the Romans and is the object of **insequantur**. Translate *as they were returning*, literally *(them) taking themselves back*.

8   **cum**: *whenever*. (For **cum** used with the pluperfect indicative to express actions which happened repeatedly, see LL p. 89. Compare also line 3.)

9   **eam partem nudari necesse erat**: *that part (of the circle) was inevitably exposed*, literally *it was necessary that that part was laid bare*. **eam partem nudari** and **ab latere aperto tela recipi** are Accusative and Infinitive clauses depending on **necesse erat**.

10   **ab latere aperto**: *on the open* (i.e. *right*) *side*. Since a soldier normally carried his shield on his left arm, his left side was well protected. He relied on the shield carried by the man on his right for the protection of his right side.

11   **ab eis qui cesserant** refers to the Gauls; **ab eis qui proximi steterant** refers to the Romans. Whenever a group of soldiers made a charge, a gap was left in the circle, and there would be a tendency for the soldiers on the left of the gap to move to their right to get more protection from those on their right. The effect of this was that the gap was partially filled, leaving insufficient room for those who had made the charge.

12   **nec virtuti locus relinquebatur**: *there was no room for heroic action*.

38 Gallic Treachery

(Caesar, *Bellum Gallicum* V. 34–37)

The Gallic chief Ambiorix, pretending to be a friend of the Romans, has told them that a large force of German mercenaries is on its way to attack the Roman camp which is under the command of L. Cotta and Q. Titurius Sabinus. Against his better judgment, Cotta has agreed to a proposal by Sabinus that the only safe course of action for the Romans is to abandon camp before the Germans arrive and to link up with a neighbouring legion. However, they are immediately ambushed by the forces of Ambiorix and, in the following extract, we read of the desperate struggle as they fight for their lives.

The Gauls change tactics

Galli erant et virtute et studio pugnandi pares. nostri tamen, etsi ab duce et a fortuna deserebantur, tamen omnem spem salutis in virtute ponebant; et, quotiens quaeque cohors procurrerat, ab ea parte magnus hostium numerus cadebat. qua re animadversa, Ambiorix pronuntiari iubet ut procul tela
5 coniciant neu propius accedant et, quam in partem Romani impetum fecerint, cedant: levitate armorum et cotidiana exercitatione nihil eis noceri posse: rursus se ad signa recipientes insequantur.

The Romans in difficulties

quo praecepto ab eis diligentissime observato, cum quaepiam cohors ex orbe excesserat atque impetum fecerat, hostes velocissime refugiebant. interim eam
10 partem nudari necesse erat et ab latere aperto tela recipi. rursus, cum in eum locum unde erant egressi reverti coeperant, et ab eis qui cesserant et ab eis qui proximi steterant circumveniebantur. sin autem locum tenere vellent, nec virtuti locus relinquebatur neque ab tanta multitudine coniecta tela conferti vitare poterant.

desero (3), to fail, let down	**observo** (1), to observe, obey, carry out
quisque, quaeque, quodque, each	**quispiam, quaepiam, quodpiam,** any
animadverto (3), to notice, realise	**excedo** (3), to come out from, leave
neu, and not	**velociter**, swiftly
propius, too close	**refugio** (3), to retreat, flee back
accedo (3), to approach	**nudo** (1), to lay bare, expose, leave
cedo (3), to give ground	unprotected
levitas (*f*), lightness	**revertor** (3), to return
cotidianus, daily	**circumvenio** (4), to surround, hem in
exercitatio (*f*), training, practice	**sin autem**, if on the other hand
insequor (3), to pursue	**nec…neque**, neither…nor…
praeceptum (*n*), instruction	**confertus**, packed close together

16   **cum pugnaretur**: *although the fighting lasted.* Caesar again uses the verb impersonally to emphasise the action rather than the people involved in the action. (See LL p. 57.)

    ad horam octavam: *until the eighth hour*, i.e. about two o'clock in the afternoon. The time from sunrise to sunset was divided into twelve equal "hours."

17   **nihil quod ipsis esset indignum committebant**: *they did not disgrace themselves in any way*, literally *they committed no act which would be unworthy of themselves.*

    T. Balventio . . . utrumque femur tragula traicitur: *T. Balventius had both his thighs pierced by a javelin.* The subject of the Latin is **femur**, and **Balventio** is dative to indicate the person towards whom the action was directed. Often the only convenient way of translating this type of dative is by the English possessive (*each thigh of Balventius*).

18   **primum pilum duxerat**: *had been the chief centurion.* The most senior centurions served in the first cohort of the legion; and the most senior centurion of all was called the **primipilus**, because he led the elite unit (**primus pilus**) in that cohort. (See note 1 on page 178 for more details about the promotion of centurions.)

    magnae auctoritatis: *highly respected*, literally *of great influence.* (For the genitive used to describe personal qualities, see LL p. 8.)

21   **in adversum os**: *full in the face.*

22   **Q. Titurius**: The full name of the Roman commander was Quintus Titurius Sabinus.

23   **rogatum**: *to ask.* (For the Supine used to express Purpose, see LL p. 45.)

24   **quos tribunos habebat**: *the tribunes he had.* As often happens in Latin when the relative clause precedes its antecedent (**tribunos**), the latter is placed within the relative clause.

    primorum ordinum centuriones: *centurions of the first rank*, i.e. the most senior centurions. (See also line 18.)

26   **imperatum facit**: *he obeyed the order.*

27   **longior instituitur sermo**: *the conversation was prolonged*, literally *a longer (than necessary) discussion was begun.*

29   **suo more victoriam conclamant**: *raised their customary shout of victory*, literally *hailed their victory in their usual way.*

31   **ex quibus**: *of them.* (For Linking Relative, see LL p. 26.)

Stubborn resistance by the Romans

15 tamen tot incommodis conflictati, multis vulneribus acceptis, resistebant; et,
magna parte diei consumpta, cum a prima luce ad horam octavam pugnaretur,
nihil quod ipsis esset indignum committebant. tum T. Balventio, qui superiore
anno primum pilum duxerat, viro forti et magnae auctoritatis, utrumque femur
tragula traicitur. Q. Lucanius eiusdem ordinis, fortissime pugnans, dum
20 circumvento filio subvenit, interficitur. L. Cotta legatus, omnes cohortes
ordinesque adhortans, in adversum os funda vulneratur. his rebus permotus
Q. Titurius, cum procul Ambiorigem suos cohortantem conspexisset, inter-
pretem suum Cn. Pompeium ad eum mittit rogatum ut sibi militibusque parcat.

Ambiorix responds

*In response to this appeal, Ambiorix said that, if Sabinus wished to confer with him,
he was at liberty to do so. He said he hoped that his army could be persuaded to
spare the lives of the Roman soldiers and gave his own personal guarantee that no
harm would come to Sabinus himself. Sabinus suggested to the wounded Cotta that,
if he agreed, they should withdraw from the battle and discuss terms with Ambiorix.
He was confident that he could persuade Ambiorix to spare them and their troops.
Cotta, however, said he would not go to an armed enemy, and persisted in his
refusal.*

Treachery

Sabinus, quos in praesentia tribunos militum circum se habebat, et primorum
25 ordinum centuriones, se sequi iubet. et, cum propius Ambiorigem accessisset,
iussus arma abicere, imperatum facit, suisque ut idem faciant imperat. interim,
dum de condicionibus inter se agunt longiorque consulto ab Ambiorige
instituitur sermo, paulatim circumventus interficitur.

Massacre

tum vero suo more victoriam conclamant atque ululatum tollunt; impetuque in
30 nostros facto, ordines perturbant. ibi L. Cotta pugnans interficitur cum maxima
parte militum. reliqui se in castra recipiunt unde erant egressi: ex quibus

incommodum (*n*), disadvantage
conflicto (l), to afflict, handicap
consumo (3), to use up
superior, previous
subvenio (4) (+ *dat*.), to come to the
assistance (of)
legatus (*m*), legate, lieutenant-general
adhortor (l), to encourage
funda (*f*), sling-stone

permotus, alarmed
cohortor (l), to encourage, urge on
interpres (*m*), interpreter
in praesentia, at that time
tribuni militum, military tribunes
abicio (3), to throw away
agere de (+ *abl*.), to discuss
consulto, deliberately
ululatus (*m*), wild yell, war-cry

33 **illi**: *they*, i.e. the soldiers in the camp.

34 **ad unum omnes**: *all to a man*, i.e. to the very last man.

35 **incertis itineribus**: *by ill-defined tracks.*

36 **de rebus gestis**: *about what had happened.*

L. Petrosidius aquilifer, cum magna multitudine hostium premeretur, aquilam intra vallum proiecit, ipse pro castris fortissime pugnans occiditur. illi aegre ad noctem oppugnationem sustinent; noctu ad unum omnes, desperata salute, se
35 ipsi interficiunt. pauci, ex proelio elapsi, incertis itineribus per silvas ad T. Labienum legatum in hiberna perveniunt atque eum de rebus gestis certiorem faciunt.

aquilifer (*m*), standard-bearer	**noctu**, by night
premo (3), to overwhelm, press hard	**elabor** (3), **elapsus sum**, to slip away
proicio (3), to hurl	**hiberna** (*n.pl*), winter-quarters
oppugnatio (*f*), attack	**certiorem facere**, to inform
sustineo (2), to hold off	

Points for Discussion

1 Explain in your own words the clause **etsi ab duce et a fortuna deserebantur** (lines 1–2).

2 Describe briefly the new tactics adopted by Ambiorix and how the change affected the Romans.

3 How long did the Romans keep up their resistance to the Gauls (lines 15–17)?

4 Gather as much evidence as you can from this passage to prove that Roman soldiers were highly disciplined.

5 Why do you think many of the survivors in the camp killed themselves? Can you think of any other examples, from ancient or modern times, of people committing suicide after being defeated?

6 From the information contained in this passage (both the Latin and the English), provide a short assessment of the character and ability of (*a*) Sabinus, (*b*) Cotta, (*c*) Ambiorix.

Caesar: See Notes on Authors on page 8.

line

1 **primis ordinibus**: *(promotion to) the first rank*. The legion was made up of ten numbered cohorts, each consisting of six centuries. The relatively small size of the century (anything from 50 to 100 men) made it possible for a strong team-spirit to develop, and this was further helped by the fact that each century was led by an experienced veteran, called a centurion – a kind of sergeant-major whose authority was never questioned by the soldiers. It was the cohesiveness of the century which made the legion such an effective fighting force. The most experienced centurions (**primi ordines**) were concentrated in the First Cohort – an elite unit comprising five double-centuries. The First Cohort also contained such specialists as secretarial staff, engineers and technicians, priests and perhaps medical orderlies.

3 **quinam anteferretur**: *about which of them should be given preference*. (For Deliberative Questions, see LL p. 108.)

   de loco: *over (the matter of) promotion*

4 **cum acerrime pugnaretur**: *when the fighting was at its fiercest*, literally *it was being fought most fiercely*. (For verbs used impersonally, see LL p. 57.)

5 **locum tuae probandae virtutis**: *opportunity for proving your courage*. He implies that the opportunity is already there; so why hold back? (For this use of the Gerundive, see LL p. 61.)

7 **quae pars ... in eam**: *into the part which*. As often happens in Latin, the relative clause precedes the antecedent; and, so that the reader may know immediately what the relative clause describes, the author brings the noun **pars** forward into the relative clause.

8 **ne Vorenus quidem sese vallo continet**: *nor indeed did Vorenus remain within the rampart*.

9 **omnium existimationem**: *what everyone would think*, literally *the opinion of all*.

11 **hunc** refers to the wounded Gaul, **illum** to Pullo.

12 **regrediendi facultatem**: *an opportunity to retreat*. (For Gerund, see LL p. 60.)

14 **conanti dextram moratur manum**: *hindered his right hand as he tried* ...

   impeditum: *when he was struggling (to draw his sword)*, literally *(him) hampered*.

39 Two Brave Rivals

(Caesar, *Bellum Gallicum* V. 44)

Among Roman soldiers, rivalry for promotion could lead to near-hostility. In this story a Roman camp is being besieged by the Nervii and two rival centurions leave the camp to fight with the enemy, each trying to show how much braver than the other he is.

erant in ea legione fortissimi viri centuriones, qui iam primis ordinibus appropinquarent, T. Pullo et L. Vorenus. hi perpetuas controversias inter se habebant quinam anteferretur; omnibusque annis de loco summis simultatibus contendebant. ex his Pullo, cum acerrime ad munitiones pugnaretur, "quid
5 dubitas," inquit "Vorene? aut quem locum probandae virtutis tuae spectas? hic, hic dies de nostris controversiis iudicabit."

haec cum dixisset, procedit extra munitiones, quaeque pars hostium confertissima visa est, in eam irrumpit. ne Vorenus quidem sese vallo continet, sed omnium veritus existimationem subsequitur. tum, mediocri spatio relicto,
10 Pullo pilum in hostes mittit, atque unum ex multitudine procurrentem traicit. quo percusso et exanimato, hunc scutis protegunt hostes, in illum tela universi coniciunt; neque dant regrediendi facultatem. transfigitur scutum Pulloni, et verutum in balteo defigitur. avertit hic casus vaginam, et gladium educere conanti dextram moratur manum; impeditum hostes circumsistunt.

perpetuus, never-ending	**protego** (3), to protect
controversia (*f*), argument	**universi**, all
simultas (*f*), rivalry	**transfigo** (3), to pierce
quid? why?	**verutum** (*n*), spear
confertus, dense, thick	**balteum** (*n*), sword-belt
veritus, fearing	**defigo** (3), to fix, stick
subsequor (3), to follow closely	**averto** (3), to turn aside, knock out
mediocris, relatively small	of place
traicio (3), to pierce, transfix	**casus** (*m*), mishap, blow
percutio (3), to strike through	**vagina** (*f*), scabbard
exanimatus, unconscious	**circumsisto** (3), to surround

15   **laboranti**: *as he struggled*, picking up **illi** earlier in the sentence.

   hunc refers to Vorenus; **illum** (line 16) refers to Pullo.

16   **transfixum**: Supply **esse**.

18   **cupidius**: *over-enthusiastically.*

   deiectus: *he was pushed down and . . .* , literally *having been thrown down.*

21   **fortuna utrumque versavit**: *each of them suffered a reversal of fortune*, literally *fortune whirled each of them around.*

   alter alteri: *the one to the other.* These two words are to be taken with both **inimicus** (*the one a rival to the other*) and **auxilio salutique esset** (*the one helped and saved the other*). (For Predicative Datives (**auxilio** and **saluti**), see LL p. 13.)

22   **virtute anteferendus**: *more to be praised for his valour*, literally *deserving to be preferred from (the point of view of) valour.* (For Gerundives, see LL p. 61.)

15 succurrit inimicus illi Vorenus et laboranti subvenit. ad hunc se confestim a
Pullone omnis multitudo convertit; illum veruto transfixum arbitrantur.
occursat ocius gladio comminusque rem gerit Vorenus atque, uno interfecto,
reliquos paulum propellit. dum cupidius instat, in locum deiectus inferiorem
concidit. huic rursus circumvento fert subsidium Pullo, atque ambo incolumes,
20 compluribus interfectis, summa cum laude sese intra munitiones recipiunt.

   sic fortuna in contentione et certamine utrumque versavit ut alter alteri
inimicus auxilio salutique esset, neque diiudicari posset uter utri virtute
anteferendus videretur.

subvenio (4) (+ *dat*.), to help
confestim, immediately
se convertere, to turn
arbitror (1), to think
occurso (1), to rush against, attack
ocius, quickly, speedily
comminus, at close quarters
rem gerere, to carry on the fight
propello (3), to drive away, ward off
insto (1), to press on, press forward

inferior, lower
concido (3), to fall
rursus, in turn
circumvenio (4), to surround
subsidium (*n*), help
ambo, both
se recipere, to return
contentio (*f*), rivalry, contest
certamen (*n*), struggle
diiudico (1), to distinguish, decide
   between

Points for Discussion

1 To whom do the words **multitudine** (line 10) and **multitudo** (line 16) refer?

2 Why do you think the two rivals helped each other?

3 "Competition and rivalry bring out the best in people."
   "Competition and rivalry bring out the worst in people."

   Discuss these two points of view. Are they necessarily irreconcilable?

Virgil: See Notes on Authors on page 15.
Metre: Hexameter (see p. 255.)

line

1   **acerrimus armis**: *a very valiant warrior*, literally *most keen in arms.*

2   **Hyrtacides**: *a son of Hyrtacus.* The ending **-ides** (meaning *son of*) corresponds to the Scottish "Mac" (e.g. MacDonald) and the Irish "O'" (e.g. O'Neill).

    comitem Aeneae: *as a companion to Aeneas.*

    Ida venatrix: *the huntress Ida*, a mountain nymph who was the mother of Nisus.

3   **iaculo celerem**: *because he was an expert* (literally *swift*) *with the javelin.* Experts can do things quickly.

4   **iuxta**: Supply a verb such as **erat** or **stabat** – *stood next to him.*

    quo pulchrior alter non fuit Aeneadum: *most handsome of all the followers of Aeneas*, literally *more handsome than whom there was not another of the followers of Aeneas.*

5   **Troiana neque induit arma**: The words **pulchrior alter** must be understood with this clause – *and all who put on Trojan armour*, literally *nor did (another more handsome) put on Trojan armour.*

6   **ora puer prima signans intonsa iuventa**: The literal meaning is *a boy exhibiting unshaven cheeks in the first (stages of) manhood.* Translate *a boy whose unshaven cheeks proclaimed the onset of manhood.*

7   **amor unus**: *a common bond of affection.*

    ruebant: *they used to charge.*

A Vatican stamp issued in 1981 to commemorate the 2000th anniversary of Virgil's death in 19BC

see p 15

Honour and Glory

40 Nisus and Euryalus

(Virgil, *Aeneid IX*, selections from lines 176–445)

When Aeneas and his followers eventually reached Italy after their escape from Troy, they were welcomed by Latinus, king of Latium, the country near the mouth of the River Tiber. That was not the end of their troubles, however. Latinus promised his daughter Lavinia in marriage to Aeneas, but this did not please Turnus, king of the Rutulians, to whom she had previously been betrothed. To prevent the marriage, Turnus waged war against Aeneas. The following episode occurred during this war. Aeneas had gone to seek help from Evander, king of the neighbouring city of Pallanteum. During his absence, the Rutulians set siege to the Trojan camp. It was important to get that news through to Aeneas.

Two devoted friends, Nisus and Euryalus, are on guard-duty at the camp.

    Nisus erat portae custos, acerrimus armis,
    Hyrtacides, comitem Aeneae quem miserat Ida
    venatrix iaculo celerem levibusque sagittis;
    et iuxta comes Euryalus, quo pulchrior alter
5   non fuit Aeneadum Troiana neque induit arma,
    ora puer prima signans intonsa iuventa.
    his amor unus erat pariterque in bella ruebant.
    tum quoque communi portam statione tenebant.

iaculum (*n*), javelin	**iuventa** (*f*), youth
sagitta (*f*), arrow	**pariter**, side by side
induo (3), to put on	**bellum** (*n*), battle, warfare
signo (1), to show	**communis**, shared
intonsus, unshaven	**statio** (*f*), sentry-duty

9   **fiducia rerum**: *over-confidence*, literally *confidence in things*.

11   **procubuere = procubuerunt**: *they lie prostrate*, literally *they have fallen forward*.

    porro: *then*, as used in the next stage of an argument.

12   **quid dubitem**: *what I am contemplating*.

    animo: *in my mind*. Prepositions are frequently omitted in poetry. (Cf. **armis** in line 1.)

13   **Aenean acciri**: *that Aeneas should be recalled* – an Accusative and Infinitive depending on **exposcunt**. This is followed by another Accusative and Infinitive (**mitti viros**). (For the Greek accusative form **Aenean**, see page 262.)

    populusque patresque: a poetic equivalent of **senatus populusque Romanus** (SPQR).

14   **qui certa reportent**: *to bring him a reliable report*. (For this type of Purpose clause, see LL p. 44.)

15   **si tibi promittunt**: Nisus seems to suggest that he will ask some material reward for his friend, but want only the glory (**facti fama**, *the fame of the deed*) for himself.

16   **videor reperire posse**: *I think I can find*. Understand **mihi** with **videor** – literally *I seem (to myself) to be able to find*.

17   **Pallantea**: *of Pallanteum*. Pallanteum was reputed to have stood on the Palatine Hill, the future site of Rome.

18   **cetera animalia**: *all other living creatures*.

19   **laxabant curas et corda**: English would probably require to use a different translation for **laxabant** with each of the objects.

20   **Teucrum (= Teucrorum)**, *of the Trojans*.

    delecta iuventus: *a chosen band of warriors*, in apposition to **ductores primi.** Although **iuvenis** and **iuventus** are normally translated as *youth*, the Romans used them to describe a far wider age-group than we do. They were used of males fit to bear arms (i.e. from late teens to mid-forties).

21   **summis regni de rebus**: *on matters of supreme importance to the state*.

22   **quid facerent**: *(debating) what they should do*. (For Deliberative Question, see LL p. 38.)

24   **castrorum et campi medio**: *in the assembly area in the middle of the camp*, literally *in the middle of the camp and of the open area*.

25   **admittier orant**: *begged to be admitted*. **admittier** is an archaic form of the present infinitive passive. The **-ier** ending gave way to **-i** in the second century BC.

26   **rem magnam pretiumque morae fore**: An Accusative and Infinitive giving their reason for asking to be heard. Understand a verb of speaking (following **orant**), and supply **esse** with **rem magnam**. Translate *(and said) that it was an important matter and it would be worth interrupting (the debate to hear it)*, literally *it would be the value of the delay*.

    Iulus (scanned as three syllables) was the son of Aeneas.

Nisus explains his plan to Euryalus – to go through the enemy lines and summon help from Aeneas.

"cernis quae Rutulos habeat fiducia rerum:
10   lumina rara micant, somno vinoque soluti
procubuere, silent late loca. percipe porro
quid dubitem, et quae nunc animo sententia surgat.
Aenean acciri omnes, populusque patresque,
exposcunt, mittique viros qui certa reportent.
15   si tibi quae posco promittunt (nam mihi facti
fama sat est), tumulo videor reperire sub illo
posse viam ad muros et moenia Pallantea."

1999

The Trojan leaders are holding a council-of-war when Nisus and Euryalus ask to be admitted.

cetera per terras omnes animalia somno
laxabant curas et corda oblita laborum.
20   ductores Teucrum primi, delecta iuventus,
consilium summis regni de rebus habebant,
quid facerent, quisve Aeneae iam nuntius esset.
stant longis adnixi hastis et scuta tenentes
castrorum et campi medio. tum Nisus et una
25   Euryalus confestim alacres admittier orant,
rem magnam pretiumque morae fore. primus Iulus
accepit trepidos ac Nisum dicere iussit.

cerno (3), to observe, see
rarus, sparse, far apart
mico (1), to shine, flicker
solutus, relaxed
sileo (2), to be silent
late, far and wide
percipio (3), to perceive, learn
sententia (*f*), idea, plan
-que ... -que ..., both ... and ...
patres (*m.pl*), the elders
exposco (3), to insist
tumulus (*m*), mound, hillock
sub (+ *abl.*), under, at the foot of

moenia (*n.pl*), walls, battlements
laxo (1), to relax, soothe, shed
cor, cordis (*n*), heart, mind
obliviscor (3), **oblitus** (+ *genitive*), to forget
ductor (*m*), leader
consilium (*n*), council
-ve, or
adnixus (+ *dat.*), leaning (on)
una, together
confestim, immediately
alacer, eager(ly)
trepidus, excited

28 **quos euntes**: *them as they went.*

30 **nec non et**: The two negatives cancel each other out to produce a very strong affirmative – *and (Iulus) too.*

31 **ante annos**: *beyond his years*, i.e. you would not have expected this in one so young.

   curam: *sense of responsibility.*

32 **portanda**: *to take*, literally *to be taken*. (For the Gerundive, see LL p. 61.)

35 **inimica**: not just *belonging to the enemy* but also *hostile to them* in that it was to bring about their own death. This is clear from the use of **tamen** which contrasts their own deaths, as yet unmentioned, with the havoc they were to wreak on the enemy before that (**ante**).

   multis futuri exitio: *destined to bring destruction on many.* (For Predicative Dative, see LL p. 13.)

36 **somno vinoque**: *in drunken sleep*, literally *in sleep and wine.* (For Hendiadys, see page 259.)

37 **fusa**: *sprawling.* This is the perfect participle passive of **fundo** (3), *to pour.*

   arrectos currus: *tilted chariots*, i.e. with the pole sticking up in the air, as happens with a two-wheeled vehicle when the horses are unyoked.

   litore: For the omission of the preposition, compare lines 1 and 12.

39 **vina**: *wine-flasks.*

   locutus: Supply **est**.

40 **audendum (est) dextra**: *we must act boldly*, literally *it must be dared with our right hand.* (For the Gerundive used impersonally, see LL p. 62.)

41 **ne qua manus**: *so that no band.* (For Purpose clauses, see LL p. 44.)

42 **consule longe**: *keep a sharp lookout on all sides.*

43 **haec vasta dabo** (= **haec vastabo**), *I will cause havoc here.*

44 **vocem premit**: *said not a word more*, literally *checked his voice.*

45 **altis**: *piled high.*

46 **toto proflabat pectore somnum**: *was breathing heavily as he slept*, literally *breathed forth sleep from his whole chest* – an apt description of drunken sleep.

47 **rex idem**: *himself a king*, literally *the same man, a king.*

   augur: An augur, or seer, foretold the future both by inspecting the entrails of animals which had been sacrificed to the gods and by interpreting various natural signs such as the flight of birds.

The Trojan leaders agree to their plan. Nisus and Euryalus start to make their way through the sleeping enemy encampment.

      protinus armati incedunt; quos omnis euntes
      primorum manus ad portas, iuvenumque senumque,
30   prosequitur votis. nec non et pulcher Iulus,
      ante annos animumque gerens curamque virilem,
      multa patri mandata dabat portanda. sed aurae
      omnia discerpunt et nubibus inrita donant.
      egressi superant fossas noctisque per umbram
35   castra inimica petunt, multis tamen ante futuri
      exitio. passim somno vinoque per herbam
      corpora fusa vident, arrectos litore currus,
      inter lora rotasque viros, simul arma iacere,
      vina simul. prior Hyrtacides sic ore locutus:
40   "Euryale, audendum dextra: nunc ipsa vocat res.
      hac iter est. tu, ne qua manus se attollere nobis
      a tergo possit, custodi et consule longe!
      haec ego vasta dabo et lato te limite ducam."

They attack the sleeping Rutulians wildly, killing all in their way.

      sic memorat vocemque premit, simul ense superbum
45   Rhamnetem aggreditur, qui forte tapetibus altis
      exstructus toto proflabat pectore somnum,
      rex idem et regi Turno gratissimus augur,
      sed non augurio potuit depellere pestem.

protinus, immediately
incedo (3), to move off
primores (*m.pl*), the leaders, chiefs
prosequor (3), to escort
vota (*n.pl*), prayers, good wishes
animus (*m*), thoughtfulness
gero (3), to display
virilis, manly
mandatum (*n*), instruction, message
aura (*f*), breeze, wind
discerpo (3), to scatter
inritus, useless, futile, unaccomplished
dono (1), to give
supero (1), to cross, climb over
passim, everywhere

herba (*f*), grass
lora (*n.pl*), reins, harness
rota (*f*), wheel
hac (*abl.*), this way
attollo (3), to lift, raise up
a tergo, from behind
limes, -itis (*m*), path
memoro (1), to speak
ensis (*m*), sword
tapete (*n*), rug
exstruo (3), to raise up
gratus (+ *dat.*), loved (by)
augurium (*n*), skill in prophecy

49   **temere iacentes**: *lying haphazardly*, wherever they had flopped down drunk, instead of being carefully positioned to guard their master.

51   **nactus**: *coming upon (him)*, from **nanciscor**. He was lying among the horses' feet.

52   **ceu**: *just like*, introduces a simile (see page 260.)

53   **manditque trahitque**: *mangles and carries off*. (**-que . . . -que . . .** = *both . . . and . . . .*)

54   **molle pecus**: *the soft flock*. The adjective refers to the softness of the sheep's fleece and also the feebleness of their natures.

55   **nec minor**: *likewise*. The simile has ended and the poet picks up the story of the slaughter, this time describing the exploits of Euryalus.

    et ipse: *he too*.

56   **multam sine nomine plebem**: *many ordinary people*. **sine nomine** (*without a name*) does not mean that they had no names, but that their names were not known or unimportant.

58   **ignaros**: *unawares* or *taken by surprise*.

59   **magnum post cratera**: *behind a large wine jar*. **cratera** is a Greek accusative form. (See page 262.)

60   **pectore in adverso cui**: *full in his breast*, literally *in the front of whose breast*. (For the dative (**cui**) used possessively, see LL p. 11.)

61   **adsurgenti** agrees with **cui** (line 60).

    multa morte recepit purpureum: *drew (it) out, crimson with much shedding of blood*.

63   **vina refert**: *brought up wine*. (For Poetic Plural, see page 262.)

    hic furto fervidus instat: *he (Euryalus) eagerly pressed on with his stealthy attack*.

64   **ignem deficere extremum**: *that the last flicker of the watch-fire was dying down*, literally *that the last (of the) fire was failing* – an Accusative and Infinitive depending on **videbat**.

65   **religatos rite**: *properly tethered*.

66   **talia** is the object of **ait**, *(he) said*.

67   **nimia caede atque cupidine ferri**: Supply **eum**. *That he (Euryalus) was being carried away by an excessive lust for slaughter*. Note how the two complementary ideas (*by too great slaughter and (too great) desire*) have been combined in the English translation. (For Hendiadys, see page 259.)

68   **absistamus**: *let us stop*. (For Wishes or Exhortations, see LL p. 107.)

69   **poenarum exhaustum satis est**: *we have taken our fill of vengeance*, literally *enough (of) punishment has been drained (by us)*.

    facta: Supply **est**.

tres iuxta famulos temere inter tela iacentes
50 armigerumque Remi premit aurigamque sub ipsis
nactus equis ferroque secat pendentia colla.
impastus ceu plena leo per ovilia turbans
(suadet enim vesana fames) manditque trahitque
molle pecus mutumque metu, fremit ore cruento.
55 nec minor Euryali caedes; incensus et ipse
perfurit, ac multam in medio sine nomine plebem,
Fadumque Herbesumque subit Rhoetumque Abarimque
ignaros; Rhoetum vigilantem et cuncta videntem,
sed magnum metuens se post cratera tegebat.
60 pectore in adverso totum cui comminus ensem
condidit adsurgenti et multa morte recepit
purpureum: vomit ille animam et cum sanguine mixta
vina refert moriens, hic furto fervidus instat.

Nisus calls a halt to the killing.

iamque ad Messapi socios tendebat; ibi ignem
65 deficere extremum et religatos rite videbat
carpere gramen equos, breviter cum talia Nisus
(sensit enim nimia caede atque cupidine ferri)
"absistamus," ait "nam lux inimica propinquat.
poenarum exhaustum satis est, via facta per hostes."

depello (3), to drive off, keep away
pestis (*f*), death, destruction
iuxta, nearby
famulus (*m*), attendant, retainer
armiger (*m*), armour-bearer
premo (3), to overpower
auriga (*m*), charioteer
seco (1), to cut through
pendeo (2), to hang, droop
collum (*n*), neck
impastus, hungry, starving
ovile (*n*), sheep-fold
turbo (1), to create havoc
suadeo (2), to urge on
vesanus, mad, raging
mutus, silent, dumb
fremo (3), to roar
cruentus, bloody, dripping with blood

perfuro (3), to rage furiously
subeo, -ire, to steal up on, attack
metuo (3), to fear
tego (3), to conceal, hide
comminus, at close quarters
condo (3), to bury
adsurgo (3), to rise, get up
vomo (3), to vomit up
mixtus, mixed
tendo (3), to make one's way,
    head towards
carpo (3), to crop, feed on
gramen (*n*), grass
breviter, briefly
inimicus, hostile
propinquo (1)(+ *dat.*), to approach,
    draw near

70 **ex urbe Latina:** This was the city of Laurentum. Turnus had asked the city to send him reinforcements to attack Aeneas' camp.

71 **campis:** For the omission of the preposition, see lines 1, 12 and 37.

73 **Volcente magistro:** *led by Volcens*, literally *Volcens (being) master (of the cavalry)*. (For this type of Ablative Absolute, see LL p. 30.)

75 **hos:** *them* , i.e. Nisus and Euryalus.

laevo flectentes limite: *turning off to the left*, literally *bending (their course) along the left-hand path.*

77 **immemorem:** *thoughtless*, literally *forgetful*. He hadn't thought when he took it as booty that its reflective surface might betray him.

radiisque adversa refulsit: *gleaming as it reflected the rays (of the moon)*, literally *and turned towards the rays it flashed back.*

78 **haud temere est visum:** *the sight did not go unheeded*, literally *not carelessly was it seen.*

79 **quive . . . quove:** The **-ve** has little force except to show that another question is being asked. We would probably not translate it in English.

80 **nihil illi tendere contra:** *they (i.e. Nisus and Euryalus) made no effort to reply*, literally *they attempted nothing against (this)*. **tendere** is a Historic Infinitive – often used by Roman authors in place of a past tense of the indicative when they wished to add vividness or excitement to the story. Compare **celerare** and **fidere** in line 81. (For Historic Infinitive, see LL p. 32.)

82 **obiciunt sese:** *blocked their escape*, literally *placed themselves in the way.*

ad divortia nota: *at the places where they knew the paths crossed*, literally *at the well-known separations (of the paths).*

83 **hinc atque hinc:** *on all sides*, literally *on this side and on that.*

84 **ilice:** *holly-oak*, a dark-leaved, evergreen oak. The botanical name for the holly-tree is **ilex.**

85 **horrida** (*bristling*) is nominative agreeing with **silva.**

complerant = compleverant.

86 **rara per occultos lucebat semita calles:** *here and there* (**rara**), *the path showed up* (**lucebat**) *among the indistinct tracks*. There were two kinds of path in the wood: the tracks made by animals (**calles**) and a man-made path (**semita**) which had become overgrown and barely distinguishable from the animal tracks.

87 **onerosa praeda:** *the heavy plunder* (nominative case), referring to the plunder he had picked up during the slaughter. The stolen helmet had already given them away!

88 **fallit timor regione viarum:** *fear made him lose his way among the paths*, literally *fear deceived (him) in the direction of the paths.*

They snatch any plunder they can, and Euryalus puts on a captured helmet. They leave the camp and think they are safe. But a squadron of Rutulian cavalry, approaching the camp under the command of Volcens, catches sight of the two friends. When challenged, Nisus and Euryalus flee for safety into the darkness.

70   interea praemissi equites ex urbe Latina,
       cetera dum legio campis instructa moratur,
       ibant et Turno regi responsa ferebant,
       ter centum, scutati omnes, Volcente magistro.
       iamque propinquabant castris muroque subibant
75   cum procul hos laevo flectentes limite cernunt;
       et galea Euryalum sublustri noctis in umbra
       prodidit immemorem radiisque adversa refulsit.
       haud temere est visum. conclamat ab agmine Volcens:
       "state, viri! quae causa viae? quive estis in armis?
80   quove tenetis iter?" nihil illi tendere contra,
       sed celerare fugam in silvas et fidere nocti.
       obiciunt equites sese ad divortia nota
       hinc atque hinc, omnemque abitum custode coronant.
       silva fuit late dumis atque ilice nigra
85   horrida, quam densi complerant undique sentes,
       rara per occultos lucebat semita calles.
       Euryalum tenebrae ramorum onerosaque praeda
       impediunt, fallitque timor regione viarum.

praemitto (3), to send ahead
legio (*f*), company of soldiers
ter, thrice, three times
scutatus, armed with a shield
subeo, -ire (+ *dat.*), to approach, draw near to
cerno (3), to see, notice
galea (*f*), helmet
sublustris, glimmering
conclamo (1), to shout out
celero (1), to hasten

fido (3) (+ *dat.*), to trust
abitus, -us (*m*), exit, way out
corono (1), to surround
late, widely
dumus (*m*), thicket
niger, dark, shady
densus, thick
sentes (*m.pl*), briars, brambles
tenebrae (*f.pl*), darkness
ramus (*m*), branch

89 **imprudens**: *not realising (he had left his friend behind).*

91 **qua regione**: *where*, literally *in what area.*

92 **perplexum**: *tangled*, because he had picked his way through the thickets of the wood. The metaphor is continued in the participle **revolvens** (*unwinding*).

93 **vestigia retro observata legit**: *he searched for his tracks and picked his way back*, literally *he picked the tracks observed backwards.*

95 **signa sequentum**: *the calls of the pursuers.* The noun **signa** refers to all the signs which indicated that people were following, such as shouts, trumpet calls, etc. Note the alliterative use of the "**s**" sound (see p. 259).

96 **nec longum in medio tempus (erat)**: *he had not long to wait*, literally *there was not much time in between.*

97 **quem iam manus omnis oppressum rapit**: *whom the entire band (of Rutulians) had overwhelmed and seized.*

98 **fraude loci et noctis**: *confused by his surroundings and the darkness.* The ablative **fraude** may simply explain one of the circumstances which brought about his capture (literally *thanks to the deception of the place and the night*): or it may be governed by **oppressum** (literally *overwhelmed by the deception of the ground and the night*), in which case **oppressum** performs a two-fold function: he was *confused* by his surroundings and *overpowered* by the Rutulians.

   subito turbante tumultu: *bewildered by the sudden uproar*, literally *the sudden uproar bewildering (him).* The eerie effect of the repeated **t**, **u** and **b** sounds captures the extent of Euryalus' fear and confusion. (See Alliteration, Assonance and Onomatopoeia on pp. 259–60.)

99 **conantem plurima frustra**: *despite many hopeless attempts (to break free)*, literally *(still) attempting very many things in vain.* Like **oppressum**, the participle **conantem** agrees with **quem** (line 97).

100 **quid faciat?** *What was he to do?* – a Deliberative Question (see LL p. 107). The present subjunctive (**faciat**) continues the sequence of Historic Presents which Virgil uses at this point to create an atmosphere of speed and excitement. (Cf. **audeat**, **inferat** and **properet**.)

101 **moriturus**: *to certain death*, literally *about to die.*

103 **adducto lacerto**: The most natural way to translate this Ablative Absolute is: *he drew his arm back.* The verb **adducere** here means literally *to draw towards (himself).* The comparative **ocius** here means simply *quickly.*

104 **Lunam**: *The Goddess of the Moon*, usually called Diana (or Artemis), who was also the goddess of hunting and the woods. In line 106, she is called **Latonia**, *daughter of Latona.*

105 **praesens nostro succurre labori**: *be with me and help me in my difficult task.* **praesens** is often used of divine help, where the god is thought to help human beings by appearing at their side. (Cf. the Biblical use *a very present help in trouble.*)

Nisus escapes, but Euryalus loses his way. Nisus retraces his steps and finds his friend surrounded by the enemy.

      Nisus abit; iamque imprudens evaserat hostes,
90   ut stetit et frustra absentem respexit amicum:
      "Euryale infelix, qua te regione reliqui?
      quave sequar, rursus perplexum iter omne revolvens
      fallacis silvae?" simul et vestigia retro
      observata legit dumisque silentibus errat.
95   audit equos, audit strepitus et signa sequentum.
      nec longum in medio tempus, cum clamor ad aures
      pervenit ac videt Euryalum, quem iam manus omnis
      fraude loci et noctis, subito turbante tumultu,
      oppressum rapit et conantem plurima frustra.

What should he do? Out of the darkness, he hurls his spears at Euryalus' captors and causes consternation by killing two of them.

100   quid faciat? qua vi iuvenem, quibus audeat armis
      eripere? an sese medios moriturus in enses
      inferat et pulchram properet per vulnera mortem?
      ocius adducto torquens hastile lacerto,
      suspiciens altam Lunam sic voce precatur:
105   "tu, dea, tu praesens nostro succurre labori,

evado (3), to evade, elude
respicio (3), to look round for
qua, where
fallax, deceptive
silens, silent
strepitus, -us (*m*), din, shouting
auris (*f*), ear
manus (*f*), band, squadron
fraus (*f*), treachery, deceit

eripio (3), to snatch away, rescue
sese = **se**
infero, to hurl, fling
pulcher, fine, noble
propero (1), to hasten, bring on quickly
torqueo (2), to poise, brandish
hastile (*n*), spear, javelin
suspicio (3), to look up
altus, high, on high
precor (1), to pray

107   **sine** is the imperative of **sinere**. Similarly, **rege** is the imperative of **regere**, *to direct*.

108   **dixerat**: This word indicates the end of the Direct Speech – a necessary device, since the poem was recited to an audience, not read by them from a book.

110   **venit aversi in tergum Sulmonis**: *struck Sulmo full in the back*, literally *came into the back of Sulmo (who was) turned away*.

111   **fisso ligno**: *with its broken shaft*.

112   **diversi**: *in every direction*. The adjective vividly describes their consternation, since they did not know where the assailant was.

      hoc acrior: *all the more fiercely*, literally *by this amount the fiercer*.

      idem: *he* (i.e. Nisus), literally *the same man*.

113   **summa ab aure**: *from just above his ear* – the position of a javelin immediately before it is thrown.

114   **Tago per tempus utrumque**: *through both Tagus' temples*. (For the Possessive Dative, see LL p. 11.)

115   **traiecto tepefacta cerebro**: *warmed in the brain it had pierced*.

116   **saevit**: *went wild with rage*, because an unseen assailant had just killed two of his men.

      teli auctorem: *the person who had thrown the spear*, literally *the source of the weapon*.

117   **nec quo**: This introduces an Indirect Question depending on **conspicit** – *and he did not see where . . .*

118   **tu tamen interea**: He turns to the captive Euryalus and makes it clear that the attack will not save him. **tamen** implies *I haven't caught the attacker yet but . . . .*

119   **amborum**: *both*, referring to the two attendants killed by Nisus.

123   **adsum qui feci**: *Here I am. I did it.*

124   **iste**: *that youth you have there!*

      ausus: Supply **est**.

125   **conscia**: *which know the truth*. Although this adjective agrees with **sidera**, it should also be taken with **hoc caelum**.

126   **tantum dilexit**: *all he did was to love*, literally *he merely loved*.

astrorum decus et nemorum Latonia custos!
hunc sine me turbare globum et rege tela per auras!"
dixerat, et toto conixus corpore ferrum
conicit. hasta volans noctis diverberat umbras
110 et venit aversi in tergum Sulmonis, ibique
frangitur, ac fisso transit praecordia ligno.
diversi circumspiciunt. hoc acrior idem
ecce aliud summa telum librabat ab aure.
dum trepidant, iit hasta Tago per tempus utrumque
115 stridens traiectoque haesit tepefacta cerebro.

But he is too late to save his friend.

saevit atrox Volcens nec teli conspicit usquam
auctorem nec quo se ardens immittere possit.
"tu tamen interea calido mihi sanguine poenas
persolves amborum" inquit. simul ense recluso
120 ibat in Euryalum. tum vero exterritus, amens,
conclamat Nisus nec se celare tenebris
amplius aut tantum potuit perferre dolorem:
"me, me, adsum qui feci, in me convertite ferrum,
o Rutuli! mea fraus omnis, nihil iste nec ausus
125 nec potuit; caelum hoc et conscia sidera testor.
tantum infelicem nimium dilexit amicum."

astrum (*n*), star
decus (*n*), glory, ornament
nemus (*n*), wood, grove
globus (*m*), band, mob
conixus, straining
ferrum (*n*), javelin
volo (1), to fly
diverbero (1), to strike (cut) through
praecordia (*n.pl*), heart
circumspicio (3), to look around
libro (l), to poise, level
trepido (1), to be confused, panic
strido (3), to whiz, whir
haereo (2), **haesi, haesum**, to stick
usquam, anywhere
se immittere, to launch oneself

ardens, blazing with anger
calidus, warm
persolvo (3), to pay in full
recludo (3), to draw (a sword)
exterritus, terrified, frantic
amens, mad, out of one's mind
nec amplius, and no longer
celo (1), to conceal, hide
perfero, to endure
converto (3), to turn, direct
nec ... nec ..., neither ... nor ...
sidus, -eris (*n*), star
testor (1), to call to witness
nimium, too much

127 **viribus adactus:** *driven home with force.*

128 **costas:** *(Euryalus') ribs.*

    pectora: *breast.* (For Poetic Plural, see page 262.)

129 **leto:** *in death.* For the omission of the preposition, compare lines 1, 12, 37 and 71.

130 **collapsa recumbit:** *sank and drooped.*

131 **veluti:** *just as* introduces a simile (see page 260).

133 **demisere = demiserunt:** *have dropped* or *have bowed down.*

    cum: *when.*

135 **in solo Volcente moratur:** *he was intent on Volcens alone,* literally *he lingers on Volcens alone.*

136 **quem:** object of **proturbant** – *they tried to fend him* (i.e. Nisus) *off.*

    hinc atque hinc: *on all sides,* literally *from this side and from that.*

138 **Rutuli clamantis in ore adverso:** *full in the face of the screaming Rutulian,* i.e. Volcens.

139 **animam abstulit hosti:** *deprived his enemy of life,* literally *took the soul away from his enemy.* (For the dative used with verbs of "Taking Away", see LL p. 10.)

141 **confossus:** *riddled with wounds,* literally *stabbed through and through.*

    ibi demum: *there and only there* or *there at last,* i.e. when he had reached his dead friend.

Nisus rushes at Volcens and falls mortally wounded as he kills him.

      talia dicta dabat, sed viribus ensis adactus
      transabiit costas et candida pectora rumpit.
      volvitur Euryalus leto, pulchrosque per artus
130 it cruor inque umeros cervix collapsa recumbit.
      purpureus veluti cum flos succisus aratro
      languescit moriens, lassove papavera collo
      demisere caput pluvia cum forte gravantur.
      at Nisus ruit in medios solumque per omnes
135 Volcentem petit, in solo Volcente moratur.
      quem circum glomerati hostes hinc comminus atque hinc
      proturbant. instat non setius ac rotat ensem
      fulmineum, donec Rutuli clamantis in ore
      condidit adverso et moriens animam abstulit hosti.
140 tum super exanimum sese proiecit amicum
      confossus, placidaque ibi demum morte quievit.

dictum (*n*), word
transabeo, -ire, to pierce, go right through
candidus, fair, white
rumpo (3), to burst through
volvo (3), to roll, keel over
artus, -us (*m*), limb
cruor (*m*), blood
umerus (*m*), shoulder
cervix (*f*), neck
purpureus, crimson, bright
succido (3), to cut down
aratrum (*n*), plough
languesco (3), to droop
lassus, weary, limp

papaver (*n*), poppy
pluvia (*f*), rain
gravo (1), to weigh down
glomero (1), to crowd, mass
comminus, at close quarters
insto (l), to press on
non setius, nonetheless
roto (1), to whirl
fulmineus, flashing, like lightning
donec, until
condo (3), to hide, bury, plunge
exanimus, lifeless
proicio (3), to throw down
placidus, peaceful
quiesco (3), to rest

142 **si quid mea carmina possunt**: *if my poetry has any power at all*, literally *if my poems can (achieve) anything*. The verb **possum** is a compound of **potis + sum**, *I am powerful*.

143 **memori aevo:** *from the memory of time*, literally *from mindful time*.

144 **domus Aeneae:** *the descendants of Aeneas*, i.e. the Romans.

Capitoli immobile saxum: *the Capitol's unshakeable rock.* The Capitol, on which were situated the Citadel and the Temple of Jupiter, symbolised the eternal destiny of Rome.

145 **pater Romanus:** The home and the head of the household (**pater**), who symbolised the home, were both greatly revered by the Romans, and the loyalty which this inspired was undoubtedly one of the main sources of Rome's strength. Here, Virgil not only pays tribute to all the "fathers" who had made Rome great over the centuries, but also probably intends it as a hidden compliment to the Emperor Augustus, regarded as the wise father of the nation.

A final eulogy from the poet.

fortunati ambo! si quid mea carmina possunt,
nulla dies umquam memori vos eximet aevo,
dum domus Aeneae Capitoli immobile saxum
145 accolet imperiumque pater Romanus habebit.

fortunatus, fortunate, happy
ambo, both
memor, mindful

eximo (3) (+ *dat.*), to take away (from)
accolo (3), to inhabit

Points for Discussion

1 Explain in your own words the meaning and significance of lines 32–33.

2 Study the sounds of the words in lines 52–54. How do they contribute to the vividness of the simile? Comment in particular on the different effect produced by **manditque trahitque** in line 53 and by the alliterative use of the "m" sound in line 54.

3 Why is daylight described as **inimica** (line 68)?

4 Pick out two parts of the text in which Virgil, while describing the glorious feats of the two heroes, hints at the disaster which is to follow.

5 Study the descriptions of the deaths of Rhoetus (lines 60–63) and of Euryalus (127–133). In what way does the language of the one passage differ from that of the other, and why do you think Virgil decided on this different treatment of the two deaths?

6 How apt do you think the simile of the flowers is in lines 131–133? Compare it for effectiveness with the simile of the hungry lion in lines 52–54. Give reasons for your answers.

7 Do you think Nisus and Euryalus could have succeeded in their attack on the enemy camp? What actually gave them away to the enemy? What contributed most to their downfall?

8 "Far from deserving eternal glory, as Virgil states in lines 142–145, Nisus and Euryalus deserved to be court-martialled." Make out the cases for the Defence and Prosecution.

Eutropius: See Notes on Authors on page 11.

line

1   **eodem tempore**: *round about the same time.* In 283 BC, two years before Pyrrhus'
invasion, the Samnites had tried, unsuccessfully, to defeat Rome by joining forces with
some marauding Gauls. This was the latest in a series of wars fought between the
Romans and the Samnites to decide which of them would control the area south-west of
Rome. It was the Samnites who had inflicted one of the most shameful defeats on the
Romans at the Caudine Forks, when the Roman armies were "sent under the yoke" after
being forced to lay down their arms. That had taken place in 321 BC; but, by the end of
the fourth century, Rome had the upper hand again. Her enemies, however, were keen
to seize every opportunity to drive her from the conquered territory.

    ultima: *furthest*, i.e. the far south of.

    quia iniuriam fecissent: *because, it was alleged, they had insulted.* The use of the
subjunctive indicates that this was the reason the Romans gave for declaring war,
whereas the indicative would have been a factual statement made by the writer. (See
LL p. 99.)

3   **poposcerunt:** Note that the verb **poscere** takes two direct objects.

    ex genere Achillis: In ancient times, important people liked to trace their family-tree
back to a god or a hero. Pyrrhus claimed to be directly descended from the son of the
Greek hero Achilles, also called Pyrrhus, who had founded the kingdom of Epirus.
(Cf. Julius Caesar who traced his lineage back to the goddess Venus through Iulus, son
of Aeneas.)

6   **duci:** *to be led* (present infinitive passive). Compare **ostendi** (line 6) and **dimitti** (line
7); and **capi** and **reverti** (lines 28 and 29).

7   **quaecumque Romanis agerentur:** *all that the Romans were doing*, literally *whatever
was being done by the Romans*. (For Dative of Agent, compare LL p. 62.)

10   **incognitos:** *because they were unfamiliar to them.* The Romans had never encountered
elephants before.

12   **quos:** This Linking Relative, together with the infinitive **iacere**, forms an Accusative
and Infinitive clause depending on **vidisset**. (For Linking Relative, see LL p. 26.)

    adverso vulnere: *with their wounds on the front of their bodies.*

13   **etiam mortuos**: *even in death.*

    tulisse ... dicitur: *he is said to have raised.*

14   **se potuisse:** *he could have been* – an Accusative and Infinitive introduced by the phrase
cum hac voce.

    sibi contigissent: *if he had had the good fortune (to have such soldiers)*, literally *had
happened to him.*

41 Rome and Pyrrhus

(Eutropius II. 11–14)

Tarentum was a flourishing Greek trading colony in the "heel" of Italy which resented Rome's expansion into southern Italy. When a squadron of Roman ships called in at Tarentum, the Tarentines sank four of them. Rome immediately sent envoys to protest, but the Tarentines ridiculed them and pelted them with rubbish. Rome declared war on Tarentum (281 BC). The Tarentines had no army of their own but, when necessary, they used their wealth to hire mercenary troops to protect themselves and their neighbours. On this occasion, they appealed for help to Pyrrhus, king of Epirus in Greece. Being eager to emulate the conquests of his ancestor, Alexander the Great, Pyrrhus willingly agreed to help them; and, in 280 BC, he crossed into Italy with 25 000 men and twenty elephants.

The first battle

eodem tempore Tarentinis, qui in ultima Italia sunt, bellum indictum est quia legatis Romanorum iniuriam fecissent. hi Pyrrhum, Epiri regem, contra Romanos auxilium poposcerunt, qui ex genere Achillis originem trahebat. is mox ad Italiam venit, tumque primum Romani cum transmarino hoste
5 dimicaverunt. missus est contra eum consul P. Valerius Laevinus, qui, cum exploratores Pyrrhi cepisset, iussit eos per castra duci, ostendi omnem exercitum tumque dimitti ut renuntiarent Pyrrho quaecumque Romanis agerentur.
    commissa mox pugna, cum iam Pyrrhus fugeret, elephantorum auxilio vicit,
10 quos incognitos Romani expaverunt. sed nox proelio finem dedit. Laevinus tamen per noctem fugit; Pyrrhus Romanos mille octingentos cepit et eos summo honore tractavit; occisos sepelivit. quos cum adverso vulnere et truci vultu etiam mortuos iacere vidisset, tulisse ad caelum manus dicitur cum hac voce: se totius orbis dominum esse potuisse, si tales sibi milites contigissent.

bellum indicere (+ *dat.*), to declare war (on)	**octingenti**, 800
traho (3), to trace	**honos** (*m*), respect
transmarinus, from across the sea	**tracto** (1), to treat
dimico (1), to fight	**occido** (3), to slay
explorator (*m*), scout	**sepelio** (4), to bury
committo (3), to join (battle)	**trux, trucis**, grim
expavesco (3), **-pavi**, to fear greatly	**vox, vocis** (*f*), voice, remark
finem dare (+ *dat.*), to put an end (to)	**orbis** (*m*), world

16 **ferro ignique:** *by fire and sword*, the expression used to describe complete destruction.

17 **terrore exercitus:** *because of the fear inspired by the (Roman) army.*

18 **de redimendis captivis:** *to negotiate the release of the prisoners*, i.e. by ransoming them. (For this use of the Gerundive, see LL p. 61.)

20 **admiratus:** Supply **est.** This verb is balanced by **contemptusque est** (line 22).

   sic leads on to the Result clause **ut ... voluerit.** The clause **ut ad se transiret** depends on **sollicitare.**

21 **voluerit:** *he tried.*

23 **qui** here introduces a Purpose clause. (See LL p. 44.)

24 **praecipuum virum** and **legatum** (line 23) both refer to Cineas.

   ita ut: ita depends on **peteret.** English would probably begin a new sentence here: *The terms were to be that ....*

26 **pax:** *the peace (terms).*

   remandatum est: *word was sent back.* On this verb depends the Accusative and Infinitive **eum ... pacem habere non posse.** (For Impersonal Passives, see LL p. 57.)

27 **iusserunt:** The order was issued *not* to the prisoners, but to the rest of the Roman people. Translate *issued a decree.*

28 **infames haberi:** *to be regarded as disgraced.* This would probably involve temporary loss of citizenship.

   potuissent: *they had allowed themselves*, literally *they had been able.* (For this use of the subjunctive to express an alleged reason, see LL p. 99.)

29 **nec ante eos ad veterem statum reverti quam si:** This also depends on **iusserunt.** **ante** is not a preposition here; **ante ... quam** (*until*) is often split up in this way (see LL p. 52). Translate *and (they gave orders that) they were not to be restored to their former status until ....* Translate the conjunction **si** by *and unless.* The use of **si** suggests there was doubt about their ability to meet the conditions laid down for clearing their names, i.e. to kill two enemy soldiers each.

30 **spolia:** *the spoils*, i.e. the armour stripped from the enemies they slew.

   ita: *with this answer.*

   a quo cum quaereret: *when (Pyrrhus) asked him*, literally *sought from him.* (For Linking Relative, see LL p. 26.)

31 **qualem Romam comperisset:** *what impression he had formed of Rome*, literally *what sort of (place) he had found Rome (to be).*

Unsuccessful peace overtures

15   postea Pyrrhus, coniunctis sibi Samnitibus, Lucanis, Bruttiis, Romam perrexit,
omnia ferro ignique vastavit, Campaniam populatus est atque ad Praeneste
venit, miliario ab urbe octavo decimo. mox terrore exercitus, qui eum cum
consule sequebatur, in Campaniam se recepit. legati ad Pyrrhum de redimendis
captivis missi ab eo honorifice suscepti sunt. captivos sine pretio Romam misit.

20   unum ex legatis Romanorum Fabricium sic admiratus, cum eum pauperem esse
cognovisset, ut quarta parte regni promissa sollicitare voluerit ut ad se transiret,
contemptusque est a Fabricio. quare, cum Pyrrhus Romanorum ingenti
admiratione teneretur, legatum misit qui pacem aequis condicionibus peteret,
praecipuum virum, Cineam nomine: ita ut Pyrrhus partem Italiae, quam iam

25   armis occupaverat, obtineret.

     pax displicuit: remandatum Pyrrho est a senatu eum cum Romanis, nisi ex
Italia recessisset, pacem habere non posse. tum Romani iusserunt captivos
omnes, quos Pyrrhus reddiderat, infames haberi, quod armati capi potuissent,
nec ante eos ad veterem statum reverti quam si binorum hostium occisorum

30   spolia rettulissent. ita legatus Pyrrhi reversus est. a quo cum quaereret Pyrrhus
qualem Romam comperisset, Cineas dixit regum se patriam vidisse; scilicet

coniungo (3), to join
pergo (3), **perrexi**, to march, make for
populor (1), to devastate
miliarium (*n*), milestone
se recipere, to withdraw
honorifice, with respect
suscipio (3), to receive
pretium (*n*), price, ransom
admiror (l), to marvel at
sollicito (l), to tempt, bribe
contemno (3), to despise, spurn

quare, therefore
aequus, fair, just
praecipuus, distinguished, exceptional
obtineo (2), to keep
displiceo (2), to displease
recedo (3), to retreat, withdraw
revertor (3), to return
bini, two each
referre, to bring back
scilicet, undoubtedly, without a doubt

32 **tales illic fere omnes esse qualis** ... : Having used **dixit** (line 31) to introduce the first Accusative and Infinitive, Latin does not need any other introductory verbs to continue the Indirect Speech. Translate *almost all (who lived) there were such as* ... , another way of saying they were all like kings. (For Correlatives, see LL p. 63.)

33 **putaretur**: Supply **esse**.

35 **certamine commisso**: Compare **commissa pugna** in line 9. Lines 35–36 are misleading. According to modern historians who have sifted through the evidence of the various ancient writers, Pyrrhus lost 3500 men and the Romans 6000. In a sense, therefore, Pyrrhus had actually inflicted a second defeat on the Romans at this Battle of Asculum (279 BC); but his own losses were so great that he was forced to withdraw (**fugatus**) to Tarentum.

36 **fugatus**: Supply **est**.

37 **interiecto anno**: *after a year had passed.*

Fabricius: See lines 20ff.

41 **Pyrrhoque dici**: This phrase depends on **iussit**. Translate *and (ordered) Pyrrhus to be told*. (For Dative Verbs used in the passive, see LL p. 57.)

42 **eum** is the object of **admiratus**.

ille est Fabricius: *That's (typical of) Fabricius.*

difficilius: *less easily*, literally *with more difficulty*.

43 **ad Siciliam**: Pyrrhus was rather disillusioned by his "victories" and also by the poor support he was receiving from his allies in the south of Italy. When an urgent appeal came from the Greek colony of Syracuse, which was being attacked by the Carthaginians, Pyrrhus crossed into Sicily (278 BC) and drove out the Carthaginians before returning to Italy in the spring of 275 BC.

44 **triumphavit**: *was given a triumph*. Normally a general had to disband his troops before entering the city; but, after a great victory, the state might decide to *give him a triumph*, which meant that he was allowed to parade his troops, with all the spoils and prisoners they had captured, through Rome along the Via Sacra to the Temple of Jupiter on the Capitoline Hill.

46 **pugnavit**: Soon after this battle, which took place in 275 BC, Pyrrhus left Italy with 8000 footsoldiers and 500 cavalry, less than a third of the army he had brought over from Greece in 281 BC.

48 **primus duxit**: *he was the first man to bring.*

49 **apud Argos**: When he returned to Greece, Pyrrhus continued his flamboyant career by seizing the throne of Macedonia and then attacking Sparta and Argos in the Peloponnese. During the attack on Argos in 272 BC, he was about to kill one of the Argive defenders when the mother of his intended victim, seeing the danger her son was in, threw a roof-tile at Pyrrhus and killed him!

civitatem: In ancient Greece, a "state" and a "city" were usually one and the same thing.

tales illic fere omnes esse, qualis unus Pyrrhus apud Epirum et reliquam Graeciam putaretur.

The tide turns

missi sunt contra Pyrrhum duces P. Sulpicius et Decius Mus consules.
35 certamine commisso, Pyrrhus vulneratus est, elephanti interfecti, viginti milia caesa hostium et ex Romanis tantum quinque milia; Pyrrhus Tarentum fugatus.
interiecto anno, contra Pyrrhum Fabricius est missus, qui prius inter legatos sollicitari non potuerat, quarta regni parte promissa. tum, cum vicina castra ipse et rex haberent, medicus Pyrrhi nocte ad eum venit promittens veneno se
40 Pyrrhum occisurum, si sibi aliquid polliceretur. quem Fabricius vinctum reduci iussit ad dominum Pyrrhoque dici quae contra caput eius medicus spopondisset.
tum rex admiratus eum dixisse fertur: "ille est Fabricius, qui difficilius ab honestate quam sol a cursu suo averti potest." tum rex ad Siciliam profectus est.
Fabricius victis Lucanis et Samnitibus triumphavit. consules deinde M'.
45 Curius Dentatus et Cornelius Lentulus adversum Pyrrhum missi sunt. Curius contra eum pugnavit, exercitum eius cecidit, ipsum Tarentum fugavit, castra cepit. ea die caesa hostium viginti tria milia. Curius in consulatu triumphavit. primus Romam elephantos quattuor duxit. Pyrrhus etiam a Tarento mox recessit et apud Argos, Graeciae civitatem, occisus est.

unus, alone
apud (+ *acc.*), in
puto (1), to think, consider
certamen (*n*), struggle, battle
tantum, only
medicus (*m*), doctor
venenum (*n*), poison
aliquid, something
polliceor (2), to promise

vincio (4), to tie up, put in chains
caput, -itis (*n*), head, life
spondeo (2), **spopondi,** to promise
fertur, is said
honestas (*f*), honour, path of honour
averto (3), to turn away
M'= Manius
consulatus (*m*), consulship

205

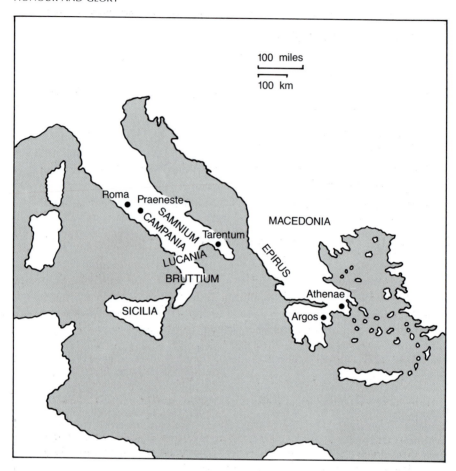

The Mediterranean area

Points for Discussion

1 When he captured Pyrrhus' scouts, how did Laevinus treat them (lines 5–8)? Why do you think he did this?

2 What unusual aid enabled Pyrrhus to turn defeat into victory in his first battle with the Romans (lines 9–10)?

3 What conclusions did Pyrrhus draw from the appearance of the Roman dead after the first battle (lines 12–14)?

4 To whom do the following Linking Relatives refer: **quos** (line 12), **a quo** (line 30) and **quem** (line 40)?

5 What condition did the Romans lay down before they would make peace with Pyrrhus (lines 26–27)?

6 Collect the present infinitives passive from lines 6 (two), 7, 28 (two), 29, 38, 40, 41 and 43, and arrange them according to their Groups.

7 State the tenses of the two participles **promissa** (line 38) and **promittens** (line 39), and explain why Eutropius used these tenses.

8 To achieve variety in his language, Eutropius uses different words for the same idea, e.g. **dicitur** (line 13) and **fertur** (line 42) both mean *is said*. Find three different words for "kill" (lines 34–49), three for "promise" (lines 37–41) and three for "battle" (lines 9–36).

9 Explain the point of Pyrrhus' statement (lines 42–43).

10 Why do you think Pyrrhus released the Roman prisoners without a ransom (lines 18–19)?

11 Why do you think Pyrrhus "marvelled at" Fabricius (line 20)? Is there some inconsistency between this statement and the fact that he attempted to bribe him? Or was it a perfectly logical thing to do?

12 Do you think that the action taken by the Romans (lines 27–30) was (a) justified, (b) advisable?

13 List what you think were the good and bad qualities of Pyrrhus.

14 Explain the expression "to win a Pyrrhic victory".

15 Do you think Eutropius is a good story-teller? Use the descriptions of Cineas' embassy (lines 22–33) and of the doctor's treachery (lines 38–41) to illustrate your answer.

line

1   **ecce!** *lo and behold!* – a stylistic feature used by the author to create dramatic effect.

3   **ad radices**: *at the foot*, literally *at the roots*.

5   **putans quod:** *thinking that*. In Medieval Latin, a **quod** clause is frequently used where Classical Latin would use an Accusative and Infinitive clause. Medieval usages are discussed in some detail in LL pages 132–7.

     alicuius gigantis: *of some giant.*

6   **audaciam sumens**: *summoning up courage.*

     cum taederet me vivere: *although I was tired of living*, literally *although to live wearied me* (see LL p. 58). The bandit had faced so many terrifying experiences already that he was tempted to give up.

7   **domumculam:** *a small house*. The use of the diminutive arouses more pity than the word **domum** would. Compare the use of **cum parvulo** (*with a tiny child*) and **muliercula** (*a poor little woman*).

8   **unam** agrees with **mulierculam**. In Medieval Latin, **unus** is frequently used for the indefinite article "a". The author may have placed **cum parvulo** between **unam** and **mulierculam** to emphasise "mother and child" as an entity.

10   **quantum distem:** *how far away I was.*

     triginta milibus: *thirty miles.*

11   **a terra habitabili:** *from civilisation*, literally *from a habitable land.*

12   **quas striges vocant:** *whom they (people) call witches.*

     raptam fore = raptam esse.

Marvel and Mystery

42 Tale of the Witches

The following story is taken from a long work of prose fiction written by John de Alta Silva, a Cistercian monk who lived around AD 1200. The story describes one of a number of hair-raising adventures which a notorious old bandit experienced during his attempts to escape to his home after being captured in an unsuccessful raid on a wild part of the country.

Horrific discovery

et ecce in vallem quandam tenebrosam horribilemque profunditate sua oculos dirigens, conspicio a longe fumum quasi de clibano consurgentem. notans igitur locum festinanter de monte descendi; et ecce ad montis radices tres latrones recenter suspensos repperio. horrui illico nimio terrore correptus,
5 coepique haesitare et desperare de salute, putans quod in alicuius gigantis habitationem incidissem. tamen ex necessitate audaciam sumens, cum taederet me vivere, progredior invenioque domumculam ostium apertum habentem, in qua unam tamen cum parvulo mulierculam ad prunas sedere conspexi.
       intro autem domum, accedo ad eam, saluto interrogoque quid ibi sola agat, si
10 virum habeat quantumve ab hominum habitatione distem. illa vero, triginta milibus a terra habitabili me remotum esse affirmans, subinfert cum lacrimis se cum filio nocte transacta a sinu viri sui ab eis quas striges vocant raptam fore

vallis (*f*), valley	**salus, -utis** (*f*), safety
tenebrosus, dark	**habitatio** (*f*), dwelling
horribilis, terrifying	**incido** (3), to stumble on, come upon
profunditas (*f*), depth	**domumcula** (*f*), small house
dirigo (3), to direct	**ostium** (*n*), door
a longe, far off	**pruna** (*f*), coal, (*pl.* fireside)
fumus (*m*), smoke	**accedo** (3), to approach
quasi, as if	**saluto** (l), to greet
clibanus (*m*), furnace	**interrogo** (1), to ask
consurgo (3), to rise up	**quid agat**, what she is doing
festinanter, quickly	**-ve**, or
latro (*m*), robber	**vero**, in truth, but
recenter, recently	**removeo** (2), to remove
suspensus, hanged	**affirmo** (1), to state, say
repperio (4), to find	**subinfero**, to add
horreo (2), to shudder	**transactus**, previous, last
illico, immediately	**sinus, -us** (*m*), embrace
nimius, extreme, very great	**strix** (*f*), witch
correptus, seized	**rapio** (3), to carry off
haesito (l), to hesitate	

13 **iussam ut coqueret:** Whereas in Classical Latin **iubere** is normally used with an infinitive, it may be used in Medieval Latin with an Indirect Command clause. Translate *ordered to cook.*

14 **sero strigibus devorandum:** *to be eaten later by the witches.* (For uses of the Gerundive, see LL p. 61.)

15 **super mulieris casu:** *for* (literally *over*) *the woman's misfortune.*

    cum ipsa: *with (the woman) herself.*

16 **liberaturum:** Supply **esse.**

18 **medium**: *the middle (one).* The participle (**depositum**) agrees with this direct object.

21 **in frusta concisum:** *cut into pieces.*

22 **in concavo ligno:** *in a hollow log.*

23 **et ... et ... :** *both ... and ....*

    dum venirent: *when they came.*

    si opus esset: *if necessary.*

25 **quasi:** *what appeared to be,* literally *as it were.*

27 **quae:** *they.* (For Linking Relative, see LL p. 26.)

28 **illud** refers to **nescioquid** (line 26).

    intervallo facto: *after some time (had elapsed).*

30 **Thyesteam cenam:** *a meal like the one served to Thyestes.* Atreus, king of ancient Argos, discovered that his wife had been raped by his own brother, Thyestes. For that crime he banished Thyestes from Argos, but his thirst for revenge was still not satisfied. At a later date, therefore, he pretended to be reconciled with Thyestes and invited him to a banquet. He then secretly killed Thyestes' son and served up to Thyestes pieces of the son's flesh.

32 **qua** is a Linking Relative forming an Ablative Absolute with **respondente.** (For Linking Relative, see LL p. 26.)

    sic fuisse factum: *that this was indeed the case,* literally *that it had been done thus.*

33 **magis puto:** *I rather think.*

34 **quod ut citius probem:** *so that I may prove this more quickly.* (For Linking Relative, see LL p. 26.)

35 **de quolibet:** *from each.*

delatamque in heremum, iussam etiam ut filium coqueret coctumque proponeret
sero strigibus devorandum.

Rescue plan

15 ad haec ego, super mulieris casu motus misericordia, filium cum ipsa me
liberaturum promitto, et quamquam lassitudine nimia nimiaque inedia affectus
essem, quamquam etiam de mea desperarem salute, recucurri tamen ad illos tres
latrones quos pendentes transieram; depositumque eorum medium qui
pinguissimus erat attuli mulieri, monens ut, filio mihi commisso, coctum
20 latronem lamiis apponeret.
       concessit illa filiumque mihi tradens latronem in frusta concisum igni
superposuit. porro ego, parvulum optime in concavo abscondens ligno, me
prope domum abscondi, volens et monstra dum venirent videre et, si opus esset,
succurrere mulieri.

The witches' banquet

25 ecce autem, sole iam Hesperias tingente undas, intueor de montibus quasi
quasdam simias innumerabiles cum strepitu magno descendere, nescioquid
cruentum post se trahentes. quae intrantes domum maximum accendunt rogum
illudque cruentum inter se dentibus carpentes devorant. intervallo deinde facto,
ollam nefandam ab igne deponunt frustaque cocti latronis inter se dividentes
30 sibi Thyesteam peragunt cenam.
       hoc facto, illa quae inter ceteras potentior videbatur mulierem interrogat
utrum eius filium an alium devorassent. qua sic fuisse factum respondente:
"magis" ait lamia "puto quod, filio reservato, unum illorum trium nobis
apposueris latronum. quod ut citius probem, ite!" ait tribus strigibus; "deferte
35 mihi de quolibet latronum frustum carnis!"

defero, to carry away
heremus (*m*), wilderness
propono (3), to place before, serve
misericordia (*f*), pity
lassitudo (*f*), weariness, exhaustion
inedia (*f*), hunger
recurro (3), to run back
pendeo (2), **pependi**, to hang
depono (3), to take down
pinguis, fat
affero, -ferre, attuli, allatum, to
    bring to
committo (3), to entrust
lamia (*f*), witch
appono (3), to place before, serve
concedo (3), to agree
superpono (+ *dat.*), to place upon
porro, next
abscondo (3), to hide

monstrum (*n*), monster, strange creature
Hesperius, western
tingo (3), to colour
intueor (2), to see
simia (*f*), ape, monkey
strepitus (*m*), noise, din
nescioquid, something
cruentus, bloody, dripping with blood
accendo (3), to light
rogus (*m*), fire
dens (*m*), tooth
carpo (3), to pluck, tear at
devoro (1), to eat
olla (*f*), pot
nefandus, disgusting, revolting
perago (3), to finish off
ait, (she) said
reservo (1), to keep safe
caro, carnis (*f*), flesh

38 **cicatrix et fossa:** The **fossa** was the hollow that was left after part of his buttock had been gouged out; the **cicatrix** was the scar that covered this wound.

40 **me submitto:** *I lowered myself.*

41 **pannis lineis:** *with strips of linen cloth.*

instar rivuli: *like a stream.*

42 **magis:** Take closely with **sollicitus** (line 43) – *more worried.*

quam defendendam susceperam: *whom I had undertaken to keep safe.* (For this use of the Gerundive, see LL p. 61.)

43 **quam:** *than.*

44 **nimiam:** Take **nimiam** with all three nouns – **inediam, vigilias, lassitudinem.**

45 **defectum cordis patiens:** *fainting,* literally *suffering a failure of heart.*

49 **ad suspendium:** *to my hanging-place.*

52 **omnium:** Take with **ora.**

ad me devorandum: *to devour me.* (For this use of the Gerundive, see LL p. 61.)

53 **nescio cuius occultae virtutis sibi contrariae perterritae maiestate:** *terrified by the power* (**maiestate**) *of some* (**nescio cuius**) *hidden force* (**occultae virtutis**) *that was hostile to them* (**sibi contrariae**).

54 **velut:** *just like,* one of the words which commonly introduces a simile (see p. 260).

Self-sacrifice

hoc ego audiens festinus praecucurri meque inter duos latrones medium manibus suspendo. subsecutae illico striges duo frusta de natibus latronum abscidunt, tertium de femore meo (ut adhuc cicatrix et fossa indicat) tollentes et post haec ad suam principem revertuntur.

40   graviter igitur sauciatus, de ligno in quo pependeram me submitto; locumque vulneris pannis lineis circumligans, sanguinem, qui instar rivuli in terram defluebat, stagnare volui nec potui. magis tamen de salute mulieris (quam sub fide mea defendendam susceperam) quam de me ipso sollicitus ad meas redii latebras, crebro ibi ob nimium sanguinis fluxum nimiamque inediam, vigilias,

45   lassitudinem defectum cordis patiens.

    illa vero lamiarum princeps singula latronum frusta degustans, cum meam quoque carnem ore cruento temptasset, "ite" ait "citius latronemque medium apportate, quia recentes et optimae sunt carnes eius."

A narrow escape

hoc ego audito ad suspendium redii meque iterum inter latrones suspendo.

50   veniunt iterum ministrae tenebrarum meque depositum a ligno per manus ac pedes perque capillos supra vepres ac cautes ad domum usque protrahunt. iamque singulae super me dentes acuebant iamque avida omnium ad me devorandum hyabant ora, cum ecce, nescio cuius occultae virtutis sibi contrariae perterritae maiestate, cum clamore magno velut quaedam tempestas

55   per ostium, per tectum perque foramina domus diffugiunt, me intacto cum muliere relicto.

festinus, quick(ly)
praecurro (3), to run ahead
suspendo (3), to hang
subsequor (3), to follow
nates (*f.pl*), rump, buttock
abscido (3), to cut off
femur (*n*), thigh
adhuc, still
tollo (3), to take away, remove
princeps (*f*), leader, mistress (of a coven of witches)
revertor (3), to return, go back
graviter, seriously
sauciatus, wounded
lignum (*n*), branch
circumligo (1), to bind
defluo (3), to flow down
stagno (1), to stem, stop
fides (*f*), protection
sollicitus, worried
latebrae (*f.pl*), hiding-place
crebro, often, frequently
ob (+ *acc*.), on account of
fluxus (*m*), flow, loss

vigiliae (*f.pl*), lack of sleep
singuli, one each, one by one
degusto (1), to taste
tempto (1), to try out, sample
citius, (more) quickly
recens, fresh
ministra (*f*), attendant, servant
tenebrae (*f.pl*), darkness
capilli (*m.pl*), hair
vepres, -is (*m*), briar-bush
cautes, -is (*f*), rock
usque, all the way
protraho (3), to drag towards
super (+ *abl*.), over
acuo (3), to sharpen
avidus, greedy
hyo (1), to gape, be wide open
contrarius (+ *dat*.), opposed (to), hostile (to)
tectum (*n*), roof
foramen (*n*), crack, opening
diffugio (3), to disperse, scatter
intactus, unharmed, untouched

57 **effugatas ... subsequitur:** Besides following the darkness and putting it to flight, the approach of dawn drove the witches away since it was dangerous for them, as with vampires and other such creatures of the night, to be caught up by daylight.

Safe at last

statim autem post duarum vel trium horarum spatium effugatas noctis tenebras ministrasque tenebrarum rutilans diei aurora subsequitur. et ego, muliere arrepta ac parvulo, solitudinem pertransiens vix tandem post quadraginta dies,
60 herbarum radicibus ac foliis arborum interim victitans, ad homines perveni, mulierem et parvulum suis reddidi.

effugo (1), to put to flight	**quadraginta**, forty
rutilo (1), to glow, be rosy	**radix** (*f*), root
aurora (*f*), dawn	**folium** (*n*), leaf
arripio (3), to take charge of	**victito** (1) (+ *abl.*), to feed on, live off
solitudo (*f*), desert, wilderness	**sui** (*m.pl*), their own family

Points for Discussion

1 What regular happening is described in the phrase **sole iam Hesperias tingente undas** (line 25)? Do you think there is any reason why the author did not simply say **solis occasu?** What, if anything, has the author achieved by his choice of words?

2 Produce a good translation of the words **ad homines perveni** (line 60).

3 Four different words/expressions are used to describe the witches. Quote the appropriate words from the text.

4 Summarise the main incidents in the story.

5 In lines 44–45, you were told to take **nimiam** with the three nouns **inediam**, **vigilias** and **lassitudinem**. The Latin is ambiguous, however, and it may be that **vigilias** and **lassitudinem** should be taken with **defectum cordis** as objects of **patiens**. Which of these alternatives do you prefer? Give reasons for your preference.

6 What events in this story do you find incredible, and why?

7 Do you think there is a moral in the story?

Pliny: See Notes on Authors, page 13.

line

2　**si attenderes acrius**: *if you listened more carefully.* (See LL p. 54.)

　longius reddebatur: *could be heard quite far off*, literally *was returned farther away.* (See LL p. 55.)

3　**macie et squalore confectus**: *in a wretched state of emaciation and filth,* literally *badly affected by emaciation and filth.*

4　**promissa barba** (*with flowing beard*) and **horrenti capillo** (*with tousled hair*) are ablatives describing the old man. (For Ablative of Description, see LL p. 15.)

　cruribus: *on his legs.*

6　**inhabitantibus**: a present participle used with the force of a noun – *by those who lived there.* Although the Dative of the Agent is most commonly used with the Gerundive (see LL p. 62), it is also used frequently in poetry. Here, it is to be taken with **noctes vigilabantur**: *sleepless nights were spent by the occupants,* literally *nights were spent in wakefulness.*

7　**sequebatur** has two subjects: **morbus** and **mors**.

8　**oculis inerrabat**: *haunted them,* literally *wandered in front of their eyes.*

　longior causis: *longer-lasting than the causes.* (For Ablative of Comparison, see LL p. 16.)

9　**deserta**: Supply **est** with **deserta** and **relicta**.

　illi monstro: *to that ghost.* The noun **monstrum** was used in religious language for any evil omen.

10　**seu quis ... vellet**: *(to see) whether anyone might want.*

　ignarus tanti mali: *unaware of such an evil (presence).*

12　**titulum**: *the notice* posted beside the house advertising it, i.e. the "For Sale" notice.

13　**suspecta vilitas**: Supply **est**. The literal meaning is *the cheapness was suspected,* i.e. he was suspicious of the low price.

　immo tanto magis: *in fact, all the more eagerly.*

15　**iubet sterni**: *he ordered a bed to be made up,* literally *he ordered it (bedding) to be spread.*

　in prima parte: This was the part of the house nearest the front door, whereas the living-quarters were farther inside. (See **interiora** in line 16.)

43 A Ghost Story

(Pliny, *Letters* VII. 27)

erat Athenis spatiosa et capax domus, sed infamis et pestilens. per silentium
noctis sonus ferri et, si attenderes acrius, strepitus vinculorum longius primo,
deinde e proximo reddebatur. mox apparebat idolon, senex macie et squalore
confectus, promissa barba, horrenti capillo. cruribus compedes, manibus
5 catenas gerebat quatiebatque.
    inde inhabitantibus tristes diraeque noctes per metum vigilabantur. vigiliam
morbus et, crescente formidine, mors sequebatur. nam interdiu quoque,
quamquam abscesserat imago, memoria imaginis oculis inerrabat, longiorque
causis timoris timor erat. deserta inde domus totaque illi monstro relicta.
10 proscribebatur tamen, seu quis emere, seu quis conducere ignarus tanti mali
vellet.
    venit Athenas philosophus Athenodorus; legit titulum auditoque pretio, quia
suspecta vilitas, percunctatus omnia docetur; ac nihilo minus, immo tanto
magis conducit.
15 ubi coepit advesperascere, iubet sterni sibi in prima domus parte; poscit

spatiosus, spacious
capax, roomy
infamis, with a bad reputation
pestilens, haunted
sonus (*m*), sound, clanking
strepitus (*m*), noise, rattling
vincula (*n.pl*), chains
primo, at first
e proximo, (from) close at hand
idolon (*n*), ghost
compedes (*f.pl*), shackles, fetters
catena (*f*), chain
quatio (3), to shake
inde, after that, then
tristis, miserable
dirus, fearful

vigilia (*f*), insomnia
morbus (*m*), illness
cresco (3), to increase
formido (*f*), fear
interdiu, during the day
abscedo (3), to go away
imago (*f*), apparition, ghost
proscribo (3), to advertise for sale
seu ... seu ..., whether ... or ...
conduco (3), to rent
philosophus (*m*), philosopher
percunctor (1), to make enquiries
doceo (2), to inform, tell
nihilo minus, none the less
advesperascere, to grow dark

16 **pugillares stilum lumen:** *writing-tablets, pen and lamp.* Pliny frequently lists items in this way without any connecting word. (Cf. line 17.) A writing-tablet was a small wooden board with a thin coating of wax spread over it. The **stilus** was a pointed piece of metal used to scratch words on the wax. The **lumen** would be an oil-lamp.

suos: *his attendants.*

in interiora: *into the inner (parts of the house).*

ad scribendum: *to writing.* (For the Gerund, see LL p. 60.)

17 **vacua mens:** *an idle mind,* i.e. having nothing to occupy it.

audita simulacra: *imagined sounds,* literally *heard images.* Another possible interpretation is *the visions about which he had heard.*

19 **quale ubique:** *as everywhere (else).*

silentium: Supply **est.**

concuti ferrum: *iron was rattled.* Here, and in the next few lines, a series of present infinitives (Historic Infinitives) is used to heighten the excitement for the reader. (Cf. **moveri, tollere, remittere, offirmare, praetendere, crebrescere, adventare, audiri.**) Note that the subjects of these infinitives are in the nominative case. Translate the infinitives as if they were past tense indicative verbs, active or passive as required. (For Historic Infinitive, see LL pp. 32–33.)

20 **non remittere stilum:** *he did not lay aside his pen,* i.e. *he did not stop writing.*

auribus praetendere: Supply **animum.** Literally *he stretched (his mind) in front of his ears* as a kind of screen. Translate *he shut his ears.*

21 **iam ... iam ... :** *at one moment ... at another ....*

ut in limine: *as if in the doorway .*

22 **narratam sibi effigiem:** *the ghost which had been described to him.*

23 **stabat:** The subject is the ghost.

similis vocanti: *similar to someone beckoning.* (For the present participle used as a noun, compare **inhabitantibus** in line 6.)

hic contra: *he* (i.e. *Athenodorus*) *in response.*

ut exspectaret: an Indirect Command depending on **significat** (*made a sign*).

24 **illa:** *it,* referring to **effigiem** in line 22.

scribentis capiti catenis insonabat: *rattled its chains over his head as he continued to write,* literally *sounded with its chains to the head of him writing.*

25 **innuentem:** literally *the beckoning one* (i.e. the ghost) is the object of **respicit.** (For the present participle used as a noun, compare lines 6 and 23.)

nec moratus: *and without any delay,* literally *and not having delayed.*

pugillares stilum lumen; suos omnes in interiora dimittit; ipse ad scribendum animum oculos manum intendit, ne vacua mens audita simulacra et inanes sibi metus fingeret.

initio, quale ubique, silentium noctis; dein concuti ferrum, vincula moveri.
20 ille non tollere oculos, non remittere stilum, sed offirmare animum auribusque praetendere. tum crebrescere fragor, adventare, et iam ut in limine, iam ut intra limen audiri. respicit, videt agnoscitque narratam sibi effigiem.

stabat innuebatque digito similis vocanti. hic contra ut paulum exspectaret manu significat, rursusque ceris et stilo incumbit. illa scribentis capiti catenis
25 insonabat. respicit rursus innuentem, nec moratus, tollit lumen et sequitur. ibat

intendo (3), to apply, concentrate
inanis, empty, groundless
fingo (3), to form, imagine
initio, at first
dein, then
offirmo (1), to strengthen
animus (m), concentration
crebresco (3), to become frequent,
    increase
fragor (m), din, clanking

advento (1), to approach
intra (+ acc.), inside
respicio (3), to look round at
agnosco (3), to recognise
effigies (f), image, apparition
innuo (3), to make a sign, beckon
digitus (m), finger
cerae (f.pl), writing-tablets
incumbo (3) (+ dat.), to apply oneself (to)

27 **desertus:** *(when) left on his own.*

folia concerpta ponit: *he gathered leaves and placed them*, literally *he placed gathered leaves.*

signum (*as a sign*) is used in apposition to **herbas et folia concerpta**. In other words, he used grass and leaves to mark the spot.

29 **magistratus:** *the city officials.* They would be involved because, for religious and health reasons, corpses should not be buried inside the city boundaries. They would also, of course, be involved if a murder had been committed.

monet ut iubeant: *advised (them) to give orders.*

30 **inserta catenis et implicata:** *all tangled up in chains*, literally *inserted in chains and wound round.*

quae corpus reliquerat: *which the body had left.* The antecedent of **quae** is **ossa**; **corpus** refers to the flesh and the organs which had decomposed because the body had been in the ground a long time (**aevo terraque putrefactum**) and left only the bare bones.

31 **exesa vinculis:** *eaten away by the chains.* **nuda** and **exesa** both agree with **quae**, which refers to the bones.

collecta (*gathered together*) agrees with **ossa** (understood).

32 **rite conditis:** *which had been properly buried.* It was believed that the soul or spirit of a dead person (**manes**, *m.pl*) could not rest until it had been laid to rest (**conditis**) with the appropriate rites (**rite**).

manibus caruit: *was free from the ghost.*

illa lento gradu, quasi gravis vinculis. postquam deflexit in aream domus, repente dilapsa deserit comitem. desertus herbas et folia concerpta signum loco ponit.

30   postero die adit magistratus, monet ut illum locum effodi iubeant. inveniuntur ossa inserta catenis et implicata, quae corpus aevo terraque putrefactum nuda et exesa reliquerat vinculis. collecta publice sepeliuntur. domus postea rite conditis manibus caruit.

lentus, slow	**herba** (*f*), grass
gradus (*m*), step	**folium** (*n*), leaf
quasi, as if	**concerptus**, gathered together
deflecto (3), to turn aside	**effodio** (3), to dig up
area (*f*), courtyard	**aevum** (*n*), age, time
repente, suddenly	**publice**, at public expense
dilabor (3), to vanish	**sepelio** (4), to bury

Points for Discussion

1 Write down as full a description of the ghost as you can.

2 Describe, in order, the succession of things that happened to the previous occupants (lines 6–11).

3 Explain why different tenses are used in the Ablative Absolutes **crescente formidine** (line 7) and **audito pretio** (line 12).

4 Do you think the previous tenants were justified in fearing the ghost? Give reasons for your answer. Why did it not frighten Athenodorus?

5 By what means does Pliny increase the excitement and pace of the narrative in lines 19–22? Why do you think he reverts to indicative verbs (**respicit, videt agnoscitque**) in the final sentence of this paragraph?

6 Find four places in the passage where the present participle is used with the force of a noun.

7 What do you think Athenodorus might have been writing (lines 16–18)? Why do you think Athenodorus signalled to the ghost to wait? What do you think he might have written after his signal? What would you have done in this situation?

8 What finally convinced Athenodorus that the ghost should be taken seriously?

9 Do you find this story believable? Justify your answer.

10 At the beginning of the letter from which this story is taken, Pliny asks Sura (the recipient of his letter) whether he thinks that ghosts actually exist or whether he believes they are merely figments of our fears and imagination. Do you think that this story helps us to answer Pliny's question?

Pliny: See Notes on Authors on page 13.

line

1   **Hipponensis:** Hippo was a settlement (**colonia**) on the north coast of Africa, not far from Carthage. It had been given to veteran soldiers as a reward for their faithful service. It is chiefly remembered for its connection with its fourth century bishop, St Augustine, a Christian writer famed for his *Confessions*. (See "Addicted to the Games" on page *32*.)

2   **in modum fluminis:** *like a river*.

   nunc infertur mari, nunc redditur stagno: *at one time flows into the sea, at another is carried back into the lagoon*. There is little or no tide in the Mediterranean, but the change in the water level would be noticeable at this point because of the narrowness of the channel.

3   **omnis hic aetas piscandi studio tenetur:** *here, people of all ages* (literally *every age*) *are very keen on fishing* (literally *are held by an enthusiasm for fishing*). The three Gerunds (**piscandi**, **navigandi** and **natandi**) are all genitive. (See LL pp. 60 and 159.)

4   **quos otium lususque sollicitat:** *who are attracted by sport and have time to pursue it,* literally *whom leisure and sport attract.*

   his gloria et virtus altissime provehi: *For these (boys), swimming really far out to sea is the height of daring,* literally *to be carried into very deep water* (**altissime**) *(is) glory and courage for these* (*boys*). Note that the two nouns (**gloria et virtus**) convey one idea in English – *the height of daring*. (For this Figure of Speech, called Hendiadys, see page *259*.)

5   **qui longissime ut litus ita simul natantes reliquit:** *who has left farthest behind him both the shore and his fellow-swimmers* (literally *those swimming along with him*). **ut … ita …** means literally *as … so …* and is used to link two related words or ideas; hence the meanings *both … and …* or *not only … but also.*

6   **audentior ceteris:** *more daring than the others.* (For Ablative of Comparison, see LL p. 16.)

   in ulteriora tendebat: *used to swim out farther than the rest.* Note how Pliny makes **ceteris** apply to both of the comparatives by placing it between them.

7   **praecedere puerum:** *swam in front of the boy.* **praecedere** is a Historic Infinitive, used when the author wants to add vividness and excitement to a description (see LL p. 32). Here it is the speed and agility of the dolphin which Pliny wishes to capture. There are six other Historic Infinitives in this sentence; they should all be translated as past tenses of the indicative. Note how Pliny reverts to the indicative for the last two verbs in the sentence (**flectit** and **reddit**), since these two actions were much more leisurely.

8   **subire:** Not just *went under*, but *took him on its back.*

   trepidantem: *the frightened boy.*

   in altum: *into the open sea*, literally *into the deep.*

9   **reddit:** Supply **eum.**

44 The Boy and the Dolphin

(Pliny, *Letters* IX. 33)

Boy riding on a dolphin, 520 BC

est in Africa Hipponensis colonia mari proxima. adiacet navigabile stagnum;
ex hoc in modum fluminis aestuarium emergit, quod nunc infertur mari, nunc
redditur stagno. omnis hic aetas piscandi, navigandi atque etiam natandi studio
tenetur, maxime pueri, quos otium lususque sollicitat. his gloria et virtus
5 altissime provehi: victor ille qui longissime ut litus ita simul natantes reliquit.

hoc certamine puer quidam audentior ceteris in ulteriora tendebat. delphinus
occurrit, et nunc praecedere puerum, nunc sequi, nunc circumire, postremo
subire, deponere, iterum subire, trepidantemque perferre primum in altum, mox
flectit ad litus redditque terrae et aequalibus.

adiaceo (2), to lie near	**lusus** (*m*), play
stagnum (*n*), lagoon	**sollicito** (1), to attract, appeal to
aestuarium (*n*), channel, tidal flow	**certamen** (*n*), contest, competition
emergo (3), to come forth, emerge	**delphinus** (*m*), dolphin
nato (1), to swim	**flecto** (3), to turn, veer
maxime, especially	**aequalis** (*m*), companion

10   **concurrere**: *flocked together.* Again, Pliny uses a series of Historic Infinitives (**concurrere** ... **narrare**), this time to convey the excited hubbub of the spectators (see LL p. 32).

11   **narrare:** Part of the thrill of being an eye-witness is being able to tell others about it.

      obsident litus: *they mobbed* (literally *besieged*) *the shore.*

12   **inter hos ille: hos** refers to **pueri**, and **ille** is the boy who is the hero of the occasion.

      sed cautius: Supply a suitable verb in English. (Cf. **delphinus rursus** in the next sentence.)

      ad tempus: The dolphin obviously came at a set time each day.

13   **quasi invitet et revocet:** *as if it were inviting (him) and calling (him) back.*

14   **varios orbes implicat expeditque**: *did all sorts of somersaults*, literally *tied and untied different circles.*

15   **hoc**: Supply **fecit**. The repetition of **hoc** links the three phrases.

      tertio: Supply **die**. With **pluribus** supply **diebus**.

      donec homines subiret timendi pudor: *until men began to feel ashamed of being afraid*, literally *until shame of fearing came over men.* They were reluctant to admit it at first.

      innutritos mari: *bred to the sea*, i.e. the sea was part of their lives.

16   **pertrectant praebentem:** Supply **se** with **praebentem** – *it allowed itself to be stroked*, literally *they stroked (it) offering (itself).*

18   **fertur:** *was carried (out to sea)*, as can be deduced from **refertur** which follows.

      agnosci se, amari (se) are both Accusative and Infinitive clauses depending on **putat**: *he thought he was recognised (by the dolphin) and liked (by it).*

19   **huius** ... **illius**: *of the one (i.e. the boy)* ... *of the other (i.e. the dolphin).*

      nec non: The double negative produces a very strong positive – *and what is more.*

20   **hortantes monentesque:** *shouting encouragement and advice.*

      una: *along with (it).*

22   **patiebatur:** *allowed (to be done to itself).*

      alterum illum ducebat: *it used to escort the other one*, i.e. the first dolphin.

      ducebat reducebat: Understand **et** between these two verbs. Pliny puts them side by side to convey the idea of speed.

      ut (*as*) **puerum ceteri pueri:** Supply **ducebant, reducebant**.

10   serpit per coloniam fama; concurrere omnes, ipsum puerum tamquam
miraculum adspicere, interrogare, audire, narrare. postero die obsident litus,
prospectant mare. natant pueri, inter hos ille, sed cautius. delphinus rursus ad
tempus, rursus ad puerum. fugit ille cum ceteris. delphinus, quasi invitet et
revocet, exsilit, mergitur, variosque orbes implicat expeditque.

15   hoc altero die, hoc tertio, hoc pluribus, donec homines innutritos mari subiret
timendi pudor. accedunt et alludunt et appellant, tangunt etiam pertrectantque
praebentem. crescit audacia experimento. maxime puer, qui primus expertus
est, adnatat, insilit tergo, fertur referturque, agnosci se, amari putat, amat ipse;
neuter timet, neuter timetur; huius fiducia, mansuetudo illius augetur. nec non
20   alii pueri dextra laevaque simul eunt hortantes monentesque. ibat una (id
quoque mirum) delphinus alius, tantum spectator et comes. nihil enim simile
aut faciebat aut patiebatur; sed alterum illum ducebat reducebat, ut puerum
ceteri pueri.

serpo (3), to creep, spread
fama (*f*), rumour, story
tamquam, as if
miraculum (*n*), marvel
adspicio (3), to look at
interrogo (1), to question
prospecto (1), to look out at
caute, cautiously
exsilio (4), to leap out
mergo (3), to dive
plures, several

alludo (3), to play with
cresco (3), to increase
experimentum (*n*), experience
insilio (4), to leap upon
neuter, neither
fiducia (*f*), confidence
mansuetudo (*f*), gentleness, tameness
augeo (2), to increase
laevus, left
tantum, only

24 **incredibile:** Supply **est.** On this depend the two Accusative and Infinitive clauses:

delphinum	**in terram quoque**		**extrahi**	**solitum** (esse)
(delphinum)	**harenis siccatum in mare**	**revolvi**	(solitum esse).

tam verum quam priora: *as true as the earlier (happenings).* (For Correlatives, see LL p. 63.)

25 **extrahi solitum (esse)... in mare revolvi:** *got into the habit of dragging itself out (of the water to bask in the sun) and of rolling back into the sea.* Both infinitives (**extrahi** and **revolvi**) are governed by **solitum (esse).** Pliny describes what the dolphin did as incredible, since the Romans believed that dolphins died the moment they left the water.

harenis siccatum: *after drying itself on the sands.*

26 **omnes magistratus:** These were the Roman officials who, when they visited a community, expected to have all their expenses met by that community.

quorum adventu et mora: *by whose arrival and lengthy stay.*

27 **modica res publica:** *the modest resources of the community.*

28 **placuit:** *it was decided,* the usual word describing a resolution of a body such as a senate or council.

interfici ad quod coibatur: *that the creature which was drawing the crowds should be killed,* literally *that (the object) to which there was a gathering should be killed.*

incredibile, tam verum tamen quam priora, delphinum in terram quoque
25 extrahi solitum harenisque siccatum, ubi incaluisset, in mare revolvi.
confluebant omnes ad spectaculum magistratus, quorum adventu et mora
modica res publica novis sumptibus atterebatur. postremo locus ipse quietem
suam secretumque perdebat: placuit occulte interfici ad quod coibatur.

incalesco (3), to grow warm
confluo (3), to flock
sumptus (m), expense
attero (3), to wear away, exhaust

quies (f), peace
secretum (n), seclusion
occulte, secretly

Points for Discussion

1 One of the techniques commonly used by Pliny is the repetition and/or
balancing of words and phrases to produce a specific effect, e.g.

(a) **rursus ad tempus, rursus ad puerum** (lines 12and 13).

Here, the balanced phrases create the impression of repeated action. Find
two similar examples in lines 15–23.

(b) Similarly, Pliny brings out the idea of mutual feelings in

se amari putat, amat ipse (line 18).

Find two other examples in lines 15– 23 which convey mutual feelings.

2 Pliny frequently uses pairs of words to describe something, each word in the
pair having a slightly different shade of meaning from the other. What
different shades of meaning can you identify in the following pairs?

otium lususque (line 4), **gloria et virtus** (line 4),

hortantes monentesque (line 20), **quietem secretumque** (line 27).

3 What English word is derived from the verb **serpere** (line 10)? Do you think it
is an appropriate verb to associate with **fama**? Give reasons for your answer.

4 Many of the verbs used by Pliny in this passage are compounds created by
adding prefixes to simple verbs. Give the meanings of the following:

circumire (line 7), **subire** (line 8), **coire** (line 28)
praecedere (line 7), **accedere** (line 16)
provehi (line 5), **prospectare** (line 12)
inferre (line 2), **perferre** (line 8), **referre** (line 18).

5 What arguments do you think might have been put forward by the local
inhabitants for and against the decision to kill the dolphin? How would you
have voted?

6 Retell in English any other story you know in which man and beast strike up a
close friendship (e. g. Arion and the Dolphin, or Androcles and the Lion), and
identify those aspects of the stories which are similar/different.

Martial: See Notes on Authors on page 12.
Metre: Elegiac Couplet (See p. 257.)

Martial: See Notes on Authors on page 12.
Metre: Elegiac Couplet (See p. 257.)

line

1   **nubere:** This is the verb used of a woman marrying a man. Literally it means *to put on the (saffron) veil for someone*, which explains why it governs the dative case.

      sapisti = sapivisti: *you have shown good sense.*

2   **ducere:** This is the verb used of a man marrying a woman. It sometimes appears in a fuller form: **in matrimonium ducere** or **uxorem ducere.**

      et: also.

Wit and Humour

45 An Enigma

(Martial, *Epigrams* XII. 47)

> difficilis facilis, iucundus acerbus es idem:
>   nec tecum possum vivere nec sine te.

iucundus, pleasant
acerbus, bitter
nec... nec..., neither... nor...

Points for Discussion

1 What do you think Martial means in line 1?

2 Do you think that the title is a good one or not? Say why.

46 Two Sensible People

(Martial, *Epigrams* IX. 5)

> nubere vis Prisco; non miror, Paula; sapisti.
>   ducere te non vult Priscus; et ille sapit.

Points for Discussion

1 How do you think Paula would have felt after reading line 1?

2 How do you think she would have felt after reading line 2?

3 What do you think was Martial's own attitude towards Paula?

Martial: See Notes on Authors on page 12.
Metre: Elegiac Couplet (See p. 257.)

line

2 **nubere:** Note the subtle change from **ducere**, used of a man marrying a woman, to **nubere** (+ *dat.*), used of a woman marrying a man.
3 **sit:** *let (her) be.* (See LL p. 107.)
4 **non aliter:** *in no other way.*

Boy with goose, Capitolino Museume, Rome

47 EQUALITY?

(Martial, *Epigrams* VIII. 12)

> uxorem quare locupletem ducere nolim
>   quaeritis? uxori nubere nolo meae.
> inferior matrona suo sit, Prisce, marito:
>   non aliter fiunt femina virque pares.

quare, why
locuples, rich
inferior, lower (in status), less important

matrona (*f*), wife
maritus (*m*), husband

Points for Discussion

1 The Romans had two different expressions for "marrying". What do you think this tells us about Roman attitudes?

2 What do you think Martial is implying when he uses **nubere** in line 2 rather than **ducere**? What does **nubere** suggest the husband's role would be in such a marriage? What, according to Martial, would bring this about?

3 In your view, is there a contradiction between lines 3 and 4? Discuss what Martial says in the context of (*a*) the Roman world and (*b*) modern times.

Martial: See Notes on Authors on page 12.
Metre: Hendecasyllabics (See page *258*.)

line

1   **Catulli:** See the poems called "Lesbia's Pet" and "The Songbird Dies" (on pages *41* and *43)*.

3   **omnibus puellis:** The idiom in English would tend to be *than any girl.* (For Ablative of Comparison, see LL p. 16.)

6   **hanc loqui:** *that she (Issa) is speaking* – an Accusative and Infinitive depending on **putabis.**

8   **collo nixa:** *resting against (her master's) neck.*

9   **ut:** *(in such a way) that* or *(so lightly) that.*

10   **desiderio ventris:** *by the call of nature*, literally *by the necessity of the belly* (i.e. *bladder).*

12   **suscitat:** Supply *her master.*

        blando pede: *by rubbing her foot gently against him*, literally *with caressing foot.*

14   **hanc ne lux rapiat suprema totam:** *so that her last day (i.e. death) may not take her completely (totam) away.* The position of **hanc** permits it to be the object of both **rapiat** and **exprimit** (line 15).

15   **picta tabella:** *in a painting*, literally *with a painted board.* Publius was both the owner and the painter of Issa.

16–17   **in qua ... ipsa:** *in which you will see such a good likeness of Issa that it is more lifelike than the puppy itself*, literally *that not even (Issa) herself is so like herself.*

18   **pone:** an imperative – *put* or *compare.*

19   **veram:** *real* or *alive.*

48 Issa

(Martial, *Epigrams* I. 109)

Issa est passere nequior Catulli,
Issa est purior osculo columbae,
Issa est blandior omnibus puellis,
Issa est carior Indicis lapillis,
5   Issa est deliciae catella Publi.
hanc tu, si queritur, loqui putabis;
sentit tristitiamque gaudiumque.
collo nixa cubat, capitque somnos
ut suspiria nulla sentiantur.
10   et desiderio coacta ventris
gutta pallia non fefellit ulla,
sed blando pede suscitat toroque
deponi monet et rogat levari.
hanc ne lux rapiat suprema totam,
15   picta Publius exprimit tabella,
in qua tam similem videbis Issam,
ut sit tam similis sibi nec ipsa.
Issam denique pone cum tabella:
aut utramque putabis esse veram,
20   aut utramque putabis esse pictam.

passer (*m*), songbird
nequior, naughtier, more mischievous
purus, pure, innocent
osculum (*n*), kiss
columba (*f*), dove
blandus, charming, gentle
Indicus, Indian
lapillus (*m*), gem, pearl
deliciae (*f.pl*), pet
catella (*f*), puppy
queror (3), to whimper, whine
-que ... -que ..., (both) ... and ...

tristitia (*f*), sadness
cubo (1), to lie
suspirium (*n*), breath, breathing
coactus, compelled
gutta (*f*), drop
pallium (*n*), cover
fallo (fefelli), to foul (stain) secretly
suscito (1), to rouse, alert
torus (*m*), couch
levo (1), to lift up
exprimo (3), to portray, paint
denique, in short, in fact

Boy training a monkey to do tricks, from a Pompeian wall-painting

Points for Discussion

1   As you read the first four lines of this poem, who or what did you think Issa was? What effect do you think Martial was trying to create?

2   What is your reaction to Publius' decision to paint his pet?

3   Compare the **Issa** poem with Catullus' poems "Lesbia's Pet" and "The Song-bird Dies" on pages *41* and *43*.

(a)   Do you think Martial wrote this poem because he thought that Publius' puppy was a better pet than Lesbia's bird, or because he wanted to show that he was as clever a poet as Catullus? Can you suggest another possible reason?

(b)   Select the two lines from the pair of Catullus poems and the two from the Issa poem which make the greatest impact on you. Give reasons for your choice.

4   Several Roman authors refer to the keeping of pets. For example, in writing about the death of a young boy, Pliny (*Letters* IV. 2) says the following:

"The boy used to have several Gallic ponies for riding and driving, as well as dogs of all sizes, nightingales, parrots and blackbirds. His father had them all slaughtered around his funeral pyre."

Again, when someone taunts him over his fondness for a young boy, Martial (VII. 87) produces the following response:

"If my friend Flaccus can delight in a long-eared lynx, if Canius appreciates a dark-skinned boy, if Publius is aflame with love for a tiny lap-dog, if Cronus loves a long-tailed monkey as ugly as himself, if a mischievous mongoose delights Marius, if Lausus fancies a talking magpie, if Glaucilla twines a clammy snake round her neck, if Telesilla has erected a monument over her nightingale, why should Martial who sees that these monsters are the delight of their owners not love the handsome face of Labycas, Cupid's boy?"

(a)   What do the above extracts, Martial's **Issa** poem and Catullus' two **passer** poems tell us about Roman attitudes to pets? How does this compare with their attitude to the **bestiae** in the arena?

(b)   What are the most popular types of pets today?

(c)   How does the British attitude to pets and other animals compare with that of the Romans?

Catullus: See Notes on Authors on page *10*.
Metre: Hendecasyllabic (See page *258*.)

line

1 **mi Fabulle**: *My Dear Fabullus.* **mi** is the vocative of **meus**.

2 **paucis**: Take with **diebus**.

   si tibi di favent: *if you are lucky*, literally *if the gods favour you*.

3 **si attuleris**: *if you bring*. Note that the future perfect is translated by the present tense in English. (See LL p. 52.)

4 **cenam**: The position of the word is chosen deliberately to surprise the reader. Food is the last thing one would expect to be asked to bring if invited to dinner.

   non sine (literally *not without*) is much more emphatic than **cum** (*with*). It introduces a list of things that are to be brought in addition to the food. Translate *as well as*.

5 **sale**: Since it appears between **vinum** and **cachinnis**, it is deliberately ambiguous. Here it means *wit*, which adds flavour to a social occasion, just as *salt* (the normal meaning of **sal**) brings out the flavour in food.

   omnibus cachinnis: The plural suggests a series of stories that provoke loud laughter. Translate *your entire fund of uproariously funny stories*.

6 **venuste noster**: *my charming friend*. The adjective **venustus** is from the same root as Venus (goddess of love).

8 **sacculus**: *little purse*. Note again Catullus' use of a diminutive, this time to poke fun at his impecunious state.

   plenus aranearum: *full of cobwebs* (a common way of saying one was hard-up). Its position at the end of the sentence produces an amusing anticlimax. (Cf. the position of **cenam** in line 4.) His friend would realise why he was hard-up: he had probably spent all his money on Lesbia.

9 **contra**: *in return*, i.e. what Catullus *can* supply is. . . .

   meros amores: *pure, unadulterated friendship and affection*, i.e. *a hearty welcome*. The noun **merum** was the word for *pure wine*, which was so potent that it was usually mixed with water before being drunk.

10 **seu quid suavius elegantiusve est**: *or something that is more delightful or more to your taste*.

11 **puellae**: A reference to his lady-love, Lesbia. (See introduction to Passage 7, page 39.)

12 **donarunt = donaverunt**: *have bestowed, have given*.

   Veneres Cupidinesque: *the gods and goddesses of love*.

13 **quod**: Begin a new sentence and translate as *this*.

14 **ut** introduces an Indirect Command depending on **rogabis**. As often in poetry, it does not appear as the first word in the clause. Take **totum** with **nasum**.

49 Come Dine with Me

(Catullus 13)

cenabis bene, mi Fabulle, apud me
paucis, si tibi di favent, diebus,
si tecum attuleris bonam atque magnam
cenam, non sine candida puella
5 et vino et sale et omnibus cachinnis.
haec si, inquam, attuleris, venuste noster,
cenabis bene: nam tui Catulli
plenus sacculus est aranearum.
sed contra accipies meros amores
10 seu quid suavius elegantiusve est.
nam unguentum dabo, quod meae puellae
donarunt Veneres Cupidinesque,
quod tu cum olfacies, deos rogabis
totum ut te faciant, Fabulle, nasum.

ceno (1), to dine
atque, and also
candidus, fair, pretty
cachinnus (*m*), loud laughter, mirth
inquam, I say

elegans, tasteful
-ve, or
unguentum (*n*), perfume
olfacio (3), to smell
nasus (*m*), nose

Points for discussion

1 What is unusual about this invitation to dinner?

2 Which of the things on offer, if any, would tempt you along to the dinner?

3 The guest, Fabullus, is expected to bring everything for the dinner. The only contribution Catullus offers to make is **unguentum** (line 11). What do you think the **unguentum** is?

   (*a*) Is it an actual perfume?

   (*b*) Is it Lesbia herself?

   (*c*) Is it her fragrance clinging to Catullus or to the room?

   (*d*) Is it something else?

4 Do you think **totum nasum** (line 14) is meant to be taken seriously or as a joke? Compare this line with the English expression "He is all ears" and with the following poem from Martial:

   **Tongilianus habet nasum; scio, non nego. sed iam
      nil praeter nasum Tongilianus habet.**

   In what way is line 14 closer in sense to the English expression than to the theme of Martial's poem?

237

Catullus: See Notes on Authors on page *10.*
Metre: Elegiac Couplet (See p. *257.*)

line

1   **chommoda**: Arrius was not a "Roman cockney" but an upstart (possibly an orator) who constantly made his audience cringe with his affected form of speech. The sarcasm in this poem is directed, not at the uneducated person who speaks ungrammatically, but at the person who, in trying to appear very sophisticated, succeeds only in highlighting his ignorance.

     commoda (*n.pl*) means *advantages, opportunities*; Arrius might have made these "*hadvantages*" or "*hopportunities*". (Compare someone pronouncing the "h" in "honours".)

3   **sperabat**: In this context, **sperabat** means, not *hoped*, but *liked to think.*

4   **cum dixerat**: *whenever he said.* (For Frequentative **cum**, see LL p. 89.)

     quantum poterat: *as distinctly as he could.*

5   **credo**: *I (can well) believe* or *I suppose.*

     sic: *that is how . . .*, literally *in this way.* Note that all the people mentioned are on his mother's side of the family.

     liber: It would appear that Arrius' uncle was the first member of the family to be "free-born". His parents would have been "freedmen", and prior to that the family would have been slaves. It is thus another sarcastic gibe at the upstart Arrius.

7 .   **hoc misso**: an Ablative Absolute. Arrius was sent to Syria on official business.

     requierant omnibus aures: *everyone's ears got a rest.* **requierant** is a contracted form of **requieverant** (from **requiescere** (3), *to rest*). The dative (**omnibus**) is often used in this way to indicate the person affected, though it can usually be translated as if it were a genitive. (See LL p. 11.)

8   **audibant = audiebant.**

     eadem haec: *these same words.*

     leniter et leviter: *(pronounced) smoothly and lightly,* i.e. without the aspirated "h" which grated on the ears.

9   **sibi**: The verb **metuere** is used in two ways: firstly, governing the accusative and meaning *to be afraid of*; secondly, governing the dative and meaning *to fear for.* The two uses are combined here to indicate that people's ears no longer had to worry about the effect Arrius' grating aitches would have on them.

     talia verba: *such words,* i.e. words which were maltreated in this way by Arrius.

10   **horribilis**: *dreadful.* The root **horr–** suggests *roughness which makes one shudder* – no doubt a pun on the aspirated "h" of Arrius and the effect it had on those who heard it.

11   **Ionios fluctus . . . esse**: An Accusative and Infinitive depending on what is said in line 10. The *Ionian Sea* lay between the toe of Italy and Greece.

50 A Man called 'Arry

(Catullus 84)

chommoda dicebat, si quando commoda vellet
    dicere, et insidias Arrius hinsidias,
et tum mirifice sperabat se esse locutum,
    cum quantum poterat dixerat hinsidias.
5   credo, sic mater, sic liber avunculus eius,
    sic maternus avus dixerat atque avia.
hoc misso in Syriam, requierant omnibus aures:
    audibant eadem haec leniter et leviter,
nec sibi postilla metuebant talia verba,
10   cum subito affertur nuntius horribilis:
Ionios fluctus, postquam illuc Arrius isset,
    iam non Ionios esse sed Hionios.

si quando, if ever, whenever
mirifice, marvellously well
avunculus (*m*), uncle (mother's brother)
maternus, maternal
avia (*f*), grandmother

postilla, after that, afterwards
metuo (3), to fear
affero, to bring
isset = **ivisset**

Points for Discussion

1 List the three examples given in the poem of Arrius' affected speech. Can you think of similar affectations in speech in modern times?

2 Suggest English adjectives to describe what you think was Catullus' attitude towards Arrius.

Martial: See Notes on Authors on page *12*.
Metre: Hendecasyllabics (See page 258.)

line

1   **quae**: Supply **ea**, *the things which*.

2   **Martialis**: The poem is addressed to his namesake, Julius Martialis, not to himself.

4   **non ingratus ager**: *land which gives a good return*, literally *a field which is not ungrateful* (i.e. for the work that is put into it).

    focus perennis: *a hearth where there is always a fire burning*, literally *an everlasting hearth*. The continuing life of the household was symbolised by the fire burning on the altar and by the fire in the hearth on which they depended for cooking.

5   **toga rara**: *few official duties*, literally *a toga seldom worn*. The **toga** was a heavy cumbersome garment which citizens wore only when they were in the public eye.

6   **vires ingenuae**: *the constitution of a free man*. The free man would be fit because of a proper diet and the exercise he took as part of his daily routine at the Baths. This way of life is implicitly contrasted with the inferior condition of slaves.

7   **simplicitas**: *uprightness* or *honesty*. The word is used to describe wood with a straight grain and, here, refers to a character which is free from deviousness.

8   **sine arte mensa**: *plain meals*, literally *a table without art* (i.e. without any effort to impress).

10 **torus**: The *marriage-bed* is a way of referring to the sexual relationship between husband and wife. Martial says that the ideal is achieved when the wife enjoys the love-making, but is still faithful and virtuous.

12 **quod sis esse velis**: *Wish to be what you are!*, i.e. *be content with being yourself*. The present subjunctive (**velis**) expresses a wish or a command. (See LL p. 107, and compare **malis**, **metuas** and **optes**.)

    nihil malis: *seek nothing in preference (to that)*.

13 **nec metuas**: *and do not fear*.

    summum diem: *death*, literally *the last day*.

Attitudes and Values

51 Recipe for a Happy Life

(Martial, *Epigrams* X. 47)

vitam quae faciunt beatiorem,
iucundissime Martialis, haec sunt:
res non parta labore sed relicta;
non ingratus ager, focus perennis;
5 lis numquam, toga rara, mens quieta;
vires ingenuae, salubre corpus;
prudens simplicitas, pares amici,
convictus facilis, sine arte mensa;
nox non ebria sed soluta curis,
10 non tristis torus et tamen pudicus;
somnus qui faciat breves tenebras:
quod sis esse velis nihilque malis;
summum nec metuas diem nec optes.

beatus, happy
iucundus, pleasant, dear
res, rei (*f*), property
partus, acquired
relictus, inherited
perennis, everlasting, unfailing
lis (*f*), lawsuit, court case
quietus, untroubled, without a care

salubris, healthy
par, equal, well-matched
convictus (*m*), company, companionship
facilis, easy, agreeable
ebrius, drunken
solutus, released, free
pudicus, chaste, virtuous
tenebrae (*f.pl*), darkness, night

Points for Discussion

1 What does Martial mean when he says that the friends are equal/well-matched (line 7)?

2 What is the point Martial is making in line 11?

3 Quote from the poem the Latin phrases which match the following expressions:
   (*a*) Inherited wealth
   (*b*) Productive farming
   (*c*) Life without stress
   (*d*) Contentment with one's lot.

4 Discuss what you consider to be the importance of the **focus** (*hearth*)
   (*a*) to a person living in ancient Rome
   (*b*) to our ancestors of, say, a century ago
   (*c*) in a modern house.
   What do "focus" and "focal point" mean in English? How do you think they acquired these meanings?

5 Which items in Martial's list do you agree/disagree with? What would be your recipe for a happy life?

6 As far as you can judge from this poem, what sort of person do you think Martial was? Quote from the poem to support your answer.

Gellius: See Notes on Authors on page *11*.

line

1   This story was one of the fables told by the Greek writer Aesop (sixth century BC).

    id ferme temporis ut: *usually around the time when.* The phrase **id temporis** means *at that time*; the adverb **ferme** makes the time slightly less specific. (For Partitive Genitive, see LL p. 9.)

2   **pullis iam iam plumantibus**: *and the chicks are almost ready to fly.* The verb **plumare** means literally *to grow feathers.* The repetition of the word **iam** emphasises just how close they were to being able to fly off.

    ea cassita: *the lark in the fable.*

    in sementes tempestiviores: *in crops that had ripened earlier (than usual).* The accusative is used with the preposition **in** because of the notion of "motion" contained in the verb **congerere**, which literally means *to bring together* or *heap up*, but here means *to build a nest.*

4   **cibum quaesitum**: *to search for food.* The supine (**quaesitum**) expresses Purpose. (See LL p. 45.)

5   **si quid rei novae fieret**: *if anything new was done (occurred).*

    uti = ut, introducing another Indirect Command depending on **monet**. (Gellius frequently uses **uti** for **ut**; compare lines 13, 15.)

8   **die crastini**: *tomorrow* – Gellius is fond of this type of unusual expression where other authors would simply have used **cras**.

9   **fac amicos eas et roges**: *see that you go and ask our friends.* The subjunctive frequently is used after **fac**, with no introductory **ut**, to express a command. (Cf. **roges veniant ... dent ... adiuvent**.)

    operam mutuam dent: *work for us in the knowledge that we will later help them,* literally *offer shared work*, i.e. *work that will be returned.*

11 **circumstrepere orareque matrem**: These are Historic Infinitives used instead of indicatives to express excitement (see LL pp. 32–3). Translate *twittered around their mother and begged (her).*

13 **qui** introduces a Purpose clause (see LL p. 44). For the form **uti**, see line 5.

14 **otioso animo esse**: *to be easy in mind*, i.e. *not to panic.*

    messim ad amicos reicit: *depends on friends to take in the harvest*, literally *turns over the harvest to friends.*

17 **in pabulum**: *to gather food.*

18 **it ... eunt**: Note how the verb **ire** is used with two different meanings here.

19 **magnam partem**: *mainly, to a large extent.*

    quin potius imus: *why do we not rather go?*

52 A Wise Bird

(Aulus Gellius, *Noctes Atticae*, II. 29)

avicula est parva; nomen est cassita. habitat nidulaturque in segetibus, id ferme temporis ut appetit messis pullis iam iam plumantibus. ea cassita in sementes forte congesserat tempestiviores; propterea frumentis flavescentibus pulli etiam tunc involucres erant. dum igitur ipsa iret cibum pullis quaesitum, monet eos ut,
5 si quid ibi rei novae fieret dicereturve, animadverterent idque uti sibi, ubi redisset, nuntiarent.

dominus postea segetum illarum filium adulescentem vocat et "videsne" inquit "haec ematuruisse et manus postulare? idcirco die crastini, ubi primum diluculabit, fac amicos eas et roges veniant operamque mutuam dent et messim
10 hanc nobis adiuvent." haec ubi ille dixit, discessit.

atque ubi redit cassita, pulli tremibundi, trepiduli circumstrepere orareque matrem ut iam statim inque alium locum sese asportet; "nam dominus" inquiunt "misit qui amicos roget uti luce oriente veniant et metant."

mater iubet eos otioso animo esse: "si enim dominus" inquit "messim ad
15 amicos reicit, crastino seges non metetur neque necessum est hodie uti vos auferam."

die postero mater in pabulum volat. dominus quos rogaverat opperitur. sol fervit, et fit nihil; it dies, et amici nulli eunt. tum ille rursum ad filium "amici isti magnam partem" inquit "cessatores sunt. quin potius imus et cognatos

avicula (*f*), small bird	**ubi primum**, as soon as
cassita (*f*), lark	**diluculat**, it grows light, day dawns
nidulor (l), to build a nest	**opera** (*f*), work, services
seges, -etis (*f*), cornfield, crop	**tremibundus**, trembling with fear
appeto (3), to draw near	**trepidulus**, anxious, agitated
messis (*f*)**,** reaping, harvest	**sese** = se
forte, as it happened, by chance	**asporto** (l), to carry away
propterea, therefore	**meto** (3), to reap
flavesco (3), to grow yellow	**aufero**, to carry away
etiam tunc, even at that moment, still	**volo** (l), to fly, fly off
involucer, unable to fly	**opperior** (4), to wait for
-ve, or	**fervo** (3), to grow hot
animadverto (3), to notice, take note	**rursum**, again
adulescens (*m*), young man	**iste**, that
ematuresco (3), **-ui**, to ripen	**cessator** (*m*), idler, slacker
postulo (l), to call for	**cognatus** (*m*), relative (by blood)
idcirco, therefore	

20 **assint** = present subjunctive of **adesse**. Translate this Indirect Command *to be here*, or even *to come*.

ad metendum: *to take in the harvest*. (For the Gerund used to express Purpose, see LL pp. 45 and 60.)

22 **ferme**: Note again how this word tones down the statement. Translate **nullos ferme** as *hardly any*. (Cf. line 1.)

23 **ad laborem capessendum**: *to undertake hard work*. (For the Gerundive used to express Purpose, see LL pp. 45 and 60.)

nihil cunctentur: *they do not delay at all*.

25 **in pastum**: to get food. (Cf. **in pabulum**, line 17).

opera supersederunt: *failed to carry out the work*. Note that **supersedere** governs the ablative case.

26 **valeant amici**: literally *let our friends fare well*, i.e. *goodbye to our friends!*

27 **egomet**: The suffix **-met** is used in Latin to emphasise the word, whereas in English we would tend to use voice-stress. Compare its use in line 28 to link **nos** and **ipsi**.

29 **id** is the object of **dixisse**.

tempus est cedendi et abeundi: *it is time to give in and move away*. **cedendi** and **abeundi** are genitives of the Gerund. (See LL p. 60.)

30 **dubio procul**: *without doubt*, literally *far from doubt*.

quod futurum dixit: *what he said would happen*. This whole expression is the subject of **fiet**.

in ipso vertitur: *it* (i.e. the outcome) *depends on the man himself*.

31 **cuia**: The adjective (**cuius, cuia, cuium**), agreeing with **res**, is used instead of the more normal genitive **cuius**.

unde petitur: *from whom (assistance) is sought*.

A lark feeding its chicks in a nest

20   adfinesque nostros oramus ut assint cras tempori ad metendum?"

itidem hoc pulli pavefacti matri nuntiant. mater hortatur ut tum quoque sine metu ac sine cura sint; cognatos adfinesque nullos ferme tam esse obsequibiles ait ut ad laborem capessendum nihil cunctentur et statim dicto oboediant: "vos modo" inquit "advertite, si modo quid denuo dicetur."

25   alia luce orta avis in pastum profecta est. cognati et adfines opera, quam dare rogati sunt, supersederunt. ad postremum igitur dominus filio: "valeant" inquit "amici cum propinquis. afferes prima luce falces duas; unam egomet mihi et tu tibi capies alteram et frumentum nosmetipsi manibus nostris cras metemus."

id ubi ex pullis dixisse dominum mater audivit, "tempus" inquit "est cedendi
30   et abeundi; fiet nunc dubio procul quod futurum dixit. in ipso enim iam vertitur cuia res est, non in alio unde petitur." atque ita cassita nidum migravit, seges a domino demessa est.

adfinis (*m*), relative (by marriage)	**supersedeo** (2) (+ *abl.*),
tempori, early, in good time	to refrain (from), leave undone
itidem, in the same way	**ad postremum**, finally, at last
pavefactus, alarmed	**propinquus** (*m*), relative
obsequibilis, obedient	**affero**, to bring
ait, she said	**falx** (*f*), sickle
dictum (*n*), instruction, request	**nidus** (*m*), nest
oboedio (4) (+ *dat.*), to obey	**migro** (1), to move away
denuo, anew, afresh	**demeto** (3), to reap

Points for Discussion

1 In line 8, what is meant by **manus postulare**?

2 (a) The adjective **mutuus** (line 9) implies some sharing of services. What arrangement is the farmer depending on? How would he play his part?

    (b) What is meant by "mutual" in the following English expressions: "mutual understanding", "a mutual friend", "mutual benefits", "mutual insurance", "mutual admiration society"?

3 In line 26, is "goodbye to our friends" a friendly remark? What do you think is the tone of the remark? Suggest a more natural English expression.

4 The moral of the story is summed up in lines 30–31. Explain in your own words what it is. What English proverb would most aptly describe this tale? Suggest an alternative title for the passage.

5 Throughout the passage, Gellius uses different words with the same or similar meanings, e.g.

food: **cibus** (l. 4), **pabulum** (l. 17) and **pastus** (l. 25)
tomorrow: **die crastini** (l. 8), **crastino** (l. 15), **die postero** (l. 17), **cras** (l.20)
fearful: **tremibundus** (l. 11), **trepidulus** (l. 11), **pavefactus** (l. 21)
relation: **cognatus** (l. 19), **adfinis** (l. 20), **propinquus** (l. 27)
dawn: **luce oriente** (l. 13), **alia luce orta** (l. 25), **prima luce** (l. 27).

Why do you think Gellius does this? What advantages and disadvantages do you see in this feature of the author's style?

Phaedrus: See Notes on Authors on page *13*.
Metre: Iambic Senarius (See page *258*.)

line

5   **venantum = venantium**: *of the hunters*, literally *of those hunting*. (For this use of the present participle, see LL p. 28.) Since this word probably refers to the men and the dogs, **vocibus** will mean *shouts and barking*.

10   **edidisse dicitur**: *it is said to have uttered.*

11   **qui**: *for I*. (For Linking Relative, see LL p. 26.)

12   **utilia quam**: *how useful.*

      quae: Supply **ea** – *the things which*. (Cf. **quae** in line 13.)

13   **quantum luctus habuerint**: *how much grief (they) have brought*, literally *how much of grief they have held*. The subject of **habuerint** is the whole clause – **quae laudaram**. (For Partitive Genitive, see LL p. 9.)

Stag beset by hounds – marble group from the House of the Stags in Herculaneum

53 The Stag at the Spring

(*a*) (Phaedrus I. 2)

ad fontem cervus, cum bibisset, restitit
et in liquore vidit effigiem suam.
ibi, dum ramosa mirans laudat cornua
crurumque nimiam tenuitatem vituperat,
5   venantum subito vocibus perterritus
per campum fugere coepit, et cursu levi
canes elusit. silva tum excepit ferum,
in qua, retentis impeditus cornibus,
lacerari coepit morsibus saevis canum.
10   tunc moriens vocem hanc edidisse dicitur:
"o me infelicem! qui nunc demum intellego
utilia mihi quam fuerint, quae despexeram,
et quae laudaram, quantum luctus habuerint."

fons (*m*), fountain, spring
cervus (*m*), stag
resto (1), **restiti**, to stop, stand still
liquor (*m*), water
effigies (*f*), reflection
ramosus, with many branches
cornu (*n*), antler
crus, cruris (*n*), leg
nimius, excessive
tenuitas (*f*), thinness
vitupero (1), to find fault with
cursus, -us (*m*), running
levis, light, effortless

eludo (3), **elusi, elusum**, to elude, give
  (someone) the slip
excipio (3), to receive, welcome
ferus (*m*), wild beast
retineo (2), to hold back, hold fast
impeditus, hindered
lacero (1), to tear to pieces
morsus, -us (*m*), bite
tunc, then
demum, at last
despicio (3), **-xi**, to despise
laudaram = laudaveram

line

3   **fuga**: *by fleeing.*

4   **venantibus**: *for the hunters*. For this use of the present participle as the equivalent of a noun, compare the note on line 5 of the poem. (See also LL p. 28.)

5   **quae**: For the omission of **ea**, compare lines 12–13 of the poem.

    deceptiosa: *deceitful*. The antlers seemed something to be proud of, but in fact they were the cause of the stag's downfall.

(*b*) (Anonymous)

Many of the ancient fables were revived and retold by Christian writers in the Middle Ages because of the moral message they contained. Below is one such version told by an unknown author:

cervus, bibens de fonte, sua cornua magna ut vidit, nimium laudare coepit, crura vero tenuia vituperavit. quod cum faceret, venatoris vocem audivit et canes repente latrare. fuga cervus per campum dicitur evasisse molossos. at ubi silva eum suscepit, magnitudo cornuum venantibus eum retinuit. tunc mortem suam
5 videns, ait " quae mihi erant utilia vituperavi et deceptiosa laudavi!"

nimium, too much	**evado** (3), to escape
tenuis, thin	**molossus** (*m*), hunting hound
venator (*m*), hunter	**suscipio** (3), to receive
repente, suddenly	**ait**, he said
latro (l), to bark	

Points for Discussion

1 Two meanings have been given for **vocibus** in line 5 of the poem. How did your translation of **vocem** in line 10 differ from this?

2 Describe in your own words the stag's flight as contained in the words **retentis impeditus cornibus** (line 8 of the poem).

3 Discuss the irony of the words **silva eum suscepit** (prose, line 3) and **silva excepit ferum** (poem, line 7).

4 (*a*) Pick out the words and phrases used by each of the authors to describe (i) the stag's antlers, (ii) its legs, (iii) its flight out in the open. How do the authors differ from each other?

   (*b*) What other points of detail are included in the poem, but are missing from the prose version? Why do you think the prose writer has omitted these details?

5 What is the moral that both authors draw from the fable? Do you agree with them? From your own experience, can you produce other examples which support or contradict this view?

6 Which version of the story do you prefer, and why?

Horace: See Notes on Authors on page *11*.
Metre: Lesser Asclepiad (See page *258*.)

line

1   **aere perennius**: *more enduring than bronze*. (Compare **regali situ altius** in line 2.)
The erection of bronze statues and plaques is a common way of commemorating the
achievements of great men and women; but such memorials are often destroyed in the
course of time. Horace claims that his poetry will not be affected in this way. The
ablative (**aere**) with a comparative adjective or adverb is a common way of expressing
comparison (*than*) (see LL p. 16).

    Horace deliberately placed this poem at the end of his third book of Odes, intending it
to be his farewell to lyric poetry. Only the intervention of the Emperor Augustus
persuaded him to produce a fourth book of Odes, roughly a decade later.

3   **edax**: *destructive*, literally *eating away*. The adjective **edax** is from the same root as the
verb **edere**, *to eat*.

    impotens: Supply **sui** – literally *lacking in power over oneself*. Translate *violent* or
raging.

4   **innumerabilis**: Note that it is the years, rather than the chain, which are *countless*. (For
Transferred Epithet see page *261*.)

5   **series**: *succession*. The word is used of *a chain of things all strung together*.

6   **omnis** is nominative, referring to the subject of **moriar**.

    mei: *of me* (genitive of **ego**).

7   **Libitinam**: Libitina was the Goddess of Funerals.

    usque crescam: *I shall keep on growing*, literally *I shall grow continuously*.

8   **Capitolium**: *the Capitol*. The Capitoline Hill was the most sacred place in Rome. On it
were situated the Citadel and the Temple of Jupiter, both of which symbolised for the
Romans the indestructibility of Rome. In one of the most solemn of the state
ceremonies, the chief priest (**pontifex maximus**) went up with a Vestal Virgin (**virgine**)
to the Temple to offer prayers to Jupiter for the eternal greatness of Rome.

54 Immortality

(Horace, *Odes* III. 30)

> exegi monumentum aere perennius
> regalique situ pyramidum altius,
> quod non imber edax, non Aquilo impotens
> possit diruere aut innumerabilis
> 5 annorum series et fuga temporum.
> non omnis moriar multaque pars mei
> vitabit Libitinam: usque ego postera
> crescam laude recens, dum Capitolium
> scandet cum tacita virgine pontifex.

exigo (3), to complete, fashion
regalis, royal
situs, -us (*m*), structure, building
pyramis, -idis (*f*), pyramid
imber (*m*), rain
Aquilo (*m*), North Wind

diruo (3), to destroy
tempus, -oris (*n*), time, age
posterus, future, belonging to posterity
recens, fresh
dum, while, as long as
scando (3), to climb

Horace

Points for Discussion

1 Why do you think Horace uses the adjective **edax** to describe "rain" in line 3? We have suggested the general adjective *destructive* in this context. Can you think of more specific adjectives that might be used to describe the effect of rain on (*a*) stone, (*b*) metal, (*c*) mountain-sides, (*d*) trees?

2 What does Horace mean by saying that his poetry is "loftier" than the pyramids? In what way is his claim similar to the inscription about Sir Christopher Wren (**si monumentum requiris, circumspice**) which can be seen in St Paul's Cathedral?

3 What was the main duty of the Vestal Virgins in Rome?

4 **non omnis moriar** (line 6): What do you think Horace means by this?

5 Besides the destructive elements mentioned by Horace, what other things might endanger memorials made of materials such as marble and bronze? Do you agree with him that great poetry is more likely to survive? What sorts of dangers might threaten its survival?

6 Study the following lines of Percy Bysshe Shelley (1792–1822):

Ozymandias of Egypt
I met a traveller from an antique land
Who said: Two vast and trunkless legs of stone
Stand in the desert. Near them on the sand,
Half sunk, a shatter'd visage lies, whose frown
And wrinkled lip and sneer of cold command
Tell that its sculptor well those passions read
Which yet survive, stamp'd on these lifeless things,
The hand that mock'd them and the heart that fed;
And on the pedestal these words appear:
"My name is Ozymandias, king of kings:
Look on my works, ye Mighty, and despair!"
Nothing beside remains. Round the decay
Of that colossal wreck, boundless and bare,
The lone and level sands stretch far away.

(*a*) What do you think is the main message of this poem?

(*b*) What has it in common with the poem by Horace?

(*c*) Which lines of Horace impress you most? Which in Shelley's poem? Give reasons for your answers.

7 Do you think that memorials mean much to future generations? From your own neighbourhood, name one memorial which has some meaning for you, and one which has none. What sort of people and events do you think should be commemorated, and what form(s) should the memorials take?

8 What sort of memorial would you like to have for yourself?

An Introduction to Latin Metres

arma virumque cano Troiae qui primus ab oris
I sing of arms and the man who (came) first from the shores of Troy.

It was probably not the eye of a reader but the ear of a listener that first encountered this opening line of Virgil's *Aeneid*, for the poet would introduce his work to the public by reading it to an audience. Moreover, reading aloud was the norm among the Romans; so neither their poetry nor their prose was ever intended for the eye alone. If then justice is to be done to Latin poetry, "vocal reading" is essential.

Word-Stress

In most languages, in a word of two or more syllables, one syllable is more vigorously pronounced than the others. In English, this natural word-stress is so strong that words which are identically spelled can have different meanings because different syllables are stressed, e.g. ínvalid and inválid.

Latin words also have a stress-accent, though not as strong as that of English. Obviously, we cannot now reproduce the exact sound of classical Latin, but we do know that Latin word-stress operated as follows:

(*a*)   In two-syllable words, the stress falls on the first syllable, e.g. **ámo,   rípa.**

(*b*)   In longer words, the stress falls
    (i)   on the penult (the second-last syllable) when the penult is long,
       e.g. **amábo,   supérbus**;
    (ii)   on the ante-penult (the syllable before the second-last) when the
       penult is short, e.g. **amábimus,   amavérimus.**

English and Latin Verse

In English poetry, the "beat" depends on a pattern of accented and unaccented syllables, e.g.

    Í must dówn to the séas agaín, to the lónely séa and the ský.

Although Latin words also have a stress accent, the Romans based their poetry not on stress but on length of syllable, for which the technical term is *quantity*; and their metres are sound patterns of "long/heavy" syllables (marked –) and "short/light" syllables (marked ˇ). Musical notation, in which a crotchet (♩) lasts the same length of time as two quavers (♪ ♪), helps us to appreciate the difference between long and short syllables, e.g.

arma vi|rumque ca|no Tro|iae qui|primus ab|oris.

253

The above line is made up of six "bars" (called *feet*). When we mark the quantities of the syllables in a line and divide the line into feet, we are said to "scan" the line, and the process is called *scansion*.

Quantity

To scan a line of Latin verse, we must be able to distinguish long syllables from short syllables:

1. Some syllables are long because the vowel in the syllable is naturally long, e.g.

   canō, quōs, prīmus, cētera, animō, nōmen.

   Here, good pronunciation habits are of great assistance because most long vowels are not only longer but have a different sound from their shorter counterparts. For example, note the difference in the **-i -** sounds in

   regĭs (*you rule*) – as in the English word "hiss"
   audīs (*you hear*) – as in the English word "cease".

2. Some syllables in which the vowel is pronounced as short are nevertheless scanned as long because the whole syllable takes longer to say. This happens when the vowel is immediately followed by two consonants, whether these consonants are in the same word or not ("long by position"), e.g.

   the **-e-** of **fert** is short, but the syllable is scanned as long;
   the **-u-** of **bonus** is short, but the syllable **-nus** would be scanned long in **bonus vir.**

   However, when the second consonant was **l** or **r**, the poet could treat the syllable as long or short as he pleased, e.g.

   pātrem or **pătrem.**

   No notice was taken of the letter **h** (which was not regarded as a consonant) or of the letter **u** in a **qu** combination.
      Sometimes the letter **i** is treated as a consonant (e.g. **iustus** – two syllables), sometimes as a vowel (e.g. **varĭus** – three syllables).

3. Diphthongs, i.e. two vowels which are sounded as one (**ae, oe, au, eu, ei, ui**) are long, e.g.

   puellāē, āūrum, pōēna.

   However, when two vowels occur together without forming a diphthong, the first vowel is usually short, e.g.

   pŭella, ăit, Italĭam.

Elision

When a word ends in a vowel, a diphthong or a syllable ending in **-m**, that ending is *elided* (i.e. "knocked out") if it occurs immediately before a word beginning with a vowel (or an **h**). Opinions differ as to whether the elided syllable was omitted or pronounced rapidly and lightly. In any case, for the purposes of scansion, it is treated as if it was not there. Elisions are marked as follows:

difficil(e) est   **vestr(um) est**

I. THE DACTYLIC HEXAMETER

There are many verse patterns in Latin poetry. One of the commonest is the Hexameter, which has six feet (Greek **hex** = *six*), each foot being

either a **Dactyl** (– ◡ ◡ = ♩ ♪ ♪)

(Greek **dactulos** = *a finger*, which has one long joint and two short ones)

or a **Spondee** (– – = ♩ ♩)

(Greek **spondeios** = *the solemn (foot)*).

In a Hexameter, the first four feet can be any mixture of Dactyls and Spondees, the fifth foot is almost always a Dactyl, and the sixth foot is always a spondee (– –) or a Trochee (– ◡).

(Note: The last syllable of the line is often called the **syllaba anceps** (*the doubtful syllable*) because a short syllable can replace a long one. When that happens, the end-of-line pause "takes up the slack", i.e. ♩ ♩ = ♩ ♪ 𝄾 .)

The normal pattern for a Hexameter therefore is:

$$
\left.\begin{array}{c} - \ - \\ - \ \smile\smile \end{array}\right| \left.\begin{array}{c} - \ - \\ - \ \smile\smile \end{array}\right| \left.\begin{array}{c} - \ - \\ - \ \smile\smile \end{array}\right| \left.\begin{array}{c} - \ - \\ - \ \smile\smile \end{array}\right| - \ \smile\smile \left| \begin{array}{c} - \ - \\ - \ \smile \end{array}\right.
$$

By varying the pattern, the poet can produce different sound effects and moods, e.g.

speed and excitement in

quādrŭpĕ|dāntĕ pŭ|trēm sŏnĭ|tū quătĭt |ūngŭlă |cāmpūm

toil and struggle in

ērrā|bānt āc|tī fā|tīs mărĭ|(a) omnĭă| cīrcūm

Caesura

Because the Hexameter is so long, there is usually at least one slight breathing pause within each line. Such a pause is called a *caesura* and is indicated in scansion by the sign$_\wedge$, e.g.

ārmă vī|rūmquĕ că|nō $_\wedge$ Trō|iāe quī |prīmŭs ăb | ōrīs

The caesura normally occurs between words in either the third or the fourth foot, but it may occur also in other feet – usually to produce some special dramatic effect.

A very good illustration of quantity, elision, caesura and variation in the pattern of dactyls and spondees is provided in the three lines in which Virgil describes the spirits of the dead waiting to cross the River Styx (see pp. 75 and 81):

mātrēs | ātquĕ vī|rī, $_\wedge$ dē|fūnctăquĕ| cōrpŏră | vītā

māgnănĭ |m(um) herō|ŭm, $_\wedge$ pŭĕ|r(i) īnnūp|tāequĕ pŭ|ēllāe

īmpŏsĭ|tīquĕ rŏ|gīs iŭvĕ|nēs $_\wedge$ ān|t(e) ōră pă|rēntūm.

mothers and husbands, the lifeless bodies of great-hearted heroes, boys and unwed girls, and young men laid on pyres before their parents' eyes.

Word-Stress and Verse-Beat

In English poetry, word-stress and verse-beat sometimes coincide, e.g.

The cúrfew tólls the knéll of párting dáy.   (Gray's Elegy)

Often, however, if the verse-beat were allowed to dominate, the result would be absurd. For example, note the different effects produced in the following line from Shakespeare's *Merchant of Venice*:

    (*a*) The quálitý of mércy ís not stráined.
    (*b*) The quálity of mércy is nót strained.

In (*a*), which pays attention to only the verse-beat, the effect is almost comical; in (*b*), where natural word-stress is allowed to come into play, the result is sheer poetry.

Equally, in Latin poetry, word-stress (marked ´) and verse-beat sometimes clash with each other. Sometimes the clash is slight, e.g. in the following line, only in the word **viri**:

mātrēs| ātquĕ ví|rī dē|fūnctăquĕ | córpŏră | vītā.

Sometimes the clash is more marked:

īmpŏsĭ|tīquĕ rŏ|gīs iŭvĕ|nēs ān|t(e) ōră pă|rēntūm.

Notes:

(*a*) On its own, **impositi** would have the word-stress **impósiti**, but the attachment of **-que** changes the stress to **impositíque**, with a subsidiary stress on the first syllable.

(*b*) Prepositions such as **ante**, when occurring immediately before the word they govern, virtually coalesce with that word and lose their own word-stress.

(*c*) The word-stress and the verse-beat nearly always coincide in the last two feet of the Hexameter.

Rhythmic Reading

When you become more expert in speaking Latin verse, you will learn how to combine the various elements – long and short syllables, word-stress and verse-beat. To begin with, however, you may find it helpful to stress the first syllable of each foot as in the following English mock-hexameter:

Dówn in a deép dárk déll sat an óldców múnching a beánstálk.

Once you have established a basic feel for the pattern, you will find it easier to reach a compromise between the various elements and to appreciate how the interplay between quantity and stress creates the immense variety of the Hexameter.

II. THE ELEGIAC COUPLET

When a Dactylic Hexameter is followed by a five-foot Pentameter line (Greek **pente** = *five*) to form a couplet, the combination is called an Elegiac Couplet. This couplet was used initially for an elegy or a lament, but it was soon extended to a great variety of poem types.

quōd mărĕ $\,\big|\,$ nōn nŏ$\big|$vīt, $_\wedge$ quaē $\big|$ nēscĭt Ă$\big|$rĭŏnă $\big|$ tēllūs?

cārmĭnĕ $\big|$ cūrrēn$\big|$tēs $\|$ īllĕ tĕ$\big|$nēbăt ă$\big|$quās.

It will be seen that the Pentameter is actually made up of two $2\frac{1}{2}$-foot sections. The first two feet admit both dactyls and spondees, but the line invariably ends

$$-\ \smile\ \smile\ \big|\ -\ \smile\ \smile\ \big|\ - \qquad \text{(dactyl and dactyl and long)}$$

III. OTHER METRES

(a) *Hendecasyllabic* – an eleven-syllable line (Greek **hendeka** = *eleven*), e.g.

lūgē|t(e),⁻o Vĕnĕ|rēs Cŭ|pīdĭ|nēsquĕ

ēt quān|t(um)⁻ēst hŏmĭ|nūm vĕ|nūstĭ|ōrŭm.

The only variations are
$\quad$ ‾ ˘ | ‾ ˘ ˘ | ‾ ˘ | ‾ ˘ | ‾ ‾
$\qquad\qquad\qquad$ ‾ ‾ $\qquad$ ‾ ˘

(b) *Lesser Asclepiad* – a metre based on the Choriambus foot (- ˘ ˘ -), e.g.

ēxē|gī mŏnŭmēn|t(um)⁻aerĕ pĕrēn|nĭŭs

rēgā|līquĕ sĭtū | pȳrămĭd(um)⁻al|tĭŭs

(c) *Sapphic* – a four-line stanza named after Sappho (a Greek poetess of the sixth century BC who used it in her poems) and made up of three Lesser Sapphic lines and an Adonic, e.g.

īllĕ |mī pār| ēssĕ dĕ|ō vĭ|dētŭr,	Lesser Sapphic
īllĕ,| sī fās |ēst, sŭpĕ|rārĕ	dīvōs	Lesser Sapphic
quī sĕ|dēns ād|vērsŭs ĭ|dēntĭ|dēm tē	Lesser Sapphic
spēctăt ĕt	aūdĭt	Adonic

(d) *Iambic Senarius.* The iambic foot, or iambus (˘ -), is the basis of various Latin metres. One of these is the Senarius which in its pure form consists of six iambic feet, as in the following line from Catullus:

phăsē|lŭs īl|lĕ quēm| vĭdē|tĭs, hōs|pĭtēs
That yacht which you see, friends.

However, the form of Senarius used by Phaedrus allows other metrical units such as dactyls, spondees and anapaests (˘ ˘ -) to be substituted for the iambus in any foot except the last, which must be iambic, e.g.

ād fŏn|tēm cēr|vūs cūm |bĭbīs|sēt rēs|tĭtīt

ĕt īn |lĭquō|rĕ vĭ|dĭt ĕf|fĭgĭem |sŭām

(e) The *Scazon* (Greek **skazon** = *limping*) or *Choliambus* (Greek **choliambus** = *lame iambic*) is an iambic line which reverses the iambic movement in the last foot by putting a trochee (- ˘) instead, e.g.

mĭsēr | Cătūl|lĕ, dē|sĭnās | ĭnēp|tīrĕ

Figures of Speech

Note. The decision to allocate an example to one Figure of Speech rather than to another is somewhat arbitrary, since some examples could be used to illustrate more than one Figure of Speech.

1   ALLITERATION occurs when words beginning with the same sound or letter appear in close succession, e.g. "He left with a last, long, lingering look." It is a common Figure of Speech in Latin poetry. Sometimes it is used to convey meaning through the sound of the words (see also ASSONANCE and ONO-MATOPOEIA), sometimes the poet uses it for its own sake as a stylistic feature, since it was expected in Latin poetry, e.g.

> **Phaëthon penitus penitusque patentes palluit** (Passage 31, line 44)
> **pestem perniciemque** (Passage 18, line 8)
> **ante annos animumque** (Passage 40, line 31)
> **strepitus et signa sequentum** (Passage 40, line 95)
> **molle pecus mutumque metu** (Passage 40, line 54)
> See also the repeated use of "**m**" sounds in Passage 20.

2   ASSONANCE is the term used to describe a succession of identical or similar vowel sounds, e.g. "double trouble." Latin examples in this book include:

> **ceteraque armata conscia turba manu** (Passage 32(b), line 18)
> **suos pollice chorda sonos** (Passage 32(b), line 26)
> **subito turbante tumultu** (Passage 40, line 98)

(See also ALLITERATION and ONOMATOPOEIA.)

3   HENDIADYS is the use of two words to express what is essentially one idea (e.g. "fear and trembling", "house and home", "nice and warm"). Latin examples include:

> **ius et moderamen**: *power and control* (i.e. "controlling power") (Passage 31, line 9)
> **dolorem cruciatumque**: *pain and torture* (i.e. "excruciating pain") (Passage 2, line 26)
> **somno vinoque**: *in sleep and wine* (i.e. "in drunken sleep") (Passage 40, line 36)
> **Creten longumque exsilium**: *Crete and long exile* (i.e. "long exile in Crete") (Passage 30, lines 1–2)
> **vinclis et carcere**: *by prison and chains* (i.e. "by prison chains")

4   METAPHOR: In a simile, one thing is said to be *like* another. In a metaphor, one thing is said to *be* something else which it only resembles. For example:

> "The investigator was like a terrier hunting its prey" (simile)
> "He became a terrier hunting his prey" (metaphor).

Latin examples include the accounting metaphors in Passage 10 (line 11) and Passage 16 (line 2), and the medical metaphor in Passage 18 (line 8).

5   ONOMATOPOEIA: The sound of the word(s) suggests what is being described (e.g. "quack-quack" or Tennyson's "the murmuring of innumerable bees"). Poets use this device a great deal when they wish to create a certain mood or atmosphere. Latin examples include:

tintinant (bells ringing)
pipiabat (bird chirping)
corripuere viam pedibusque per aëra motis (horses galloping)
subito turbante tumultu (confused shouting)

(See also ALLITERATION and ASSONANCE.)

6   SIMILE: In the simplest form of simile, one thing is said to be *like* another or *as* another, e.g. "trembling like a leaf", "like a bull in a china-shop", "as light as a feather." Compare:

(*a*) Catullus' answer (Passage 11) when asked how many kisses might satisfy him:

    quam magnus numerus Libyssae harenae: *as many as the grains of Libyan sand* (line 3) and
    quam sidera multa: *as many as the stars* (line 7)

(*b*) **iacebant sicut messis in campo**: *(the dead) lay like crops in a field* (Passage 33, line 55)

(*c*) **utque labant curvae iusto sine pondere naves**
    perque mare instabiles nimia levitate feruntur
    just as ships that are not fully laden toss about as they cross the sea and are unstable because they are too light (Passage 31, lines 35–6)

(*d*) the shooting star in Passage 31, lines 106–7: and the dying swan in Passage 32(b), lines 27–28.

    In poetry, similes tend to be much longer than those used in prose. Besides comparing one thing to another, the poet often develops the comparison in some detail. In Latin, similes are usually introduced by a word such as **velut(i)**, **qualis** or **ceu**; and another word (such as **sic**, **talis** or **haud secus**) marks the end of the simile.

    For example, in lines 52–55 of Passage 40, Euryalus' attack on the Rutulians is compared with the attack of a hungry lion on a sheep-fold:

impastus ceu plena leo per ovilia turbans
(suadet enim vesana fames) manditque trahitque
molle pecus mutumque metu, fremit ore cruento.
nec minor Euryali caedes; incensus et ipse
perfurit ....

Just as a starving lion, driven on by ravenous hunger, creates havoc in a crowded sheep-pen as it mangles and carries off the fleecy flock which has fallen silent through fear; and it roars from its mouth that is dripping with blood; no less was the slaughter inflicted by Euryalus in his furious rampage.

7   TRANSFERRED EPITHET (epithet = adjective): In this figure of speech, an adjective which describes one noun is attached to another noun, e.g. in "The ploughman homeward plods his weary way" it is really the ploughman, not the way, which is weary. Compare the Latin examples:

(a) **gemina teguntur lumina nocte** (Passage 7, lines 11–12) means literally *my eyes are covered in twin darkness* (**gemina** is ablative agreeing with **nocte**), although the poet is clearly thinking of "two eyes".

(b) **innumerabilis annorum series**: *the succession of countless years*, literally *the countless succession of years* (Passage 54, lines 4–5).

Language Notes

For an explanation of most grammatical points, pupils have been directed to the student handbook *The Latin Language*, published by Oliver and Boyd (referred to as "LL" in the notes). The following three points are not mentioned in that book:

1 POETIC PLURAL, i.e. where the plural form of a noun is used instead of the singular. Latin poets frequently use this device to help them fit words into the metre. For example, in Passage 40 (line 128), **candida pectora** is used since **candidum pectus** cannot be fitted into a Hexameter.

2 SINGULAR FOR PLURAL: Singular forms are sometimes used in place of plural for similar reasons, e.g. in Passage 21 (line 15), **deformis harundo** is used instead of **deformes harundines**, *unsightly reeds*, which would not scan, and **arbor** for **arbores** in Passage 31, line 72.

3 GREEK ACCUSATIVE: These are particularly common in proper names. There are two forms:
   (*a*) **-n** e.g. **Aenean** (Passage 40, line 13)
            Creten (Passage 30, line 1)
            Eurydicen (Passage 21, line 27)
   (*b*) **-a.** e.g. **Ariona** (Passage 32(b), line 1)
            aëra (Passage 31, line 30).

Vocabulary

N.B. Where only the present indicative active and the Group Number of verbs have been given, you may assume that the endings of the other principal parts (where they exist) follow the set patterns for Principal Parts:

Group 1: **-o, -are, -avi, -atum**
Group 2: **-eo, -ere, -ui, -itum**
Group 4: **-io, -ire, -ivi, -itum**

A

a, ab (+ *abl.*), by, from, away from
abeo, -ire, -ii, -itum, to go away, leave
abicio (3), **-ieci, -iectum**, to throw away, throw down
abitus, -us (*m*), exit, way out
ablego (l), to keep out of the way
abluo (3), **-ui, -utum**, to wash
abrumpo (3), **-rupi, -ruptum**, to break off
abscedo (3), **-cessi, -cessum**, to go away
abscido (3), **-cidi, -cisum**, to cut off
abscondo (3), **-condi, -conditum**, to hide
absens, -entis, absent
absisto (3), **-stiti**, to stop
absorbeo (2), to swallow up, drown
absum, -esse, afui, to be absent, distant from
absumo (3), **-sumpsi, -sumptum**, to use up, consume
abutor (3), **-usus sum** (+ *abl.*), to abuse, maltreat
ac, and, moreover
accedo (3), **-cessi, -cessum**, to go to, come to, approach
accendo (3), **-cendi, -censum**, to set fire to, light
accerso (3), **-ivi, -itum**, to send for, summon
accidit (3), **accidit**, it happens
accio (4), to summon, recall
accipio (3), **-cepi, -ceptum**, to receive, get
accipiter, -tris (*m*), hawk
accolo (3), **-colui, -cultum**, to inhabit
accommodo (l), to fit on, attach
accurate, carefully
acer, acris, acre, fierce, keen, sharp, sore
acerbus, -a, -um, bitter
acervus, -i (*m*), heap
acies, -ei (*f*), line of battle, battle
Achilles, -is (*m*), Achilles, a celebrated Greek hero

acriter, fiercely, carefully
acuo (3), **-ui, -utum**, to sharpen
ad (+ *acc.*), to, towards, at, near
    ad unum, (all) to a man
addo (3), **-didi, -ditum**, to add
adduco (3), **-duxi, -ductum**, to lead to, take to, draw towards
adeo (*adverb*), to such a degree
adeo, -ire, -ii, -itum, to go to, come near, approach
adfero, *see* **affero**
adficio, *see* **afficio**
adfinis, -is (*m*), relative (by marriage)
adflicto (l), to batter, damage
adfligo (3), -xi, -ctum, to damage, wreck
adhortor (l), to encourage
adhuc, still
adiaceo (2), to lie near
adigo (3), **-egi, -actum**, to drive, drive home
adimo (3), **-emi, -emptum** (+ *dat.*), to take away (from)
adiungo (3), **-iunxi, -iunctum**, to join, bring close to
adiuvo (1), **-iuvi, -iutum**, to help
adludo, *see* **alludo**
administro (l), to manage, organise, carry out
admirandus, -a, -um, surprising, wonderful
admiratio, -onis (*f*), admiration
    admirationi esse (+ *dat.*), to cause amazement (to)
admiror (1), to be amazed, wonder, marvel at
admitto (3), **-misi, -missum**, to send to, let in, admit
admodum, very, quite, merely
admoneo (2), to warn, advise
admoveo (2), **-movi, -motum**, to bring near, move towards, apply

adnato (l), to swim towards
adnitor (3), **-nixus sum** (+ *dat*.), to lean upon
adno (l), to swim up, swim towards
adolescens, *see* **adulescens**
adorior (4), **-ortus sum**, to attack
adoro (l), to address, worship
adpareo, *see* **appareo**
adprehendo, *see* **apprehendo**
adquiesco (3), **-evi, -etum**, to take a rest
adsiduus, -a, -um, constant, repetitive
adsigno, *see* **assigno**
adspicio, *see* **aspicio**
adstringo, *see* **astringo**
adsuetus, *see* **assuetus**
adsum, -esse, adfui, to be present
adsurgo (3), **-surrexi, -surrectum**, to rise, get up
adulescens, -entis (*m*), young man, youth
adulor (1), to fawn upon, flatter
aduro (3), **-ussi, -ustum**, to burn, scorch
advenio (4), **-veni, -ventum**, to reach, come to, arrive (at)
advento (l), to approach
adventus, -us (*m*), arrival, approach
adversus, -a, -um, facing, opposite, unfavourable
   adverso vulnere, with wounds on the front of the body
   in adversis, in adversity
adversus (+ *acc*.), opposite, against
adverto (3), **-verti, -versum**, to keep watch, take note
advesperascit (3), **-avit**, it grows dark
aedificium, -i (*n*), building
aeger, -gra, -grum, sick, feeble, sorrowful
aegre, barely, scarcely, with difficulty
   aegre ferre, to be annoyed at
Aeneadae, -um (*m.pl*), followers of Aeneas
Aeneas, -ae (*m*), Aeneas, the leader of the Trojans who escaped from Troy and eventually settled in Italy.
aëneus, -a, -um, made of bronze
aequalis, -is (*m*), companion
aeque, equally
aequinoctium, -i (*n*), equinox
aequo (l), to be equal to, equal
aequor, -oris (*n*), sea
aequoreus, -a, -um, of the sea
aequus, -a, -um, equal, fair, just
   aequo animo, patiently, calmly
aër, aëris (*m*), air (*acc*. **aëra**)
aes, aeris (*n*), bronze, money

aestimatio, -onis (*f*), calculation
aestimo (l), to judge, consider, value
aestuarium, -i (*n*), channel, estuary, tidal flow
aestuosus, -a, -um, hot, sultry, sweltering
aestus, -us (*m*), heat, tide
aetas, -atis (*f*), age, generation
aeternus, -a, -um, everlasting, for ever
aether, -eris (*m*), heaven, air (*acc*. **aethera**)
Aethiopes, -um (*m.pl*), Ethiopians
aevum, -i (*n*), age, generation, time
affero, -ferre, attuli, allatum, to bring, bring to
afficio (3), **-feci, -fectum**, to treat, affect
affirmo (l), to declare, state, say
Africa, -ae (*f*), Africa (Roman province, roughly equivalent to modern Tunisia and Libya)
ager, agri (*m*), land, field, territory
aggredior (3), **-gressus sum**, to attack, set about, begin
agitator, -oris (*m*), driver
agito (l), to move, drive
agmen, -inis (*n*), marching-column
agna, -ae (*f*), lamb
agnosco (3), **-novi, -nitum**, to recognise
ago (3), **egi, actum**, to do, drive
   age! agite! come now!
   agere de (+ *abl*.), to discuss, treat about
   iter agere, to steer a course
ait, he (she) says, said
ala, -ae (*f*), wing
alacer, -cris, -cre, eager(ly)
ales, -itis (*f*), bird
alienus, -a, -um, of another, someone else's, inappropriate
alioqui, otherwise
alipes, -pedis, winged
aliqui, -qua, -quod, some, any
   aliquo facto, somehow or other
aliquis, -quis, -quid, someone, something, some
aliter, otherwise
   non aliter, in no other way
alius, -a, -ud, other, another
allevo (l), to lift up
alligo (l), to bind, hem in, imprison
alloquor (3), **-locutus sum**, to address, speak to
alludo (3), **-lusi, -lusum**, to play with
alte, high, high up
alter, -a, -um, another, a second
   alter ... alter ..., the one ... the other ...

altum, -i (*n*), the deep, the sea, the open sea

altus, -a, -um, high, deep, lofty, on high

alumnus, -i (*m*), foster-child

amans, -antis (*m*), a lover

ambitio, -onis (*f*), ambition

ambitiosus, -a, -um, ambitious, self-seeking

ambo, -ae, -o, both

amburo (3), **-ussi, -ustum**, to burn up, scorch

amens, -entis, out of one's mind, mad

amica, -ae (*f*), (girl) friend, mistress

amicitia, -ae (*f*), friendship, love

amictus, -us (*m*), cloak

amiculum, -i (*n*), cloak

amicus, -i (*m*), friend

amicus, -a, -um, friendly

amitto (3), **-misi, -missum**, to lose

amo (1), to love

amor, -oris (*m*), love

amplexus, -us (*m*), embrace

amplius, more, further

   nec amplius, and no longer

amplus, -a, -um, lavish

an, whether, or

ancora, -ae (*f*), anchor

   ancoram iacere, to drop anchor

angustus, -a, -um, narrow, small

anima, -ae (*f*), breath, soul, spirit

animadverto (3), **-verti, -versum**, to notice, take note of, realise, perceive, see

animal, -alis (*n*), animal, living creature

animus, -i (*m*), mind, spirit, will, heart, thoughtfulness, consciousness, concentration

   aequo animo, patiently, calmly

   otioso animo esse, to be easy in mind

annus, -i (*m*), year

ante (+ *acc.*), before, in front of

ante (*adverb*), before, in front, beforehand

antea, before, previously

antefero, -ferre, -tuli, -latum, to prefer

antequam, before

anulus, -i (*m*), ring

aperio (4), **-ui, apertum**, to open

apertus, -a, -um, open

apocrisiarius, -i (*m*), delegate, deputy, representative

Apollo, -inis (*m*), Apollo, god of the sun

appareo (2), to appear, become evident

appello (1), to call, name, give a name to

appeto (3), **-ivi, -itum**, to draw near to, peck

appono (3), **-posui, -positum**, to place before, serve

apporto (1), to bring

apprehendo (3), **-endi, -ensum**, to seize, take, arrest

appropinquo (1) (+ *dat.*), to draw near (to), approach

apricus, -a, -um, sunny

apud (+ *acc.*), among, at the house of, in, before, at, in the eyes of

aqua, -ae (*f*), water, stream

aquila, -ae (*f*), eagle

aquilifer, -i (*m*), standard-bearer

Aquilo, -onis (*m*), North Wind

aranea, -ae (*f*), cobweb

arator, -oris (*m*), farmer, ploughman

aratrum, -i (*n*), plough

arbitrium, -i (*n*), will, whim, judgment

arbitror (1), to think

arbor, -oris (*f*), tree

arceo (2), to keep away

arcesso (3), **-ivi, -itum**, to send for, summon

ardeo (2), **arsi, arsum**, to burn, blaze, be on fire

   ardens, blazing with anger

arduus, -a, -um, lofty, steep, towering above

area, -ae (*f*), courtyard

arena, -ae (*f*), sand, desert

areo (2), to be dry

argumentum, -i (*n*), proof

aridus, -a, -um, dry, parched

ariolus, -i (*m*), soothsayer

arma, -orum (*n.pl*), arms, weapons

armamenta, -orum (*n.pl*), (ship's) tackle, gear

armiger, -i (*m*), armour-bearer

armo (1), to arm

arrectus, -a, -um, tilted

arripio (3), **-ripui, -reptum**, to take control of

arrogantia, -ae (*f*), arrogance, arrogant behaviour

ars, artis (*f*), art, cunning, trick, skill

articulum -i (*n*), part, point, moment

artus, -us (*m*), limb

arx, arcis (*f*), citadel

   summa arx, the highest point

as, assis (*m*), an *as* (small coin), penny, cent

ascendo (3), **-scendi, -scensum**, to climb, climb up to, get up

asper, -a, -um, rough, harsh, cruel

aspicio (3), **-spexi, -spectum**, to look at, catch sight of, take notice of
asporto (1), to carry away, carry off
assigno (l), to assign, allot
assuetus, -a, -um, usual, accustomed
ast, but
astringo (3), **-strinxi, -strictum**, to bind
astrum, -i (*n*), star
at, but
Athenae, -arum (*f.pl*), Athens
atque, and, and also
atrox, atrocis, fierce, terrible, shocking
attendo (3), **-tendi, -tentum**, to pay attention to, listen to
attero (3), **-trivi, -tritum**, to wear away, exhaust
attollo (3), to lift, raise up
auctor, -oris (*m*), author, originator, the source of
auctoritas, -atis (*f*), authority, power, influence
audacia, -ae (*f*), daring, boldness, courage
audacter, boldly
audax, -acis, bold, daring
audeo (2), **ausus sum**, to dare
audio (4), to hear, listen, listen to
aufero, -ferre, abstuli, ablatum, to take away, carry away
augeo (2), **auxi, auctum**, to increase
augur, -uris (*m*), augur, seer
augurium, -i (*n*), (power of) augury, prophecy
aura, -ae (*f*), breeze, air, wind
auriga, -ae (*m*), charioteer
auris, -is (*f*), ear
aurora, -ae (*f*), dawn
Ausonis, -idis, Ausonian, Italian
Ausonius, -a, -um, Ausonian, Italian
ausum, -i (*n*), enterprise, deed of daring
aut, or
   aut . . . aut . . ., either . . . or . . .
autem, however, but, moreover
autumnus, -i (*m*), autumn
auxilior (l), to help, aid
auxilium, -i (*n*), help, assistance
avaritia, -ae (*f*), greed, avarice
avarus, -a, -um, greedy, grasping
ave! hail!
Avernus, -i (*m*), (Lake) Avernus, near an entrance to the Underworld, used also of the Underworld itself
averto (3), **averti, aversum**, to turn away, turn aside, divert
avia, -ae (*f*), grandmother

avicula, -ae (*f*), small bird
aviditas, -atis (*f*), greed
avidus, -a, -um, greedy
avis, -is (*f*), bird
avius, -a, -um, pathless, unfrequented
avunculus, -i (*m*), uncle (mother's brother)
avus, -i (*m*), grandfather
axis, -is (*m*), axle

B

baculum, -i (*n*), stick, crook
balineum, -i (*n*), bath(s)
balteum, -i (*n*), sword-belt
barba, -ae (*f*), beard
barbarus, -i (*m*), barbarian
basiatio, -onis (*f*), kiss, kissing
basio (l), to kiss
basium, -i (*n*), kiss
beatus, -a, -um, happy, blessed
bellum, -i (*n*), war, warfare, battle
   bellum indicere (+ *dat.*), to declare war (upon)
   bellum inferre (+ *dat.*), to make war (upon)
bellus, -a, -um, beautiful, pretty, neat, dainty
bene, well
beneficium, -i (*n*), (act of) kindness, favour
bestia, -ae (*f*), beast
bibo (3), **bibi**, to drink
biduum, -i (*n*), (period of) two days
bini, -ae, -a, two each
bis, twice
blaesus, -a, -um, lisping
blande, caressingly, in a fawning manner
blandimentum, -i (*n*), caress
blandus, -a, -um, charming, gentle
bonus, -a, -um, good
   bona fide, in reality, without a doubt
boreas, -ae (*m*), North Wind
brevis, -is, -e, short, brief
   brevi, in a moment, in an instant
breviter, briefly
Britannia, -ae (*f*), Britain
bruma, -ae (*f*), winter
Bruttii, -orum (*m.pl*), inhabitants of Bruttium, in the southern tip of Italy

C

caballus, -i (*m*), horse
cachinnus, -i (*m*), loud laughter, mirth

cado (3), **cecidi, casum**, to fall
caedes, **-is** (*f*), slaughter, murder
caedo (3), **cecidi, caesum**, to kill, cut to pieces, cut down
caelum, **-i** (*n*), heaven, sky, air
caeruleus, **-a, -um**, dark blue
caerulus, **-a, -um**, dark blue
Caesar, **-aris** (*m*), Caesar (title used by emperors)
caespes, **-itis** (*m*), turf
calidus, **-a, -um**, hot, warm
caligo, **-inis** (*f*), darkness, mist, vapour
callis, **-is** (*m*), path
calor, **-oris** (*m*), heat
Calymne, **-es** (*f*), modern Calymnos, an island in the Aegean near Rhodes
Campania, **-ae** (*f*), Campania, region of Italy south of Latium
campus, **-i** (*m*), plain, wide open space
candidus, **-a, -um**, white, fair, pretty, bright, dazzling
candesco (3), **-ui**, to grow white, begin to glow
caneo (2), to be white
canesco (3), to grow white
canis, **-is** (*m*), dog
canities (*f*), grey hair
cano (3), **cecini, cantum**, to sing
cantator, **-oris** (*m*), singer, minstrel
canto (1), to sing
cantus, **-us** (*m*), song, singing
canus, **-a, -um**, grey-haired
capax, **-acis**, roomy
capesso (3), **-ivi, -itum**, to undertake
capillus, **-i** (*m*), hair
   capilli, **-orum** (*m.pl*), hair
capio (3), **cepi, captum**, to take, capture, seize, to adopt (a plan)
capitalis, **-is, -e**, concerning the head (i.e. death), criminal
Capitolium, **-i** (*n*), the Capitol, Capitoline Hill in Rome
captivus, **-i** (*m*), prisoner
capto (1), to catch, snatch, try to catch
caput, **-itis** (*n*), head, life
careo (2) (+ *abl*.), to lack, be free from
caritas, **-atis** (*f*), affection
carmen, **-inis** (*n*), song, hymn, singing, verse, epitaph
caro, **carnis** (*f*), meat, flesh
carpo (3), **carpsi, carptum**, to pluck, tear at, crop, eat
   viam carpere, to make one's way
carus, **-a, -um**, dear, precious, pleasing

cassita, **-ae** (*f*), lark
castra, **-orum** (*n.pl*), camp
casus, **-us** (*m*), fortune, luck, eventuality, misfortune, mishap, blow
   casu, by chance, as it happened
catella, **-ae** (*f*), puppy
catena, **-ae** (*f*), chain
cauda, **-ae** (*f*), tail
causa, **-ae** (*f*), cause, reason, explanation
   causa (+ *gen*.), for the sake of
caute, cautiously
cautes, **-is** (*f*), rock
cavus, **-a, -um**, hollow
cedo (3), **cessi, cessum**, to yield, give in, withdraw
celer, **-is, -e**, swift, fast
celeritas, **-atis** (*f*), speed
celeriter, quickly
celero (1), to hasten
celo (1), to hide, conceal
celsus, **-a, -um**, tall, lofty, high
cena, **-ae** (*f*), dinner
ceno (1), to dine
census, **-us** (*m*), tribute (a form of tax)
centum, hundred
centumpliciter, one hundred times
centurio, **-onis** (*m*), centurion
cera, **-ae** (*f*), wax, bits of wax, writing-tablet
cerebrum, **-i** (*n*), brain
cerno (3), **crevi, cretum**, to perceive, see, notice
certamen, **-inis** (*n*), contest, struggle, battle, competition, race
certe, certainly, surely, at least
certus, **-a, -um**, certain, definite
   certiorem facere, to inform
cerva, **-ae** (*f*), deer, hind
cervix, **-icis** (*f*), neck
   cervices, **-um** (*f.pl*), neck
cervus, **-i** (*m*), stag
cessator, **-oris** (*m*), idler, slacker
ceteri, **-ae, -a**, the rest, the others
ceterum, but
ceu, just like
Charon, **-ontis** (*m*), Charon, ferryman of the rivers Styx and Acheron
charta, **-ae** (*f*), sheet of paper (papyrus), volume
chorda, **-ae** (*f*), string
chommodus, *see* **commodus**
cibarium, **-i** (*n*), food, rations
cibus, **-i** (*m*), food
cicatrix, **-icis** (*f*), scar

Cineas, -ae (*m*), Cineas, friend and adviser of Pyrrhus
cinis, -eris (*m/f*), ash, ashes
circa (+ *acc*.), around
circensis, -is, -e, of the circus
circiter, about
circum (*adverb*), round about
circum (+ *acc*.), around
circumdo (1), **-dedi, -datum**, to surround
circumeo, -ire, -ii, -itum, to go round
circumligo (1), to bind
circumsilio (4), to hop about
circumsisto (3), **-steti**, to surround
circumspicio (3), **-spexi, -spectum**, to look around
circumstrepo (3), **—, -itum**, to twitter around
circumvenio (4), **-veni, -ventum**, to surround
Circus Maximus, the huge chariot-racing stadium in Rome; used also later for gladiatorial shows
cithara, -ae (*f*), lyre
cito, quickly
  citius, more quickly, rather quickly
civitas, -atis (*f*), state, city
clam, secretly
clamito (1), to shout out loud, bawl out, keep on shouting
clamo (1), to shout, cry
clamor, -oris (*m*), shout, shouting, noise
clare, clearly
claudo (3), **clausi, clausum**, to shut in, imprison, block
clementer, gently
clibanus, -i (*m*), furnace
coactus, *see* **cogo**
Cocytus, -i (*m*), the Cocytus, a river of the Underworld
coeo, -ire, -ii, -itum, to assemble, gather
coepi, -isse, I began
  coeptus, -a, -um, begun
coeptum, -i (*n*), task, undertaking
coerceo (2), to surround, confine, enclose
cogitatio, -onis (*f*), thought(s)
cogito (1), to think, consider, ponder over
cognatus, -i (*m*), kinsman, relative (by blood)
cognitio, -onis (*f*), identity
cognosco (3), **-novi, -nitum**, to learn, realise, find out
cogo (3), **coegi, coactum**, to compel, force, gather, collect

cohors, -ortis (*f*), cohort (tenth part of a legion)
cohortor (1), to encourage
collabor (3), **-lapsus sum**, to fall down, sink
colligo (3), **-legi, -lectum**, to collect, gather
colloco (1), to station, place, spend, employ
colloquor (3), **-locutus sum**, to converse, confer, discuss
collum, -i (*n*), neck
colonia, -ae (*f*), settlement, colony, community
color, -oris (*m*), colour
columba, -ae (*f*), dove
coma, -ae (*f*), a hair, leaf
  comae, -arum (*f.pl*), hair, mane
comes, -itis (*m*), companion, comrade
comiter, on good terms, courteously
commeatus, -us (*m*), supplies, provisions
commendo (1), to entrust
comminus, at close quarters
commisceo (2), **-ui, -mixtum**, to mix, mingle
commiseretur (2), **-itum est** (impersonal), to show pity
commiseror (1), to pity, seek pity for
committo (3), **-misi, -missum**, to entrust, commit
  proelium (pugnam) committere, to join battle
commode, conveniently, reasonably
commodus, -a, -um, advantageous, opportune
  commoda, -orum (*n.pl*), advantages, opportunities
commoveo (2), **-movi, -motum**, to move, stir up, startle
communis, -is, -e, shared, common
comparo (1), to compare, get ready, obtain, acquire
compedes, -um (*f.pl*), shackles, fetters
comperio (4), **-peri, -pertum**, to find (out)
compesco (3), **-ui**, to restrain, hold in check, curb, quench, repress
compleo (2), **-evi, -etum**, to fill, complete
complures, -es, -a, several
compono (3), **-posui, -positum**, to put together, arrange, portray
comporto (1), to bring together, collect
compos mentis, conscious
comprehendo (3), **-hendi, -hensum**, to seize, arrest, capture

concavus, -a, -um, hollow

concedo (3), **-cessi, -cessum**, to grant, agree, yield, withdraw, take refuge in

concerpo (3), **-cerpsi, -cerptum**, to pick up, gather

concido (3), **-cidi, -cisum**, to cut, cut through

concido (3), **-cidi**, to fall, collapse

concipio (3), **-cepi, -ceptum**, to take in, gather, absorb

conclamo (1), to shout out

concubina, -ae (*f*), concubine, female slave

concurro (3), **-curri, -cursum**, to flock together, rush up, gather round

concutio (3), **-cussi, -cussum**, to shake, rattle

condicio, -onis (*f*), condition, term(s), social status

condo (3), **-didi, -ditum**, to found, hide, cover, bury, plunge

conduco (3), **-duxi, -ductum**, to hire, rent

confero, -ferre, -tuli, collatum, to bring together

confertus, -a, -um, crowded together

confestim, immediately

conficio (3), **-feci, -fectum**, to overcome, distress

  confectus, -a, -um, worn out, exhausted, badly affected

confido (3), **-fisus sum**, to trust, be confident

confirmo (1), to establish

confiteor (3), **-fessus sum**, to confess, reveal

conflicto (1), to afflict, handicap

confluo (3), **-fluxi**, to flow together, flock together

confodio (3), **-fodi, -fossum**, to pierce, stab

conforto (1), to comfort, strengthen greatly

confusus, -a, -um, upset, agitated, distressed

congelo (1), to freeze

congero (3), **-gessi, -gestum**, to bring together, make a nest

conicio (3), **-ieci, -iectum**, to hurl, throw

conitor (3), **conixus sum**, to strain

coniungo (3), **-iunxi, -iunctum**, to join together

coniunx, -iugis (*f*), wife

coniuratio, -onis (*f*), conspiracy

conor (1), to try, attempt

conscendo (3), **-scendi, -scensum**, to board a ship, go on board

conscientia, -ae (*f*), guilt, conscience

conscius, -a, -um, conspiring, guilty, aware

conservus, -i (*m*), fellow-slave

consido (3), **-sedi, -sessum**, to sit down

consilium, -i (*n*), plan, advice, council, consultation, decision-making

  consilium capere, to adopt a plan

  consilium inire, to form a plan

consisto (3), **-stiti**, to stand, halt, take up a position, take a stand

conspicio (3), **-spexi, -spectum**, to catch sight of

constat, it is agreed, it is commonly believed

consterno (1), to terrify

constituo (3), **-ui, -utum**, to decide, fix, draw up

consuesco (3), **-suevi, -suetum**, to be accustomed

consuetudo, -inis (*f*), custom

consul, -ulis (*m*), consul

consularis, -is, -e, of consular rank, of an ex-consul

consulatus, -us (*m*), consulship

consulo (3), **-ui, -ltum**, to plan, take measures, look out

consulto, deliberately

consumo (3), **-sumpsi, -sumptum**, to use up

consurgo (3), **-surrexi, -surrectum**, to rise up

contemno (3), **-tempsi, -temptum**, to despise, spurn

contendo (3), **-tendi, -tentum**, to strive, struggle

contentio, -onis (*f*), struggle

contexo (3), **-ui, -textum**, to weave, compose, write

continens, -entis (*f*), mainland, the Continent

contineo (2), **-ui, -tentum**, to hold, confine, check

  se continere, to remain

contingo (3), **-tigi, -tactum**, to touch, handle, reach

  contingit, it happens, occurs

continuus, -a, -um, continuous, non-stop

contra (+ *acc.*), against, opposite

contra (*adverb*), opposite, in return, in response

contraho (3), **-traxi, -tractum**, to bring together

contrarius, -a, -um, opposite, contrary, opposed to, hostile to
  in contraria, in opposite directions

controversia, -ae (*f*), argument

contubernalis, -is (*m*), comrade, companion

contueor (2), to look at

contumelia, -ae (*f*), abuse, insult, affront

contundo (3), **-tudi, -tusum**, to pound, thump

conturbo (l), to trouble, disturb, muddle

contus, -i (*m*), pole

convenio (4), **-veni, -ventum** (+ *dat*.), to meet, assemble, gather, suit

converto (3), **-verti, -versum**, to turn, direct

convictus, -us (*m*), companionship, company, social life

convinco (3), **-vici, -victum**, to prove guilty

convivium, -i (*n*), feast, banquet, dinner-party

cooperio (4), **-perui, -pertum**, to cover over, surround

coorior (4), **coortus sum**, to arise, blow up (used of winds)

copia, -ae (*f*), supply, quantity, material, opportunity
  copiae, -arum (*f.pl*), forces

copiosus, -a, -um, well-supplied

coquo (3), **coxi, coctum**, to cook

cor, cordis (*n*), heart

coram (+ *abl*.), in the presence of, in front of, before the eyes of

Corinthius, -a, -um, Corinthian, from Corinth

Corinthus, -i (*f*), Corinth

cornix, -icis (*f*), crow

cornu, -us (*n*), horn, antler

corona, -ae (*f*), crown, garland

corono (l), to surround

corpus, -oris (*n*), body

corripio (3), **-ripui, -reptum**, to seize, launch oneself, surge forward

corrumpo (3), **-rupi, -ruptum**, to corrupt, bribe

costa, -ae (*f*), rib

cotidianus, -a, -um, daily

cotidie, daily

cras, tomorrow

crastinum, -i (*n*), tomorrow
  die crastini, tomorrow

crater, -eris (*m*), wine-jar

crebresco (3), **crebrui**, to become frequent, increase

crebro, often, frequently

credo (3), **-didi, -ditum** (+ *dat*.), to believe, entrust, suppose

cresco (3), **crevi, cretum**, to grow, increase

Crete, -ae (*f*), the island of Crete (*acc*. **Creten**)

crimen, -inis (*n*), charge, accusation

crinis, -is (*m*), a hair
  crines, -ium (*m.pl*), hair, locks

Croesus, -i (*m*), Croesus, king of Lydia in Asia Minor, famed for his riches

cruciatus, -us (*m*), torture, pain

crudelis, -is, -e, cruel

crudus, -a, -um, unripe, hardy, vigorous

cruentus, -a, -um, blood-stained, bloody, dripping with blood

cruor, -oris (*m*), blood

crus, cruris (*n*), leg

cubile, -is (*n*), bed, couch

cubo (l), **-ui, -itum**, to lie down

cuius, whose

culpa, -ae (*f*), wrong, blame, fault

cum (+ *abl*.), with

cum (+ *indicative*), when, whenever

cum (+ *subjunctive*), when, since, although

cumba, -ae (*f*), boat, skiff

cuncti, -ae, -a, all

cunctor (l), to hesitate, delay

cupide, eagerly

cupido, -inis (*f*), desire, longing for, lust

Cupido, -inis (*m*), Cupid, the god of love

cupidus, -a, -um, desirous (of), eager (to), ardent

cupio (3), **-ivi, -itum**, to want, wish, desire, long for

cur, why

cura, -ae (*f*), care, anxiety, pain, sense of responsibility

curiosus, -i (*m*), busybody

curo (l), to look after, attend to, care for, see to it (that)

curro (3), **cucurri, cursum**, to run

currus, -us (*m*), chariot

cursus, -us (*m*), course, running, race, pace
  cursum tenere, to hold one's course

curvamen, -inis (*n*), bend, curve

curvus, -a, -um, curved

custodio (4), to guard

Cynthia, -ae (*f*), Cynthia (another name for Diana, goddess of hunting)

D

damno (1), to condemn, reject, distrust, doubt

damnosus, -a, -um, damaging, deadly

damnum, -i (*n*), destruction, (business) loss

Darius, -i (*m*), Darius, king of Persia

de (+ *abl.*), down from, about, from, concerning

dea, -ae (*f*), goddess

debeo (2), to be destined, have to, owe, ought

debilis, -is -e, feeble, weakened, lame

debilito (1), to weaken

decedo (3), **-cessi, -cessum**, to withdraw, retreat, depart, end, die

deceo (2), to adorn, be in keeping with, become

deceptiosus, -a, -um, deceitful

decerno (3), **-crevi, -cretum**, to settle a dispute

decimus, -a, -um, tenth
  octavus decimus, eighteenth

declive, -is (*n*), slope, downward slope

declivis, -is, -e, sloping

decoctor, -oris (*m*), a bankrupt

decus, -oris (*n*), glory, ornament

deduco (3), **-duxi, -ductum**, to lead, bring back, accompany, escort

defectus, -us (*m*), failure

defendo (3), **-ndi, -nsum**, to defend

defero, -ferre, -tuli, -latum, to carry away, report, pass on

deficio (3), **-feci, -fectum**, to fail, die down

defigo (3), **-fixi, -fixum**, to fix, stick

deflecto (3), **-flexi, -flexum**, to turn aside

defleo (2), **-flevi, -fletum**, to weep

defluo (3), **-xi, -xum**, to flow down

deformis, -is, -e, ugly, unsightly, hideous

defunctus, -a, -um, dead, finished with, deprived of

defungor (3), **-functus sum** (+ *abl.*), to perform, finish, die

degusto (1), to taste

deicio (3), **-ieci, -iectum**, to throw down, drive down, sweep down, let down, humble

dein, then, next

deinde, then, next

deliciae, -arum (*f.pl*), darling, pet, sweetheart

deligo (1), to bind, tie
  ad ancoram deligatus, riding at anchor

deligo (3), **-legi, -lectum**, to choose

delitesco (3), **-litui**, to hide, lie in wait, cower

Delos, -i (*f*), Delos, small island in the Aegean, birthplace of Apollo and Diana

delphin, -inis (*m*), dolphin (*acc.* **delphina**)

delphinus, -i (*m*), dolphin

demano (1), to spread (down)

dementia, -ae (*f*), madness, mad folly, aberration

demeto (3), **-messui, -messum**, to cut off, reap

demitto (3), **-misi, -missum**, to send down

demo (3), **dempsi, demptum** (+ *dat.*), to take away (from), remove

demonstro (1), to point out

demulceo (2), **-mulsi, -mulctum**, to soothe, stroke, lick

demum, at last

denique, in short, in fact

dens, dentis (*m*), tooth

densus, -a, -um, thick, dense, close

denuntio (1), to tell

denuo, afresh, anew

deorsum, turned down, downwards
  usque deorsum, down as far as it can go

depello (3), **-puli, -pulsum**, to drive off, keep away

dependeo (2), to hang down

depono (3), **-posui, -positum**, to put down, take down, discard, lay aside, forget

deprecor (1), to pray against, to avert by prayer

deprehendo (3), **-hendi, -hensum**, to seize upon, catch, detect

descendo (3), **-scendi, -scensum**, to descend, go down

desero (3), **-ui, -sertum**, to desert, abandon, leave behind, let down, fail

desiderium, -i (*n*), desire, longing, necessity

desido (3), **-sedi**, to sit down, settle down

desilio (4), **-ui, -sultum**, to leap down

desino (3), **desii, desitum**, to cease, stop

despero (1), to despair

despicio (3), **-spexi, -spectum**, to look down (at), despise

destino (1), to appoint, choose, decide
  destinatus, -a, -um, fixed, firm

destringo (3), **-strinxi, -strictum**, to draw (a sword)

desum, deesse, defui, to be lacking, wanting, fail, run out

detergeo (2), **-tersi, -tersum**, to wipe away

deterreo (2), to deter

detineo (2), **-ui, -tentum**, to hold back, retain

deus, -i (*m*), god (*nom.pl* **di**)

deveho (3), **-vexi, -vectum**, to bring (to land)

devoro (l), to devour, swallow up, eat

devoveo (2), **-vovi, -votum**, to dedicate, curse

dexter, -tra, -trum, right

dextera, -ae (*f*), right hand

dextra, -ae (*f*), right hand

dicio, -onis (*f*), power, sway
   in dicionem redigere, to bring under one's sway

dico (3), **dixi, dictum**, to say, tell, speak

dictum, -i (*n*), word, instruction, request

dies, -ei (*m*), day
   dies feriatus, holiday
   die crastini, tomorrow

difficilis, -is, -e, difficult

difficulter, with difficulty

diffugio (3), **-fugi**, to flee in different directions, disperse, scatter

digitus, -i (*m*), finger

dignus, -a, -um (+ *abl.*), worthy (of)
   dignus esse, to deserve

diiudico (l), to distinguish, decide between

dilabor (3), **-lapsus sum**, to glide away, fade away, vanish

diligenter, carefully

diligo (3), **-lexi, -lectum**, to love, like

diluculat, it grows light, dawns

diluo (3), **-ui, -utum**, to dissolve, mix, remove

dimico (l), to fight

dimitto (3), **-misi, -missum**, to send away, release, send down, discharge

Diogenes, -is (*m*), Diogenes, a Greek philosopher

dirigo (3), **-rexi, -rectum**, to direct

diruo (3), **-ui, -utum**, to destroy

dirus, -a, -um, dreadful, fearful

Dis, Ditis (*m*), Dis (Pluto), god of the Underworld

discedo (3), **-cessi, -cessum**, to go away, leave

discerpo (3), **-cerpsi, -cerptum**, to scatter

disco (3), **didici**, to learn

dispersus, -a, -um, scattered

displiceo (2) (+ *dat.*), to displease

dissimulanter, pretending not to know

dissolvo (3), **-solvi, -solutum**, to melt

dissuadeo (2), **-suasi, -suasum**, to dissuade, advise against

distentus, -a, -um, swollen, stuffed full

disto (1), to be away, be distant

diu, for a long time

diverbero (l), to strike through, cut through

diversus, -a, -um, facing in different directions, in the opposite direction, far off
   in diversa, in different directions

divido (3), **-visi, -visum**, to divide, separate

divinitas, -atis (*f*), divine quality, divine aura

divortium, -i (*n*), fork in the road

divus, -i (*m*), god

do (1), **dedi, datum**, to give
   finem dare, to put an end (to)

doceo (2), **-ui, doctum**, to teach, instruct, show, tell, inform

doctus, -a, -um, learned, civilised

dolabra, -ae (*f*), axe

doleo (2), to grieve, mourn, be sorry

dolor, -oris (*m*), grief, pain, anguish, suffering

domina, -ae (*f*), mistress

dominium, -i (*n*), a master's power

dominus, -i (*m*), master, owner

domumcula, -ae (*f*), small house

domus, -us (*f*), house, home
   domi, at home

donec, until

dono (l), to give, present, dedicate

donum, -i (*n*), gift

dormio (4), to sleep

dorsum, -i (*n*), back

dubito (l), to doubt, hesitate, contemplate

dubium, -i (*n*), doubt

dubius, -a, -um, doubtful, wavering, uncertain

duco (3), **duxi, ductum**, to lead, take, think, consider, decide, marry
   in matrimonium ducere, to marry
   uxorem ducere, to marry

ductor, -oris (*m*), leader

dulce, sweetly

dulcis, -is, -e, sweet, beloved

dum, while, as long as

dumtaxat, to this extent, at least, provided that

dumus, -i (*m*), bush, thicket

duo, -ae, -o, two

duplico (l), to double

durus, -a, -um, hard, harsh, hoarse, cruel

dux, ducis (*m*), leader, general, guide

E

e, ex (+ *abl.*), out of, from

ebrius, -a, -um, drunken

ecce! lo and behold!

ecquis, ecquid, if anyone, if anything

edax, -acis, eating away, destructive

edo (3), **edi, esum**, to eat

edo (3), **edidi, editum**, to raise, give out, utter, cause

educo (3), **-duxi, -ductum**, to lead out

effero, -ferre, extuli, elatum, to carry out

efficax, -acis, powerful, effective

efficio (3), **-feci, -fectum**, to make, finish, achieve, bring about that . . .

effigies, -ei (*f*), image, ghost, apparition, reflection

effodio (3), **-fodi, -fossum**, to dig up

effugio (3), **-fugi**, to escape

effugo (l), to put to flight

effundo (3), **-fudi, -fusum**, to pour out, waste, pour along

egeo (2)(+ *abl.*), to be in need (of)

egero (3), **-gessi, -gestum**, to throw out, vomit

ego, I

egomet, I (*emphatic*)

egredior (3), **-gressus sum**, to go out, come forth, leave

eiaculo (1), to hurl out, throw out

eiecto (1), to throw out

elegans, -antis, tasteful

elephantus, -i (*m*), elephant

eloquor (3), **-locutus sum**, to speak out, pronounce

eludo (3), **-lusi, -lusum**, to mock, foil, elude, give someone the slip

ematuresco (3), **-ui**, to ripen

emereo (2), to earn

emergo (3), **-mersi, -mersum**, to come forth, emerge

eminens, -entis, high, conspicuous

en! lo!

emo (3), **emi, emptum**, to buy

enim, for

ensis, -is (*m*), sword

enuntio (l), to tell, announce, divulge

eo, to that place, on that account

eo, ire, ivi, itum, to go

eodem, to the same place

Epirus, -i (*f*), Epirus (in north-west Greece, part of modern Albania)

epistola, -ae (*f*), letter

eques, -itis (*m*), horseman, knight

　equites, -um (*m.pl*), cavalry

equitatus, -us (*m*), cavalry

equus, -i (*m*), horse

Erebus, -i (*m*), Erebus, the god of darkness; the Underworld

ergo, therefore, then, well then

Eridanus, -i (*m*), River Po (in northern Italy)

eripio (3), **-ui, -reptum**, to snatch away from, take away from, wrench from, pull out, rescue

erro (l), to wander, stray

erubesco (3), **-ui**, to blush, feel ashamed

erudio (4), to teach, train

eruditio, -onis (*f*), education

essedum, -i (*n*), chariot

et, and, also

　et . . . et . . ., both . . . and . . .

etiam, also, even

　etiam tunc, even at that moment

etiamsi, even if

etsi, although

euntis, *see* **iens**

Eurus, -i (*m*), the East Wind

evado (3), **-vasi, -vasum**, to elude, evade, escape

evenit, it happens, happened

eventus, -us (*m*), outcome, fate

evolvo (3), **-volvi, -volutum**, to roll forth, curl up from

exalto (l), to raise, elevate

exanimatus, -a, -um, petrified, paralysed

exanimis, -is, -e, lifeless, dead

excedo (3), **-cessi, -cessum**, to leave, retire, charge out

excello (3), **-ui, -celsum**, to excel, surpass

　excellens, -entis, exceptional

excido (3), **-cidi**, to fall out, fail

excipio (3), **-cepi, -ceptum**, to receive, catch, take over, welcome

excito (l), to stir, arouse, waken, urge

excrucio (l), to torture

exedo (3), **-edi, -esum**, to eat away

exemplum, -i (*n*), example

exercitatio, -onis (*f*), training

exercitus, -us (*m*), army
exhaurio (4), **-hausi, -haustum**, to exhaust, drain
exigo (3), **-egi, -actum**, to demand, complete, fashion
  censum exigere, to demand tribute
exiguitas, -atis (*f*), smallness
exilio, *see* **exsilio**
eximius, -a, -um, very great, exceptional, remarkable
eximo (3), **-emi, -emptum**, to take away
existimatio, -onis (*f*), opinion
existimo (1), to consider, think
exitium, -i (*n*), death, destruction
exitus, -us (*m*), way out, end, death, outcome
expavesco (3), **-pavi**, to fear greatly
expedio (4), to make ready, realise, untie
  expeditus, -a, -um, easy, ready, quick
expello (3), **-puli, -pulsum**, to drive out, expel
experimentum, -i (*n*), trial, experience, test
experior (4), **expertus sum**, to experience, testify, check, suffer
expleo (2), **-evi, -etum**, to fulfil
explico (1), to explain, unfold
explorator, -oris (*m*), scout
expolio (4), to smoothe
expono (3), **-posui, -positum**, to expose, leave exposed
exposco (3), **-poposci**, to insist
exprimo (3), **-pressi, -pressum**, to express, squeeze out, portray, represent, paint
exsilio (4), **-silui, -sultum**, to leap out
exsilium, -i (*n*), exile
exspatior (1), to wander from the normal path
exspectatio, -onis (*f*), expectation
exspecto (1), to wait for, expect, look for
exsto (1), to stand out, appear
exstruo (3), **-struxi, -structum**, to raise up
extendo (3), **-di, -tentum**, to stretch out
exterritus, -a, -um, terrified, frantic
extra (+ *acc.*), outside, beyond
extraho (3), **-traxi, -tractum**, to drag out, pull out
extremus, -a, -um, last, at the end, utmost

F

fabula, -ae (*f*), story, tale
facies, -ei (*f*), face

facile, easily, without difficulty
facilis, -is, -e, easy, agreeable
facilitas, -atis (*f*), readiness
facinus, -oris (*n*), crime, happening, deed
facio (3), **feci, factum**, to do, make
factum, -i (*n*), deed, action
facula, -ae (*f*), small torch
facultas, -atis (*f*), opportunity
falcatus, -a, -um, fitted with scythes
fallax, -acis, deceptive
fallo (3), **fefelli, falsum**, to deceive, tell lies, foul secretly
falx, falcis (*f*), sickle, pruning-hook
fama, -ae (*f*), story, news, rumour, report, fame, reputation
fames, -is (*f*), hunger
familiariter, on friendly terms
famulus, -i (*m*), servant, attendant, retainer
fas, allowed, lawful, right
  fas esse, to be right, legitimate, lawful
fascino (1), to cast a spell, bewitch
fatum, -i (*n*), fate, doom, destiny
  fata, -orum (*n.pl*), fate, destiny
fauces, -ium (*f.pl*), throat, narrow gorge
faveo (2), **favi, fautum** (+ *dat.*), to favour, support
favilla, -ae (*f*), ash
favor, -oris (*m*), support, popularity
fecundus, -a, -um, fruitful, rich
femina, -ae (*f*), woman
femur, -oris (*n*), thigh
fera, -ae (*f*), wild beast
fere, almost
feriatus, -a, -um, on holiday
ferinus, -a, -um, wild
ferme, almost, approximately, hardly
fero, ferre, tuli, latum, to carry, bring
  fertur, he (she, it) is said
  ferunt, they say
  feror, to be carried along
ferocia, -ae (*f*), fierceness
ferrugineus, -a, -um, dark red, rust-coloured
ferrum, -i (*n*), iron, weapon, sword, javelin
  ferro ignique, by fire and sword
ferus, -i (*m*), wild beast
ferus, -a, -um, wild, fierce
ferveo (2), **ferbui**, to be hot, boil
  fervens, -entis, hot, impetuous
fervidus, -a, -um, hot, eager(ly)
fervo (3), **fervi**, to be hot, boil, grow hot
festinanter, quickly

festinus, -a, -um, quick(ly)
fidelis, -is, -e, faithful
fides, -ei (*f*), faith, faithfulness, loyalty,
  trust, belief, protection
  bona fide, without a doubt, in reality
  vera fide, in reality
fides, -ium (*f.pl*), lyre
fido (3), fisus sum (+ *dat.*), to trust
fiducia, -ae (*f*), confidence
fidus, -a, -um, faithful, loyal
figo (3), fixi, fixum, to fix, set, place
figura, -ae (*f*), shape
filius, -i (*m*), son
findo (3), fidi, fissum, to split, crack
fingo (3), finxi, fictum, to form, imagine
finio (4), to finish, end, define
finis, -is (*m*), end
  finem dare, to put an end (to)
fio, fieri, factus sum, to be done, happen,
  occur, become
fissus, *see* **findo**
fixus, *see* **figo**
flagro (1), to scorch, burn, be on fire
flamma, -ae (*f*), flame, fire
flammifer, -era, -erum, flame-bearing,
  fiery
flavesco (3), to grow yellow
flavus, -a, -um, yellow, golden
flebilis, -is, -e, mournful, doleful, plaintive
flecto (3), flexi, flexum, to bend, turn,
  control, handle, turn off to
fleo (2), flevi, fletum, to weep
fletus, -us (*m*), weeping, tears
floreo (2), to prosper, do well
flos, floris (*m*), flower
fluctuo (1), to move up and down like
  waves
fluctus, -us (*m*), wave
fluito (1), to float
flumen, -inis (*n*), river
fluvius, -i (*m*), river
fluxus, -us (*m*), flow, loss
focilo (1), to resuscitate, bring back to life
focus, -i (*m*), hearth
foedus, -eris (*n*), treaty, agreement,
  contract, pact, bond
folium, -i (*n*), leaf
fons, fontis (*m*), fountain, spring
foramen, -inis (*n*), crack, opening
fore, *future infinitive* of **sum**
forma, -ae (*f*), shape, appearance, form
Formianus, -a, -um, of Formiae (an
  ancient city in Latium)

formido, -inis (*f*), fear, terror, horror,
  dread
fornax, -acis (*f*), furnace
forsitan, perhaps
fortasse, perhaps
forte, by chance, as it happened, it so
  happened
fortis, -is, -e, brave, strong
fortuitus, -a, -um, accidental, chance
fortuna, -ae (*f*), fate, fortune, luck, good
  fortune
fortunatus, -a, -um, fortunate, lucky,
  happy
forum, -i (*n*), forum, market-place, open
  deck
fossa, -ae (*f*), ditch, trench, gouge
fovea, -ae (*f*), pit, hole
fragor, -oris (*m*), noise, din, crash,
  thunder-crash, clanking
frango (3), fregi, fractum, to break, break
  off
frater, fratris (*m*), brother
fraternus, -a, -um, of a brother, belonging
  to a brother
fraus, fraudis (*f*), treachery, deceit
fremitus, -us, (*m*), roaring, clamour
fremo (3), -ui, -itum, to roar
freni, -orum (*m.pl*), reins
frenum, -i (*n*), bridle, bit
  frena, -orum (*n.pl*), bridle, curb, bit,
  rudder
frigidus, -a, -um, cold, trivial, boring
frigus, -oris (*n*), cold
frons, frondis (*f*), branch, twig, leaf
frumentor (1), to gather corn, forage
frumentum, -i (*n*), corn, grain, crops
fruor (3), fructus sum (+ *abl.*), to enjoy
frustra, in vain, to no purpose
frustum, -i (*n*), piece (of food or meat)
fuga, -ae (*f*), flight, fleeing
  fugam inire, to flee
fugio (3), fugi, to flee, run away, escape
fugo (1), to put to flight
fulgeo (2), fulsi, to gleam, shine
fulmen, -inis (*n*), thunderbolt
fulmineus, -a, -um, flashing, like lightning
fumo (1), to smoke, smoulder, steam
fumus, -i (*m*), smoke
funda, -ae (*f*), sling-stone
fundo (3), fudi, fusum, to pour
  fusus, -a, -um, sprawling
funis, -is (*m*), rope, cable
furor, -oris (*m*), madness, frenzy

furtivus, -a, -um, secret
furto, stealthily
furtum, -i (*n*), theft, stealth

G

galea, -ae (*f*), helmet
Gallia, -ae (*f*), Gaul
garrio (4), to chatter
gaudeo (2), **gavisus sum**, to rejoice, enjoy, be glad
gaudium, -i (*n*), joy
gelidus, -a, -um, cold, chill
gemini, -ae, -a, twin, two, twofold
gemitus, -us (*m*), groan
gena, -ae (*f*), cheek
genetrix, -icis (*f*), mother
genitor, -oris (*m*), father
gens, gentis (*f*), race, family, nation
genu, -us (*n*), knee
genus, -eris (*n*), type, kind, category, family, parentage
gero (3), **gessi, gestum**, to wage, wear, display, happen
   rem gerere, to fight
gigas, -antis (*m*), giant
glacies, -ei (*f*), ice
gladius, -i (*m*), sword
globus, -i (*m*), band, mob
glomero (l), to gather together
gloria, -ae (*f*), glory, fame
gradus, -us (*m*), step, stage
Graecia, -ae (*f*), Greece
gramen, -inis (*n*), grass
grandis, -is, -e, large, great
grates agere (+ *dat.*), to thank
gratia, -ae (*f*), favour, support, thanks, popularity, appeal
   gratiam referre (+ *dat.*), to return thanks, show gratitude
   gratias agere (+ *dat.*), to thank, give thanks (to)
gratia (+ *gen.*), because (of), for the sake (of)
gratulabundus, -a, -um, demonstrating one's joy
gratus, -a, -um, agreeable, loved by
gravis, -is, -e, heavy, weighed down, serious, dreadful, important, influential
gravitas, -atis (*f*), weight
graviter, heavily, seriously, violently
gravo (l), to burden, weigh down
gregarius, -a, -um, common, ordinary
gremium, -i (*n*), lap, bosom

gubernator, -oris (*m*), helmsman, pilot
gurges, -itis (*m*), whirlpool, stream, stretch of water, sea
gutta, -ae (*f*), drop

H

habenae, -arum (*f.pl*), reins
habeo (2), to have, hold, consider, believe
habitabilis, -is, -e, habitable
habitaculum, -i (*n*), dwelling-place, home
habitatio, -onis (*f*), habitation
habito (l), to inhabit, live in, dwell
hac, here, by this path
hactenus, thus far, so far
haereo (2), **haesi, haesum**, to stick, cling
haesito (l), to hesitate
harena, -ae (*f*), sand, arena, river-side
harundo, -inis (*f*), reed, cane, rod
hasta, -ae (*f*), spear
hastile, -is (*n*), spear, javelin
haud, not, by no means
haudquaquam, not at all
haurio (4), **hausi, haustum**, to drink up, drain
Hecuba, -ae (*f*), Hecuba, wife of Priam and queen of Troy
herba, -ae (*f*), grass
heremus, -i (*m*), wilderness
heros, -ois (*m*), hero, demi-god
Hesperia, -ae (*f*), Hesperia, the western land, Italy
Hesperius, -a, -um, western
heu! alas!
hiberna, -orum (*n.pl*), winter-quarters
hibernus, -a, -um, wintry
hic, haec, hoc, this
hic (*adverb*), here
hiemo (l), to spend the winter
hiems, hiemis (*f*), winter, wintry weather
hinc atque hinc, on this side and on that
hinnitus, -us (*m*), neighing, whinnying
hodie, today
homicidium, -i (*n*), murder, slaughter
homo, -inis (*m*), man, fellow, person
honestas, -atis (*f*), honour, path of honour
honorifice, with respect
honos, honoris (*m*), respect
hora, -ae (*f*), hour
horrendus, -a, -um, dreaded
horrens, -entis, rough, unkempt
horreo (2), to bristle, shudder
horresco (3), **horrui**, to tremble at
horribilis, -is, -e, dreadful, terrifying

horridus, -a, -um, bristling, rough
hortor (1), to encourage, urge
hospes, -itis (*m*), friend
hostis, -is (*m*), enemy
huc, (to) here, hither
   huc ... illuc ... , here and there, hither
    and thither
   modo huc ... modo illuc ... , now here,
    now there
humanitas, -atis (*f*), compassion
humanus, -a, -um, human
humilio (1), to humble, bring down to the
   ground
humilis, -is, -e, humble, lowly, humiliated
hyo (1), to gape, be wide open

I

iaceo (2), to lie
iacio (3), **ieci, iactum**, to throw
iacto (1), to throw, hurl, aim, toss about
iaculum, -i (*n*), javelin
iam, now, already
ibi, there, thereupon
(ico) (3), **ici, ictum**, to strike
ictus, -us (*m*), blow
idcirco, therefore
idem, eadem, idem, same, the same man
identidem, repeatedly, over and over again
ideo, for that (this) reason
idolon, -i (*n*), ghost
idoneus, -a, -um, suitable
ieiunus, -a, -um, fasting, not taking food
iens, euntis, *present participle* of **ire**
igitur, therefore
ignarus, -a, -um, ignorant, unawares, not
   knowing, unknown
ignis, -is (*m*), fire, heat
   ferro ignique, by fire and sword
ignoro (1), to be unaware of
ignoscendus, -a, -um, pardonable
ignosco (3), **-novi, -notum** (+ *dat*.), to
   pardon, forgive
ignotus, -a, -um, unknown
ilex, -icis (*f*), holm-oak, holly-oak
illac, by that route
illactenus, to the extent that
ille, illa, illud, that
illic, there, then
illico, immediately, at once
illuc, (to) there, to that place
   huc ... illuc ... , here and there, hither
    and thither
illucesco (3), **-luxi**, to dawn

illustris, -is, -e, bright, shining, noble
imago, -inis (*f*), likeness, ghost, apparition
imber, imbris (*m*), rain, shower
imitor (1), to copy, imitate, resemble
immanis, -is, -e, huge, brawny
immanitas, -atis (*f*), vast size
immaturus, -a, -um, premature
immemor, -oris, forgetful, thoughtless
immensus, -a, -um, immense, huge, vast
immineo (2), to hang over, threaten, be
   imminent
immitis, -is, -e, ruthless
immitto (3), **-misi, -missum**, to send into
   se immittere, to launch oneself
immo, in fact, on the contrary
   immo vero, no but in fact
immobilis, -is, -e, motionless, unshakable
immortalis, -is, -e, immortal
impastus, -a, -um, hungry, starving
impedimenta, -orum (*n.pl*), baggage
impedio (4), to hinder
impello (3), **-puli, -pulsum**, to dash
   against
impendo (3), **-ndi, -nsum**, to weigh out,
   spend
imperatum, -i (*n*), order, instruction
imperium, -i (*n*), power
impero (1), to order
impetro (1), to gain a request
impetus, -us (*m*), attack, power, strength
impleo (2), **-evi, -etum**, to fill, fulfil,
   complete
implico (1), to tangle, wind round
impono (3), **-posui, -positum**, to put upon,
   place upon, apply
impotens, -entis, weak-willed, violent,
   raging
imprimo (3), **-pressi, -pressum**, to press
   upon, imprint, stamp
imprudens, -entis, not thinking (of)
imprudentia, -ae (*f*), ignorance,
   foolishness
imus, -a, -um, lowest, innermost, the very
   heart of
in (+ *abl*.), in, on
in (+ *acc*.), into, against
inamabilis, -is, -e, revolting, hateful
inanis, -is, -e, empty, pointless, groundless
incalesco (3), **-ui**, to grow warm
incautus, -a, -um, heedless, careless
incedo (3), **-cessi, -cessum**, to enter,
   advance, move off
incendium, -i (*n*), fire

incendo (3), **-cendi, -censum**, to kindle, set on fire
incertus, -a, -um, uncertain, ill-defined, ill-formed
incido (3), **-cidi, -casum**, to drop in, stumble on, come upon
incito (1), to provoke, rouse, invite
incitatus, -a, -um, at full gallop
inclutus, -a, -um, famous
incognitus, -a, -um, unknown, unfamiliar
incola, -ae (*m*), inhabitant
incolumis, -is, -e, safe(ly), undamaged
incommodum, -i (*n*), misfortune
incredibilis, -is, -e, incredible
incubo (1), **-cubui, -cubitum**, to lie (on)
incultus, -a, -um, untrimmed, unkempt
incumbo (3), **-cubui, -cubitum** (+ *dat.*), to lean (on), apply oneself (to), devote oneself (to)
incurro (3), **-curri, -cursum**, to run on
incurso (1) (+ *dat.*), to rush (among)
incutio (3), **-cussi, -cussum** (+ *dat.*), to strike (into)
inde, from there, then, after that
indico (1), to indicate, show
Indicus, -a, -um, Indian
indignatio, -onis (*f*), indignation, displeasure
indigne, undeservedly, cruelly
indignus, -a, -um (+ *abl.*), unworthy (of)
induco (3), **-duxi, -ductum**, to spread over, lead on, persuade
indumentum, -i (*n*), garment
induo (3), **-ui, -utum**, to put on, adopt
inedia, -ae (*f*), hunger
ineo, -ire, -ii, -itum, to enter
fugam inire, to flee
ineptio (4), to be foolish, make a fool of oneself
inerro (1), to wander, haunt
inexplicabilis, -is, -e, unable to be loosened
infacetus, -a, -um, coarse, lacking in good taste
infamis, -is, -e, disgraced, with a bad reputation
infelix, -icis, unfortunate, luckless, hapless, wretched, poor
inferiae, -arum (*f.pl*), funeral rites
inferior, -oris, lower, less important
infero, -ferre, -tuli, illatum, to hurl, fling
infirmitas, -atis (*f*), weakness, illness
infirmus, -a, -um, shaky, damaged
infitias ire, to deny

infra (*adverb*), below, lower down
ingens, -entis, great, huge, enormous
ingenuus, -a, -um, free-born
ingero (3), **-gessi, -gestum**, to throw in, shovel in
ingratus, -a, -um, ungrateful, unwelcome
ingredior (3), **-gressus sum**, to go in, enter
inhabito (1), to inhabit
inhabitantes, -ium, inhabitants, occupants
inhibeo (2), to hold back
inhumanus, -a, -um, inhuman, barbarous
inimicus, -a, -um, enemy, unfriendly
iniquus, -a, -um, unjust, undeserved
initio, at first
iniuria, -ae (*f*), injury, wrong
iniuriam facere, to insult
innitor (3), **-nixus sum** (+ *dat.*), to lean (on)
innumerabilis, -is, -e, countless
innuptus, -a, -um, unwed
innuo (3), **-ui, -utum**, to give a sign, beckon
innutrio (4), to nourish, bring up (in anything)
inopinans, -antis, not expecting
inops, inopis, destitute (of), helpless
inquiro (3), **-quisivi, -quisitum**, to seek out
inquam, I say
inquit, he (she) says, said
inritus, -a, -um, useless, futile, unaccomplished
insatiabiliter, insatiably, endlessly
insequor (3), **-secutus sum**, to pursue
insero (3), **-ui, -sertum**, to push in, thrust in, insert
insideo (2), **-sedi, -sessum**, to sit on
insidiae, -arum (*f.pl*), ambush
insilio (4), **-ui**, to leap upon
insinuo (1), to insinuate into
se insinuare, to penetrate, work one's way through
insipiens, -entis, foolish
insisto (3), **-stiti**, to stand on, urge on
insono (1), **-ui**, to sound, make a sound, rattle
inspicio (3), **-spexi, -spectum**, to examine
instabilis, -is, -e, unsteady
instar (+ *gen.*), like, in the likeness (of)
instituo (3), **-ui, -utum**, to begin, decide
insto (1), **-stiti**, to press on
instruo (3), **-struxi, -structum**, to instruct, equip, fit on, draw up

insula, -ae (*f*), island
intactus, -a, -um, untouched, unharmed
intellego (3), **-lexi, -lectum**, to understand, recognise
intempestivus, -a, -um, untimely, ill-timed
intendo (3), **-tendi, -tentum**, to apply, concentrate
inter (+ *acc.*), among
intercludo (3), **-clusi, -clusum**, to shut off (from)
interdiu, during the day
interdum, sometimes, occasionally
interea, meanwhile
intereo, -ire, -ii, -itum, to be destroyed, perish
interest, it makes a difference
  nihil interest, it doesn't matter
interfector, -oris (*m*), killer
interficio (3), **-feci, -fectum**, to kill
interfundo (3), **-fudi, -fusum**, to pour between, flow between
intericio (3), **-ieci, -iectum**, to place between
interim, meanwhile
interior, -oris, inner
intermitto (3), **-misi, -missum** (+ *infin.*), to interrupt, stop (doing something), let pass, intervene
interpono (3), **-posui, -positum**, to intervene, appear
interritus, -a, -um, unafraid
interrogo (1), to ask, question, ask questions
intervallum, -i (*n*), interval
intimus, -a, -um, deep within
intono (1), to thunder
intonsus, -a, -um, unshaven
intra (+ *acc.*), inside
intremo (3), **-ui**, to tremble, shake
intro (1), to go in, enter
introduco (3), **-duxi, -ductum**, to lead inside, bring in
introgredior (3), **-gressus sum**, to enter
intueor (2), **-tuitus sum**, to look at, see
inutilis, -is, -e, useless
invado (3), **-vasi, -vasum**, to attack
invalidus, -a, -um, weak, helpless
invenio (4), **-veni, -ventum**, to find, come upon
invideo (2), **-vidi, -visum** (+ *dat.*), to envy, cast an evil eye on
invisitatus, -a, -um, not seen before, uncommon

invito (1), to invite
invitus, -a, -um, against one's will, unwilling(ly)
involucer, -cris, -cre, unable to fly
involvo (3), **-volvi, -volutum**, to wrap, envelop
iocor (1), to joke, play a game
iocosus, -a, -um, funny, pleasurable
Ionius, -a, -um, Ionian (sea)
ipse, -a, -um, -self
irrumpo (3), **-rupi, -ruptum**, to burst in, rush against
is, ea, id, that; he, she, it
istaec (*n.pl*), those events
iste, -a, -ud, that (of yours), that (man)
ita, thus, so, so much
Italia, -ae (*f*), Italy
itaque, therefore, and so
iter, itineris (*n*), route, journey, track
  iter facere, to journey, march
  iter agere, to steer a course
iterum, again
itidem, in the same way
iubeo (2), **iussi, iussum**, to order, tell, bid
iucundus, -a, -um, pleasant, delightful, dear
iudicium, -i (*n*), judgment, rational reason
iudico (1), to judge, decide
iugulo (1), to cut the throat
iugum, -i (*n*), yoke
Iulus, -i (*m*), Iulus, another name for Ascanius, son of Aeneas
iumentum, -i (*n*), beast of burden
iungo (3), **iunxi, iunctum**, to join, unite, associate
Iuno, -onis (*f*), Juno, queen of the gods
Iunonius, -a, -um, of Juno, sacred to Juno
Iuppiter, Iovis (*m*), Jupiter, king of the gods
iuro (1), to swear, take an oath
ius, iuris (*n*), law, right
iustus, -a, -um, just, fair, normal
iuvenalis, -is, -e, youthful
iuvenis, -is (*m*), youth, young man
iuventa, -a (*f*), youth (i.e. young people)
iuventus, -utis (*f*), youth, warriors
iuxta, nearby, next to

L

labellum, -i (*n*), lip
labo (1), to toss about, roll
labor, -oris (*m*), toil, hard work, task, efforts

labor (3), **lapsus sum**, to glide down, float down
laboriosus, -a, -um, elaborate
laboro (1), to be hard pressed, be in difficulties
labrum, -i (*n*), lip
lacer, -a, -um, mangled, shattered
lacero (1), to tear to pieces
lacertus, -i (*m*), arm, shoulder
lacesso (3), **-ivi, -itum**, to provoke, attack
Laconicus, -a, -um, Spartan
lacrima, -ae (*f*), tear
laetitia, -ae (*f*), pleasure, joy
laetus, -a, -um, joyful, glad, happy
laeva, -ae (*f*), left hand
laevus, -a, -um, left
lamia, -ae (*f*), witch
languesco (3), **-gui**, to droop, grow faint
lapillus, -i (*m*), gem, pearl
lasarpicifer, -a, -um, producing asafoetida
lascivus, -a, -um, playful, mischievous
lassitudo, -inis (*f*), weariness
lassus, -a, -um, weary, limp
late, widely, far and wide
latebrae, -arum (*f.pl*), hiding-place
latebrosus, -a, -um, providing a good hiding-place
lateo (2), to lie hidden, be concealed
latitudo, -inis (*f*), breadth
Latonia, -ae (*f*), Latonia, daughter of Latona (i.e. Diana)
latro, -onis (*m*), robber
latro (1), to bark
latus, -a, -um, broad, wide
latus, -eris (*n*), side
laudo (1), to praise, honour
laus, laudis (*f*), praise, honour
lavo (1), **lavi, lautum**, to wash
lavor (1), to take a bath
laxamentum, -i (*n*), relaxation
laxo (1), to relax, loosen, slacken, soothe, shed
lea, -ae (*f*), lioness
leaena, -ae (*f*), lioness
Lebinthos, -i (*f*), Lebinthus (one of the Sporadic Islands, off the coast of Asia Minor)
lectus, -i (*m*), bed, couch
legatus, -i (*m*), legate, officer, ambassador
legio, -onis (*f*), legion, company of soldiers
legitimus, -a, -um, legal, legally-binding
lego (3), **legi, lectum**, to read, pick
legens, -entis (*m*), reader
lenis, -is, -e, light, gentle

leniter, gently, smoothly
lentus, -a, -um, slow
leo, leonis (*m*), lion
lepidus, -a, -um, charming, attractive
lepus, -oris (*m*), hare
Lesbius, -i (*m*), (native) of Lesbos (a large island off the coast of Asia Minor)
letum, -i (*n*), death
levis, -is, -e, light, effortless
levitas, -atis (*f*), lightness
leviter, lightly, slightly
levo (1), to lighten, relieve, support, lift up, raise
lex, legis (*f*), law, condition, stipulation
sine lege, out of control
libellus, -i (*m*), book, little book, pamphlet
libenter, willingly, gladly, with pleasure
liber, -era, -erum, free, free-born
libere, freely
libero (1), to set free
libertas, -atis (*f*), freedom
libido, -inis (*f*), lust, caprice
Libitina, -ae (*f*), Libitina, goddess of funerals
libro (1), to balance, poise, swing
Libye, -es (*f*), Libya, Africa
Libyssus, -a, -um, Libyan, African
licet (+ *dat,*), it is permissible, it is allowable
licet (+ *subjunctive*), although
lignum, -i (*n*), log, branch
limen, -inis (*n*), threshold, doorway
limes, -itis (*m*), way, path, route, course
lineus, -a, -um, of linen
lingua, -ae (*f*), tongue
linum, -i (*n*), flax, linen, thread, twine
liquor, -oris (*m*), water
lis, litis (*f*), strife, dispute, quarrelling, court-case, law-suit
litterae, -arum (*f.pl*), letter, studies
litus, -oris (*n*), shore
locuples, -pletis, rich, wealthy
locus, -i (*m*), place
locus natalis, birth-place
longe, far
a longe, from afar, far off
longinquus, -a, -um, distant
longus, -a, -um, long, long and thin, slender, long-lasting
longum est, it would be tedious
loquax, -acis, talkative, chattering
loquor (3), **locutus sum**, to speak, talk, say

lorum, -i (*n*), thong, leather lead, leash
  lora, -orum (*n.pl*), reins
lubet, it is pleasing
Lucani, -orum (*m.pl*), Lucanians (who
  lived in southern Italy)
luceo (2), **luxi**, to shine, shine through,
  show up
luctor (1), to struggle
luctus, -us (*m*), sorrow, distress, grief
lucus, -i (*m*), grove
ludibrium, -i (*n*), mockery, laughing-stock
ludo (3), **lusi, lusum**, to play
lugeo (2), **luxi, luctum**, to mourn
lumen, -inis (*n*), light, lamp
  lumina, -um (*n.pl*), eyes
luna, -ae (*f*), moon
Luna, -ae (*f*), Luna, goddess of the moon
  (Diana)
lupus, -i (*m*), wolf
lusus, -us (*m*), play, sport, entertainment
lux, lucis (*f*), light, daylight
  prima lux, dawn
luxuriosus, -a, -um, self-indulgent
lyra, -ae (*f*), lyre, lute
lyricus, -a, -um, of a lyre, lyrical

M

M', Manius
Macedo, -onis (*m*), Macedonian
Macedonia, -ae (*f*), Macedonia, country to
  the north of Greece
macies, -ei (*f*), emaciation
madeo (2), to be wet, become wet
magis, more
magister, -tri (*m*), master, leader
magistratus, -us (*m*), magistrate, city-
  official
magnanimus, -a, -um, great-hearted
magnitudo, -inis (*f*), size
magnus, -a, -um, big, great, large
maiestas, -atis (*f*), power
maior, -oris, bigger
male, badly, with difficulty
malo, malle, malui (+ **quam**), to prefer
  (to), like better (than)
malum, -i (*n*), evil, curse, misfortune,
  disaster
malus, -a, -um, bad, evil, spiteful,
  malicious
mandatum, -i (*n*), instruction, message
mando (3), **mandi, mansum**, to mangle
manduco (1), to dine
mane, in the morning

maneo (2), **mansi, mansum**, to remain,
  endure, be left
manes, -ium (*m.pl*), shades of the dead,
  spirit of a dead person
mano (1), to drip
mansues, -etis, tame
mansuesco (3), **-suevi, -suetum**, to grow
  gentle, soften
mansuetudo, -inis (*f*), gentleness,
  tameness
manumitto (3), **-misi, -missum**, to grant
  freedom (to a slave)
manus, -us (*f*), hand, band, squadron
mare, maris (*n*), sea
maritimus, -a, -um, of the sea
maritus, -i (*m*), husband
mater, matris (*f*), mother
materia, -ae (*f*), timber, fuel
maternus, -a, -um, maternal
matrona, -ae (*f*), married woman, wife
maxime, very greatly, especially
maximus, -a, -um, biggest, greatest
medella, -ae (*f*), treatment
medicamentum, -i (*n*), medication
medicatus, -a, -um, medicated
medicina, -ae (*f*), medicine
medicus, -i (*m*), doctor
mediocris, -is, -e, relatively small
medius, -a, -um, mid-, middle of
mel, mellis (*n*), honey
melior, melius, better
mellitus, -a, -um, honey-sweet
membrum, -i (*n*), limb, joint
memor, -oris, mindful
memoro (1), to tell a story, say, speak
mens, mentis (*f*), mind, spirit, attitude,
  resolve
mensa, -ae (*f*), table
mentum, -i (*n*), chin
meo (1), to pass, flow
mereo (2) (**ut** + *subjunctive*), to deserve
  (to)
mergo (3), **mersi, mersum**, to immerse,
  dive
meridianus, -a, -um, (concerning) mid-
  day
meridie, at mid-day
Merops, -opis (*m*), Merops, reputed father
  of Phaëthon
merus, -a, -um, pure, unadulterated
Messapus, -i (*m*), Etruscan leader who was
  helping Turnus
messis, -is (*f*), reaping, harvest, harvested
  crops

Methymna, -ae (*f*), Methymna, town on the island of Lesbos
Methymnaeus, -a, -um, belonging to Methymna
metior (4), **mensus sum**, to measure
meto (3), **messui, messum**, to reap
metuo (3), **-ui, -utum**, to fear
metus, -us (*m*), fear
meus, -a, -um, my
mi = mihi
mico (1), **-ui**, to gleam, shine, flicker
Midas, -ae (*m*), Midas, king of Phrygia (in Asia Minor)
migro (1), to move away
miles, -itis (*m*), soldier
miliarium, -i (*n*), milestone
militia, -ae (*f*), military service, war, army, soldiers
mille, one thousand (*plural* **milia**)
  milia (passuum), miles
minimus, -a, -um, very small
ministerium, -i (*n*), employment, task
ministra, -ae (*f*), attendant
ministro (1), to attend to, try
minor, minus, less
  nec minus, and no less, likewise
Minos, -ois (*m*), Minos, king of Crete
mirabilis, -is, -e, wonderful
miraculum, -i (*n*), marvel
mirifice, marvellously well
mirificus, -a, -um, wonderful, strange
miror (1), to marvel, admire
mirus, -a, -um, wonderful, strange
misceo (2), **-ui, mixtum**, to mix, clash
misellus, -i (*m*), poor little wretch
miser, -era, -erum, wretched, poor, sad
miserabilis, -is, -e, pitiable, to be pitied
misereor (2), to pity, feel pity for
misericordia, -ae (*f*), pity, compassion, tender-heartedness
missus, -i (*m*), messenger
Mithras, -ae (*m*), Mithras, sun-god of the Persians
mitis, -is, -e, gentle, kindly
mitto (3), **misi, missum**, to send
mobilitas, -atis (*f*), mobility, speed, manoeuvrability
moderamen, -inis (*n*), control
moderor (1), to check
modicus, -a, -um, modest
modo, now, recently, sometimes, only just
  modo...modo..., now...now...
  si modo, if only
modus, -i (*m*), way, manner, style

modi, -orum (*m.pl*), measures, melodies
  in modum (+ *gen*.), like, after the manner (of)
moenia, -ium (*n.pl*), city-walls, battlements
moleste, in a troublesome way
mollio (4), to soften
mollis, -is, -e, soft, tender
molossus, -i (*m*), hound, hunting-dog
moneo (2), to warn, advise
monitus, -us (*m*), warning
mons, montis (*m*), mountain
monstrum, -i (*n*), monster, strange creature, portent, ghost
monumentum, -i (*n*), monument
mora, -ae (*f*), delay
morbus, -i (*m*), illness, sickness
mordeo (2), **momordi, morsum**, to bite
morior (3), **mortuus sum**, to die
mortuus, -a, -um, dead
moror (1), to delay
mors, mortis (*f*), death
  mortem obpetere, to meet death
morsus, -us (*m*), bite
mortalis, -is, -e, mortal
mos, moris (*m*), custom, fashion, manner
  mores, -um (*m.pl*), character, morals
  de more, in one's usual manner
moveo (2), **movi, motum**, to move
mox, soon
mulceo (2), **mulsi, mulsum**, to soothe, charm
mulier, -eris (*f*), woman
multiplicatus, -a, -um, greatly increased
multitudo, -inis (*f*), crowd, large numbers
multo (+ *comparative*), much (more...)
  multo post, much later
multus, -a, -um, much, many
munimentum, -i (*n*), protection
munitio, -onis (*f*), fortification (s), defence-works
munus, -eris (*n*), gift, favour
murex, -icis (*m*), shellfish, purple
murmur, -uris (*n*), murmur, growl, whimper, grumble
murus, -i (*m*), wall
musca, -ae (*f*), fly
mutus, -a, -um, silent, dumb, speechless
mutuus, -a, -um, mutual, from one another, reciprocal, in return

N

Nais, -idis (*f*), water-nymph
nam, for

namque, for, for indeed
nanciscor (3), **nactus (nanctus) sum**, to obtain, find
narro (1), to tell, relate, describe
nasus, -i (*m*), nose
natalis, -is, -e, natal, of birth, birth(-day)
nates, -ium (*f.pl*), rump, buttocks
nato (1), to swim
natura, -ae (*f*), nature, disposition, character
natus, -i (*m*), son
nauta, -ae (*m*), sailor
navigabilis, -is, -e, navigable
navigatio, -onis (*f*), crossing, sea-voyage
navigo (1), to sail
navis, -is (*f*), ship
    navis longa, warship
    navis oneraria, transport-ship
navita, -ae (*m*), sailor
-ne, (*indicates a question*)
ne (+ *subjunctive*), lest, so that ... not
ne ... quidem, not even
nebula, -ae (*f*), cloud
nec, neither, nor, and ... not
    nec amplius, and no longer
    nec ... nec ..., neither ... nor
    nec non, also, in addition
necessario, of necessity, unavoidably
necesse, necessary, unavoidable
necessitas, -atis (*f*), necessity
necessus, necessary
neco (1), to kill
nefandus, -a, -um, disgusting, revolting
nego (1), to deny, say ... not
nemo, no one
nemus, -oris (*n*), wood, grove
nepos, -otis (*m*), grandson
nequaquam, by no means
neque, and not, nor
    neque ... neque ..., neither ... nor
    neque ... nec ..., neither ... nor
nequior, -ius, naughtier, more mischievous
nequiquam, in vain, to no purpose
nescio (4), not to know
    nescio quis (quid), someone (something) or other, some, something
nescius, -a, -um (+ *infin.*), not knowing (how to)
neu, and not
neuter, -tra, -trum, neither (of two)
nex, necis (*f*), death
nexus, -us (*m*), fastening, interlacing, connection

ni = **nisi**
nidulor (1), to build a nest
nidus, -i (*m*), nest
niger, -gra, -grum, black, dark
nihil, nothing
nihilominus, nevertheless, nonetheless
nil, nothing
nimis, too much
nimium, too much
nimius, -a, -um, excessive, intense, extreme, very great
nisi, if not, unless
niteo (2), to shine, be radiant
nitor (3), **nixus sum** (+ *abl.*), to rest (upon)
no (1), to swim
nobilis, -is, -e, noble, distinguished, famous, well-known
noceo (2) (+ *dat.*), to harm
noctu, by night
nodus, -i (*m*), knot
nolo, nolle, nolui, to be unwilling, be reluctant, refuse
nomen, -inis (*n*), name
non, not
    non aliter, in no other way, even so
    non modo ... sed etiam ..., not only ... but also
    non nullus, -a, -um, some
nondum, not yet
nonne? surely?
nos, we, us
noscitabundus, -a, -um, recognising
noscito (1), to recognise
nosco (3), **novi, notum**, to know, get to know
nosmetipsi, we (*emphatic*)
noster, -tra, -trum, our
    nostri, -orum (*m.pl*), our men
nota, -ae (*f*), sign
notabilis, -is, -e, noteworthy, remarkable
noto (1), to note
notus, -a, -um, well-known, familiar
novem, nine
novi (*perfect of* **nosco**), I know
novies, nine times
novitas, -atis (*f*), newness, novelty
novo (1), to renew, change
novus, -a, -um, new, strange
nox, noctis (*f*), night
    nocte, by night
nubes, -is (*f*), cloud
nubilus, -a, -um, cloudy
    nubila, -orum (*n.pl*), clouds

nubo (3), **nupsi, nuptum** (+ *dat.*), to marry

nudo (1), to lay bare, expose, leave unprotected

nudus, -a, -um, bare, naked

nugae, -arum (*f.pl*), trifles, frivolity, childish sports, scraps of verse

nullus, -a, -um, no, none

numen, -inis (*n*), divine power, deity

numerus, -i (*m*), number

    numeri, -orum (*m.pl*), measures, notes, song

numquam, never

nunc, now

    nunc ... nunc ..., at one time ... at another

nuntio (1), to announce, tell, inform

nuntius, -i (*m*), messenger, message, news

nuptiae, -arum (*f.pl*), marriage

O

obduco (3), **-duxi, -ductum**, to cover, veil

obduro (1), to be firm, be resolute

obfero, *see* **offero**

obicio (3), **-ieci, -iectum** (+ *dat.*), to cast up to, throw to

    se obicere, to place oneself in the way

obliviscor (3), **oblitus sum** (+ *gen.*), to forget

obnoxius, -a, -um, exposed to, liable to

oboedio (4) (+ *dat.*), to obey

oborior (4), **-ortus sum**, to appear, spring up, come over

obpeto, *see* **oppeto**

obscurus, -a, -um, dark

obsequibilis, -is, -e, complying, obedient, obliging

observo (1), to observe, obey, carry out

obses, -idis (*m*), hostage

obsideo (2), **-sedi, -sessum**, to besiege, blockade, mob, throng

obstinatus, -a, -um, stubborn

obstipesco (3), **-stipui**, to be spell-bound, amazed

obsto (1), **-stiti, -statum** (+ *dat.*), to stand in the way (of), obstruct

obstruo (3), **-struxi, -structum**, to block, barricade

obtineo (2), to keep, hold, be in charge of

obvius, -a, -um, in the way, exposed

occasus, -us (*m*), falling, setting (of the sun), the west

occido (3), **-cidi, -cisum**, to kill, cut down, murder, strike

occido (3), **-cidi, -casum**, to fall, set

occulo (3), **-ui, -cultum**, to hide, conceal

occulte, secretly

occupatio, -onis (*f*), occupation, pursuit

occupo (1), to occupy, seize, jump into

    occupatus, -a, -um, occupied, busy

occurro (3), **-curri, -cursum** (+ *dat.*), to meet, approach

occurso (1), to rush against, attack

Oceanus, -i (*m*), ocean, Atlantic

ocellus, -i (*m*), (little) eye (diminutive of **oculus**)

ocius, more quickly, rather quickly, quickly,

octavus, -a, -um, eighth

octavus decimus, eighteenth

octingenti, 800

oculus, -i (*m*), eye

odi, -isse, to hate

odoratus, -a, -um, sweet-smelling, fragrant, perfumed

offero, -ferre, obtuli, oblatum, to present, offer, hold out

    sese offerre, to present oneself

offirmo (1), to strengthen

olfacio (3), **-feci, -factum**, to smell

olla, -ae (*f*), pot

olor, -oris (*m*), swan

ominosus, -a, -um, ominous

omitto (3), **-misi, -missum**, to lay aside, set down, abandon

omnino, at all, altogether

omnipotens, -entis, all-powerful

omnis, -is, -e, all, every

onerarius, -a, -um, bearing a burden

    navis oneraria, transport-ship

onero (1), to load

onerosus, -a, -um, heavy

onus, oneris (*n*), load, burden

opera, -ae (*f*), work, effort(s), services

    tua opera, thanks to you

opifex, -icis (*m*), worker, craftsman, artisan

opimus, -a, -um, rich, fat, choice

oportet (+ *infinitive*), (one) ought to

opperior (4), **-pertus sum**, to wait for

oppeto (3), **-petivi, -petitum**, to encounter, go to meet

    mortem oppetere, to meet death, die

oppidum, -i (*n*), town

opportune, suitably, fittingly

opportunus, -a, -um, suitable, opportune

opprimo (3), **-pressi, -pressum**, to overwhelm, overpower

oppugnatio, -onis (*f*), attack, assault
ops, opis (*f*), help
  opes, -um (*f.pl*), wealth
optime, very well
optimus, -a, -um, very good, excellent
opto (l), to wish, desire, yearn for, long
  for, ask
opulentus, -a, -um, rich, wealthy, opulent,
  thriving
opus, -eris (*n*), task, work
opus est (+ *abl.*), there is need of
  si opus est, if necessary
ora, -ae (*f*), coast
oraculum, -i (*n*), oracle
orator, -oris (*m*), speaker, pleader
orbis, -is (*m*), circle, world, land
Orcus, -i (*m*), Orcus, Hades, the
  Underworld, abode of the dead
ordinarius, -a, -um, ordinary, regular
ordo, -inis (*m*), rank, order, course
  in ordine, in order, in sequence, one
  after the other
origo, -inis (*f*), origin
Orion, -onis (*m*), constellation called "The
  Hunter"
orior (4), **ortus sum**, to rise
  ortus, -a, -um, sprung from
ornatus, -us (*m*), decoration, finery
orno (l), to adorn, decorate, dress, equip
oro (l), to beg
ortus, -us (*m*), rising, birth, origin, the East
os, oris (*n*), face, mouth, lips
os, ossis (*n*), bone
osculum, -i (*n*), kiss
ostendo (3), **-tendi, -tentum**, to show,
  display, point to
ostium, -i (*n*), mouth, entrance, door
otiosus, -a, -um, idle
  otioso animo, easy in mind, relaxed,
  calm
otium, -i (*n*), leisure, leisure-time, ease
ovile, -is (*n*), sheep-fold

P

pabulum, -i (*n*), food, grass, crop
pactum, -i (*n*), agreement, manner, way
  aliquo pacto, somehow or other
paene, almost
paenitet me, I regret
palatium, -i (*n*), palace
palla, -ae (*f*), palla (a long flowing robe)
Pallanteus, -a, -um, of Pallanteum

(Evander's city on the Palatine Hill)
Pallas, -adis (*f*), Pallas Athene (Minerva),
  goddess of wisdom and war
palleo (2), to turn pale
pallium, -i (*n*), cover
palma, -ae (*f*), palm (of hand), hand
palus, -udis (*f*), marsh, pool
pannus, -i (*m*), strip of cloth, cloth
papaver, -eris (*n*), poppy
par, paris, equal, well-matched
  pares, parium (*m.pl*), pairs
parco (3), **peperci (parsi)**, **parsum**
  (+ *dat.*), to spare
parens, -entis (*m*), parent, ancestor
pareo (2) (+ *dat.*), to obey
pario (3), **peperi, partum**, to achieve,
  win, acquire
pariter, equally, at the same time, side by
  side
Parmenio, -onis (*m*), Parmenio (general
  and adviser of Alexander the Great)
paro (l), to prepare, get ready
Paros, -i (*f*), Paros (one of the Cyclades
  islands off the coast of Asia Minor,
  famed for its white marble)
parricidium, -i (*n*), murder
pars, partis (*f*), part, side, direction
parum, too little, scarcely, not enough
parvitas, -atis (*f*), smallness, small number
parvulus, -a, -um, poor little
parvulus, -i (*m*), small boy
parvus, -a, -um, small, gentle, slight
passer, -eris (*m*), sparrow, finch, songbird
passim, everywhere, on all sides
pastor, -oris (*m*), shepherd
pastus, -us (*m*), food
  in pastum ire, to go for food
pateo (2), to lie open, be revealed
pater, patris (*m*), father
  patres, -um (*m.pl*), the elders
paternus, -a, -um, belonging to a father,
  of a father
patior (3), **passus sum**, to allow, let,
  suffer, endure
patria, -ae (*f*), native land, country
patrius, -a, -um, belonging to a father,
  father's
patrona, -ae (*f*), protectress, patroness
pauci, -ae, -a, few
paucitas, -atis (*f*), fewness, small
  numbers, numerical weakness
paulatim, little by little, gradually
paulisper, for a short time

paulo post, a little later
paulum, little, a little
pauper, -eris, poor
pavefacio (3), **-feci, -factum**, to terrify, alarm
paveo (2), **pavi**, to be afraid
pavimentum, -i (*n*), pavement, tiled-floor
pavor, -oris (*m*), fear
pax, pacis (*f*), peace, peace-terms
pecco (l), to do wrong
pectus, -oris (*n*), breast, chest, heart
pecunia, -ae (*f*), money
pecus, -oris (*n*), flock
peditatus, -us (*m*), infantry
pedites, -um (*m.pl*), foot-soldiers, infantry
pelagus, -i (*n*), sea
pendeo (2), **pependi**, to hang, depend on, hover, droop
penetro (l), to enter, penetrate
me penetro, I enter, make my way in
penitus, thoroughly
penna, -ae (*f*), feather, arrow, wing
penso (l), to weigh
per (+ *acc.*), through, along
per se, for their own sakes
per vim, violently
perago (3), **-egi, -actum**, to carry through, accomplish, finish off
peractus, accomplished, finished, dead
percipio (3), **-cepi, -ceptum**, to perceive, catch, learn
percunctor (l), to make enquiries
percurro (3), **-cucurri, -cursum**, to run through, run along
percutio (3), **-cussi, -cussum**, to strike, strike through
perdo (3), **-didi, -ditum**, to lose, waste, destroy, squander
perduco (3), **-duxi, -ductum**, to continue, prolong
perennis, -is, -e, long-lasting, enduring, permanent, unfailing, through the years
pereo, -ire, -ii, -itum, to perish, die
perequito (l), to ride through, drive about
perfero, -ferre, -tuli, -latum, to endure
perfundus, -a, -um, very deep
perfuro (3), to rage furiously
pergo (3), **perrexi, -rectum**, to go, march, proceed, make for
Periander, -dri (*m*), Periander (tyrant ruler of Corinth from 625–585 BC)
periculum, -i (*n*), danger, peril
perimo (3), **-emi, -emptum**, to take away, annihilate, murder

perlego (3), **-legi, -lectum**, to read through
permetior (4), **-mensus sum**, to measure through, travel
permitto (3), **-misi, -missum** (+ *dat.*), to allow
permotus, -a, -um, alarmed
pernicies, -ei (*f*), destruction
pernumero (1), to count
perosus, -a, -um, loathing, detesting
perpetior (3), **-pessus sum**, to endure
perpetuus, -a, -um, endless, unending, everlasting
in perpetuum, for ever, for all time
perplexus, -a, -um, tangled
Persa, -ae (*m*), a Persian
persevero (1), to stick to, persevere
Persis, -idis (*f*), Persia
persolvo (3), **-solvi, -solutum**, to pay in full
persto (1), **-stiti, -statum**, to be kept standing, continue standing
pertaedet, to be disgusted or weary of a thing
me pertaesum est, I became weary or bored
perterritus, -a, -um, terrified, frightened
pertranseo, -ire, -ii, to pass through, cross
pertrecto (1), to stroke
perturbatio, -onis (*f*), confusion, panic
perturbo (1), to disturb, throw into confusion
pervenio (4), **-veni, -ventum**, to arrive, reach
pervinco (3), **-vici, -victum**, to conquer completely, get the better of
pes, pedis (*m*), foot
pestilens, -entis, unhealthy, infected, haunted
pestis, -is (*f*), disease, plague, death, destruction
peto (3), **-ivi, -itum**, to seek, ask, court, woo
philosophus, -i (*m*), philosopher
Phoebus, -i (*m*), Apollo (god of the sun, called Phoebus "the bright one")
Philippus, -i (*m*), Philip, king of Macedonia (360–336 BC), father of Alexander the Great
Phryges, -um (*m.pl*), Phrygians (Phrygia was in Asia Minor)
piceus, -a, -um, pitch-black
pietas, -atis (*f*), goodness, sense of duty
piget me, I regret, loathe
pilum, -i (*n*), javelin

pinguis, -is, -e, fat
pinus, -us (*f*), pine-tree, ship (made of pine)
pipio (1), to chirp
piscis, -is (*m*), fish
piscor (1), to fish
pius, -a, -um, good, dutiful
placeo (2), to please
  placet, it pleases, it has been decided
  si tibi placet, if you please
placide, quietly, gently, calmly
placidus, -a, -um, peaceful
plaga, -ae (*f*), blow, beating
plebs, plebis (*f*), common people, ordinary people
plenus, -a, -um, full
plerique, the majority, most people
plerumque, generally
pluma, -ae (*f*), feather
plumo (1), to grow feathers, become fledged
plurimus, -a, -um, most, very much, very many
plus, pluris, more
  plures, -a, several
pluvia, -ae (*f*), rain
poculum, -i (*n*), cup
poena, -ae (*f*), punishment, vengeance
pollex, -icis (*m*), thumb
polliceor (2), **-citus sum**, to promise
pondus, -eris (*n*), weight
pone, behind
pono (3), **posui, positum**, to place, put
pontifex, -icis (*m*), high priest
pontus, -i (*m*), sea
populor (1), to devastate, ravage, destroy
populus, -i (*m*), people
porrigo (3), **-rexi, -rectum**, to hold out, stretch out
porro, then, next
porta, -ae (*f*), door, gate
portitor, -oris (*m*), ferryman
porto (1), to carry
portus, -us (*m*), harbour
  portum capere, to reach harbour
posco (3), **poposci**, to ask for, demand
possideo (2), **-sedi, -sessum**, to control, own, possess
possum, posse, potui, to be able
post (+ *acc.*), after, behind
postea, afterwards, after that
posterus, -a, -um, next, coming after, future, belonging to posterity
  postero die, on the next day

postilla, after that, afterwards
postquam, after, when
postremo, at last, finally
postremus, -a, -um, last, final
  ad postremum, at the end, finally, at last
postulaticius, -a, -um, by special request, requested
postulo (1), to demand, call for
potens, -entis, powerful
potentia, -ae (*f*), power, sway
potio, -onis (*f*), drink
potior (4) (+ *gen.*), to gain possession (of)
potis, pote, possible, able
potius, rather
prae (+ *abl.*), on account of
praebeo (2), to offer, provide, supply, expose
praecedo (3), **-cessi, -cessum**, to precede, go before
praeceps, -itis, steep, headlong, rushing headlong
  in praeceps, headlong
praeceptum, -i (*n*), order, instruction, advice
praecipue, especially
praecipuus, -a, -um, distinguished, exceptional
praecordia, -orum (*n.pl*), heart
praecurro (3), **-cucurri, -cursum**, to run ahead
praeda, -ae (*f*), booty, plunder
praedico (1), to proclaim, tell, claim, instruct
praefero, -ferre, -tuli, -latum, to bear, carry, prefer
praemitto (3), **-misi, -missum**, to send forward, send ahead
Praeneste, -is (*n*), Praeneste (town in Latium)
praeparo (1), to prepare
praesens, -entis, present, in person
praesentia, -ium (*n.pl*), present circumstances
  in praesentia, at that time
praesertim, especially
praesto (1), **-stiti, -statum**, to show, display, provide, combine
praetendo (3), **-tendi, -tentum**, to stretch in front of
praeter (+ *acc.*), except, beyond, more than
praeterea, besides
praetereo, -ire, -ii, -itum, to speed past, outstrip, pass over, say nothing about

287

praetor, -oris (*m*), praetor (Roman magistrate)
praetorius, -a, -um, of a praetor, praetorian
praevaleo (2), to be superior
preces, -um (*f.pl*), prayers
precor (1), to pray
premo (3), **pressi, pressum**, to overpower, overwhelm, check, press for, urge
prenso (1), to grasp, clutch at
pretium, -i (*n*), price, reward, ransom, payment
primo, at first
primores, -um (*m.pl*), leaders, chiefs
primum, for the first time, first
primus, -a, -um, first
  in primis, among the first
princeps, -ipis (*m*), leader, officer, emperor; (*f*) mistress (of a coven of witches)
prior, -ius, former, previous, before
priscus, -a, -um, ancient
prius, before, previously
priusquam, before
pro (+ *abl.*), on behalf of, in defence of, before, for, in place of, in return for
procedo (3), **-cessi, -cessum**, to go forward, advance
proconsularis, -is, -e, proconsular
procul, far, far off, far from, at a distance, from a distance
procumbo (3), **-cubui, -cubitum**, to fall forward, be prostrate
procurro (3), **-cucurri, -cursum**, to run forward
prodigiosus, -a, -um, monstrous
prodo (3), **-didi, -ditum**, to betray
produco (3), **-duxi, -ductum**, to lead forth, make to grow
  rem producere, to prolong the operation
proelio (1), to fight a battle
proelior (1), to fight
proelium, -i (*n*), battle
  proelium committere, to join battle
proficiscor (3), **-fectus sum**, to set out
proflo (1), to breathe heavily
profugio (3), **-fugi**, to flee, run away from
profunditas, -atis (*f*), depth
profundum, -i (*n*), sea, the deep
profundus, -a, -um, deep
progredior (3), **-gressus sum**, to go forward, advance
prohibeo (2), to prevent

proicio (3), **-ieci, -iectum**, to throw down, throw forward, hurl
proles, -is (*f*), offspring, fledgling
prolubium, -i (*n*), desire
promissum, -i (*n*), promise
promissus, -a, -um, allowed to grow long, long
promitto (3), **-misi, -missum**, to promise
promo (3), **prompsi, promptum**, to relate
pronuntio (1), to give out, announce
prope (+ *acc.*), near
prope (*adverb*), nearby, almost
propello (3), **-puli, -pulsum**, to drive away, ward off
propero (1), to hasten, bring on quickly
propinquo (1) (+ *dat.*), to approach, draw near (to)
propinquus, -a, -um, near, relative
propior, -ius, nearer
propius, closer, too close
propono (3), **-posui, -positum**, to place before, serve, declare
propositum, -i (*n*), proposal
propter (+ *acc.*), on account of
propterea, therefore
prorsus, immediately, spontaneously
proscribo (3), **-scripsi, -scriptum**, to advertise for sale
prosequor (3), **-secutus sum**, to escort
Proserpina, -ae (*f*), Proserpina (daughter of Ceres, who was carried off to the Underworld by Pluto)
prospecto (1), to look out at
prospicio (3), **-spexi, -spectum**, to look ahead
prosterno (3), **-stravi, -stratum**, to throw down on the ground
  prostratus, -a, -um, prostrate, collapsed on the ground
protego (3), **-texi, -tectum**, to protect
protinus, at once, immediately
protraho (3), **-traxi, -tractum**, to drag towards
proturbo (1), to attack, push back
provehor (3), **-vectus sum**, to go forward, sail out, put out to sea
proverbium, -i (*n*), proverb, old saying
provideo (2), **-vidi, -visum**, to arrange for, provide, be cautious
provincia, -ae (*f*), province
proximus, -a, -um, nearest, very near, very close
  e proximo, (from) close at hand
prudens, -entis, wise, sensible

prudentia, ae (*f*), good sense
pruna, -ae (*f*), coal; (*pl*) fireside
publice, officially, at public expense
pudicus, -a, -um, chaste, virtuous, pure
pudor, -oris (*m*), shame
puella, -ae (*f*), girl, lady-love
puer, -i (*m*), boy
puerilis, -is, -e, boyish, of a boy, youthful
pueriliter, childishly
pugillares, -ium (*m.pl*), writing-tablets
pugna, -ae (*f*), battle, fight
   pugnam committere, to join battle
pugno (l), to fight
pulcher, -chra, -chrum, beautiful, handsome, fine, noble
pullus, -i (*m*), chick
pulso (l), to beat, kick against
pulvinus, -i (*m*), pillow
pulvis, -eris (*m*), dust, cloud of dust
pumex, -icis (*m*), pumice-stone
punctum, -i (*n*), point, small part
puppis, -is (*f*), stern, ship
puriter, without fault, blamelessly
purpurati, -orum (*m.pl*), officials (clothed in purple)
purpureus, -a, -um, crimson, bright
purus, -a, -um, pure, innocent
puto (l), to think, consider, reckon
putrefactus, -a, -um, rotted, decomposed
pyramis, -idis (*f*), pyramid

Q

qua, where, how
quadraginta, forty
quadriiugi, -orum (*m.pl*), four-horse team
quaero (3), **quaesivi, -situm**, to seek, look for, beg for
   quaesitus, -a, -um, earned
quaeso (3), **-sivi**, to beseech
qualis, -is, -e, what sort of?
   talis ... qualis ..., such ... as
quam (+ *comparative*), than
quam! how!
quamquam, although
quando? when?
   si quando, whenever, if ever
quandoquidem, since
quantus, -a, -um, how much? how great?
quare, why, therefore
quartus, -a, -um, fourth
quasi, as if, as it were

quater, four times
quatio (3), **–, quassum**, to shakĕ, flap
quattuor, four
-que, and
   -que ... -que..., both ... and ...
quemadmodum? how?
queo, quire, quii, quitum, to be able
querela, -ae (*f*), complaint
queror (3), **questus sum**, to complain, reproach, bemoan, whimper, whine
qui, quae, quod, who, which, that
   qua regione, where
quia, because, that
quicum, with which
quid, why, what
quidam, quaedam, quoddam, a, a certain, a kind of
quidem, indeed, at least, actually, to be sure
   ne ... quidem, not even
quidni? why not?
quies, -etis (*f*), rest, quiet, peace
quiesco (3), **quievi, quietum**, to rest, go to sleep
quietus, -a, -um, quiet, untroubled, calm, without a care
quilibet, quaelibet, quodlibet, any(one) you wish
   qua lubet, in any way you can
quin, that ... not
quin? why not?
quinam, quaenam, quodnam, who, what
quinque, five
quippe, for, for in fact
quis? quid? who? what?
   quid novi? what news?
quis, quid, anyone, anything
quispiam, quaepiam, quodpiam, any
quisquam, quaequam, quicquam, anyone, anything
quisque, quaeque, quodque, each
quisquis, quidquid, whoever, whatever
quivis, quaevis, quodvis, whoever, whatever
quo, whither, where, wherever
quo (+ *subjunctive*), so that (*purpose clause*)
quod, because
quomodo, how
quondam, formerly, once upon a time
quoque, also
quot? how many?
quotiens, how often, as often (as), whenever

R

rabidus, -a, -um, raging, fierce
radius, -i (*m*), ray, spoke (of wheel)
radix, -icis (*f*), root, foot
Ramnes, -etis (*m*), Ramnes (one of the Rutuli)
ramosus, -a, -um, with many branches
ramus, -i (*m*), branch
rapidus, -a, -um, fast, swift-flowing, fierce, scorching
rapio (3), **-ui, -ptum**, to seize, snatch, carry off, carry along violently
rapto (1), to hurry along, sweep along
rarus, -a, -um, rare, sparse, far apart, seldom worn
ratio, -onis (*f*), reason, thinking, financial account
ratis, -is (*f*), boat, raft
rebellio, -onis (*f*), renewal of hostilities
recedo (3), **-cessi, -cessum**, to retreat, withdraw
recens, -entis, fresh
recenter, recently
receptus, -us (*m*), retreat
recipio (3), **-cepi, -ceptum**, to receive, take back
  se recipere, to retreat, withdraw
recludo (3), **-clusi, -clusum**, to draw (a sword)
recognitio, -onis (*f*), recognition
recondo (3), **-didi, -ditum**, to hide
recordor (1), to recall, consider
recreo (1), to renew, revive, restore
rector, -oris (*m*), driver, helmsman
rectus, -a, -um, straight
recumbo (3), **-cubui, -cubitum**, to lie down, settle
recupero (1), to recover, regain
recurro (3), **-curri**, to run back
recurvus, -a, -um, bent, curved
reddo (3), **-didi, -ditum**, to return, give back, restore, give in return
redeo, -ire, -ii, -itum, to return, go back
redigo (3), **-egi, -actum**, to reduce
  in dicionem redigere, to bring under one's sway
  in potentiam redigere, to bring under one's sway
redimo (3), **-emi, -emptum**, to buy back, ransom, release
reditus, -us (*m*), return
reduco (3), **-duxi, -ductum**, to lead back, take back

redundo (1), to overflow, come flowing back, rebound
refero, -ferre, rettuli, relatum, to bring back, recall, render, turn back
  ut refers, as you relate
reficio (3), **-feci, -fectum**, to repair
refoveo (2), **-fovi, -fotum**, to bring warmth back
refugio (3), **-fugi**, to retreat
refulgeo (2), **-fulsi**, to flash back
regalis, -is, -e, royal, regal
regio, -onis (*f*), district, region
regius, -a, -um, royal
regno (1), to rule, reign supreme
regnum, -i (*n*), kingdom, the state
rego (3), **rexi, rectum**, to rule, direct, control, steer
regredior (3), **-gressus sum**, to go back, retreat, return
reicio (3), **-ieci, -iectum**, to set aside, turn over (to)
religio, -onis (*f*), religious practice, ceremony
religo (1), to tether
relinquo (3), **-liqui, -lictum**, to leave, leave a bequest, bequeath
  relictus, -a, -um, inherited
reliquus, -a, -um, remaining, the rest of
remando (1), to send back word
remaneo (2), **-mansi**, to remain
remedium, -i (*n*), cure
  remedio esse (+ *dat.*), to be a cure, cure
remigium, -i (*n*), oar, oarage, driving power
remigro (1), to go back again
remitto (3), **-misi, -missum**, to send back, let go, lay aside
  remissus, -a, -um, loose, lenient, easy-going
removeo (2), **-movi, -motum**, to remove
  remotus, -a, -um, distant, lonely
renideo (2), to be bright, shine
renuntio (1), to announce, tell, report
reor (2), **ratus sum**, to think
  ratus, -a, -um, thinking
repagula, -orum (*n.pl*)/ bars, bolt-barriers (on a door)
repello (3), **reppuli, repulsum**, to repel, pull back, pull aside
repente, suddenly
reperio (4), **repperi, repertum**, to find, discover

repeto (3), **-petivi, -petitum**, to seek again, repeat

reporto (1), to bring back

repugno (1) (+ *dat.*), to rebel (against), reject

requiesco (3), **-quievi, -quietum**, to rest

requiro (3), **-quisivi, -quisitum**, to seek out, look for, hunt for, ask

res, rei (*f*), thing, property

   rem gerere, to fight

   rem producere, to prolong the operation

   res capitalis, a matter concerning the head, death

   res bona (*f*), possessions

   res gestae, events, what has happened

reservo (1), to keep back, keep safe

resisto (3), **-stiti** (+ *dat.*), to fight back (against)

respicio (3), **-spexi, -spectum**, to look back (at), look behind (for), look around at

respondeo (2), **-spondi, -sponsum**, to answer, reply

respublica, reipublicae (*f*), the state, community

resto (1), **restiti**, to stop in one's tracks, stand still, stop, remain

retineo (2), **-tinui, -tentum,** to hold back, hold fast

retro, back, backwards

revello (3), **-velli, -vulsum**, to pull out

revertor (3), **-versus sum**, to return, go back

revincio (4), **-vinxi, -vinctum**, to tie

revoco (1), to call back

revolvo (3), **-volvi, -volutum**, to roll back, unwind

revulsus, -a, -um, pulled down, wrenched off, torn from

rex, regis (*m*), king

rideo (2), **risi, risum**, to laugh at

rigidus, -a, -um, hard

rigor, -oris (*m*), stiffness

rima, -ae (*f*), crack

ripa, -ae (*f*), (river) bank

rite, duly, properly, with appropriate rites

ritus, -us (*m*), way, manner

rivulus, -i (*m*), stream

rogo (1), to ask, make a request

rogus, -i (*m*), funeral pyre, fire

Romanus, -a, -um, Roman

rota, -ae, (*f*), wheel

roto (1), to whirl

rubeo (2), to be red

rumor, -oris (*m*), gossip, muttering

rumpo (3), **rupi, ruptum**, to break, burst, burst through

ruo (3), **rui, rutum**, to rush, race

rursum, again

rursus, again

rutilo (1), to be rosy, glow

rutilus, -a, -um (*m.pl*), ruddy, red

Rutuli, -orum (*m.pl*), the Rutuli (a Latin tribe living to the south of Rome)

S

sacculus, -i (*m*), little purse

sacer, -cra, -crum, sacred, holy

saec(u)lum, -i (*n*), generation

saepe, often

saevio (4), to be fierce, go wild with rage

saevus, -a, -um, fierce, savage, cruel

sagitta, -ae (*f*), arrow

sal, salis (*m*), salt, wit

   sales, -um (*m pl*), banter, fun, amusement

saltus, -us (*m*), leap

salubris, -is, -e, healthy

salum, -i (*n*), the sea

salus, -utis (*f*), safety, health, well-being, means of survival

   saluti esse (+ *dat.*), to be a means of safety (to), save

saluto (1), to greet

salve! hail! greetings!

Samnites, -ium (*m pl*), Samnites (the inhabitants of Samnium, a region of southern Italy)

Samos, -i (*f*), Samos (island off the coast of Asia Minor)

sanctus, -a, -um, sacred, holy, inviolable

sane, certainly, truly, doubtless, exceedingly

sanguis, -inis (*m*), blood

sanies, -ei (*f*), pus

sano (1), to heal

sapio (3), **-ii**, to be wise, sensible

   sapiens, -entis, wise, sensible, philosophical

sat, enough

satis, enough

   satius est, it would be better

satur, -ura, -urum, full (of food)

saucio (1), to wound

saxum, -i (*n*), stone, rock

scando (3), to climb

scelestus, -a, -um, poor, wretched

scelus, -eris (*n*), crime, villainy

scilicet, undoubtedly, without a doubt
scio (4) (+ *infinitive*), to know (how to)
scindo (3), **scidi, scissum**, to cut, split
scribo (3), **scripsi, scriptum**, to write
scutatus, -a, -um, armed with a shield
scutum, -i (*n*), shield
se, himself, herself, itself, themselves
seco (l), to cut through
secretum, -i (*n*), seclusion
secretus, -a, -um, secret
sector (l), to pursue
secundus, -a, -um, second
securus, -a, -um, safe, free from anxiety
secus, otherwise, differently
sed, but
sedeo (2), **sedi, sessum**, to sit, be seated
sedes, -is (*f*), seat
sedulus, -a, -um, diligent, officious
seges, -etis (*f*), crop, cornfield, corn
sella, -ae (*f*), seat, official chair
semel, once
semen, -inis (*n*), seed
sementis, -is (*f*), a sowing, sown crops
semetipsos, themselves (*emphatic*)
   in semetipsos, with one another
semita, -ae (*f*), path, street
semper, always
senatus, -us (*m*), senate
senectus, -utis (*f*), old age
senex, senis (*m*), old man
senilis, -is, -e, belonging to an old man,
   aged, senile
senior, quite old
sensim, gradually, slowly
sensus, -us (*m*), feeling
sententia, -ae (*f*), thought, opinion, idea,
   plan
sentio (4), **sensi, sensum**, to feel, notice,
   realise, have feelings, be conscious
sentis, -is (*m*), briar, bramble
separo (l), to separate
sepelio (4), **-ivi, -pultum**, to bury
sepulcrum, -i (*n*), tomb
sequor (3), **secutus sum**, to follow
serenus, -a, -um, clear, cloudless, calm
series, (*f*), succession
sermo, -onis (*m*), talk, conversation
sero, late
serpo (3), **serpsi, serptum**, to creep,
   spread
servio (4), to be a slave
servo (l), to save, keep, protect, guard
servus, -i (*m*), slave

sese = se
setius, otherwise
seu ... seu ..., whether ... or ...
severus, -a, -um, strait–laced. over–
   critical
sextus, -a, -um, sixth
si, if
   si quando, if ever, whenever
   si quis, if anyone
   si modo, provided that, if only
sic, so, thus, in this way, in such a way
   (that)
sicco (l), to dry
siccus, -a, -um, dry
Sicilia, -ae (*f*), Sicily
Siculus, -a, -um, Sicilian
sicut, just as, as, like, just like
sidus, -eris (*n*), star, constellation
sigillum, -i (*n*), seal
significo (l), to make a sign
signo (l), to sign, mark, show, attest
signum, -i (*n*), sign, signal, standard,
   mannerism
   signa inferre, to advance
silentium, -i (*n*), silence
sileo (2), to be silent
   silens, -entis, silent
silva, -ae (*f*), wood
simia, -ae (*f*), ape, monkey
similis, -is, -e, like, similar
simplicitas, -atis (*f*), uprightness, honesty
simul, at the same time, together, along
   with
simul(ac), as soon as
simulacrum, -i (*n*), figure, effigy, statue,
   image, phantom
simulatque, as soon as
simulo (l), to pretend
simultas, -atis (*f*), jealousy, rivalry
sin, but if, if on the other hand
sincere, sincerely
sine (+ *abl.*), without
   sine lege, without control, out of control
singuli, -ae, -a, one each, one by one
singultus, -us (*m*), hiccup
sinistra, -ae (*f*), left hand
sino (3), **sivi, situm**, to allow
sinus, -us (*m*), bay, lap, bosom, embrace,
   arms
situs, -us (*m*), site, structure, building
situs, -a, -um, situated
sive, whether
   sive ... sive ..., whether ... or ...

socius, -i (*m*), comrade, ally
sol, solis (*m*), sun
  sol medius, mid-day sun
  solis occasus, the west
solacium, -i (*n*), consolation, comfort,
  solace, relief
soleo (2), **solitus sum,** to be accustomed
  solitus, -a, -um, customary, usual
solitudo, -inis (*f*), solitude, lonely place,
  wilderness, desert
sollicito (1), to rouse, tempt, bribe, attract,
  appeal to
sollicitudo, -inis (*f*), anxiety
sollicitus, -a, -um, anxious, worried
solor (1), to comfort, console
solum, only
solus, -a, -um, alone, lonely
solvo (3), **solvi, solutum,** to unravel,
  loosen, free
  navem solvere, to set sail, weigh anchor
  solutus, -a, -um, released, free,
  overcome, relaxed
somnus, -i (*m*), sleep
sonitus, -us (*m*), sound
sonorus, -a, -um, loud
sonus, -i (*m*), sound, clanking
sordidus, -a, -um, filthy
soror, -oris (*f*), sister
sors, sortis (*f*), prophecy, lot, fortune, fate,
  destiny
spargo (3), **sparsi, sparsum,** to scatter,
  splash, shower
spatiosus, -a, -um, spacious, roomy
spatium, -i (*n*), space, period, interval,
  course, track
spectaculum, -i (*n*), spectacle, show
spectator, -oris (*m*), spectator
specto (1), to watch, look at, gaze upon
specus, -us (*m/f*), cave
spero (1), to hope, like to think
spes, spei (*f*), hope
spiritus, -us (*m*), breath, breathing,
  circulation
spiro (1), to breathe
spolia, -orum (*n.pl*), spoils
spondeo (2), **spopondi, sponsum,** to
  promise
squalor, -oris (*m*), filth
stabilitas, -atis (*f*), stability, steadiness,
  firmness
stadium, -i (*n*), stade (Greek measure =
  roughly 202 yards or 185 metres)
stagno (1), to stem, stop

stagnum, -i (*n*), pool, lagoon
statim, immediately, at once
statio, -onis (*f*), sentry-post, sentry-duty,
  guard-duty
status, -us (*m*), status, condition, position
stella, -ae (*f*), star, constellation
sterno (3), **stravi, stratum,** to scatter,
  spread, lay low, cut down
sternumentum, -i (*n*), sneeze
stilus, -i (*m*), pen
stirps, stirpis (*f*), stalk, root, splinter, thorn
stiva, -ae (*f*), plough-handle
sto (1), **steti, statum,** to stand, stand by
stratum, -i (*n*), saddle
strepitus, -us (*m*), noise, din, shouting
strido (3), **-di,** to whistle, whiz, whir
stringo (3), **strinxi, strictum,** to draw (a
  sword)
strix, -igis (*f*), witch
strues, -is (*f*), heap, pile
studium, -i (*n*), zeal, enthusiasm, study
stultus, -a -um, foolish
stupefactus, -a, -um, astonished,
  astounded
stupeo (2), to be dazed, be stunned, be
  numb
Stygius, -a, -um, Stygian, of the Styx
Styx, Stygis (*f*), Styx (river of the
  Underworld)
suadeo (2), **suasi, suasum** (+ *dat.*), to urge
  on
suavis, -is, -e, delightful
sub (+ *abl.*), under
sub (+ *acc.*), down through, up to
subdo (3), **-didi, -ditum,** to place under,
  set under, go under, plunge into
subduco (3), **-duxi, -ductum,** to draw up
  (a ship), beach
subeo, -ire, -ii, -itum (+ *dat.*), to go under,
  enter, approach, attack, come over
subgero (3), **-gessi, -gestum,** to bring,
  supply
subicio (3), **-ieci, -iectum,** to place under,
  subject, expose (oneself), subdue
subigo (3), **-egi, -actum,** to drive along,
  propel
subinde, immediately after, from time to
  time
subinfero, -ferre, -tuli, to add
subito, suddenly
subitus, -a, -um, sudden
subiungo (3), **-iunxi, -iunctum,** to add
sublatus, -a, -um, raised, loud

sublimis, -is, -e, eminent, high and
mighty
sublustris, -is, -e, glimmering
submitto (3), **-misi, -missum**, to lower
subpono (3), **-posui, -positum**, to place
under
subrepo (3), **-psi, -ptum**, to creep up on,
sneak up on
subsequor (3), **-secutus sum**, to follow,
follow closely
subsidium, -i (*n*), help
subsidia, -orum (*n.pl*), reserves,
resources, the means
subvecto (l), to carry, ferry
subvenio (4), **-veni, -ventum** (+ *dat.*), to
help, come to the assistance (of)
succedo (3), **-cessi, -cessum**, to take the
place (of)
succido (3), **-cidi, -cisum**, to cut down
succurro (3), **-curri, -cursum** (+ *dat.*),
to help, occur
succutio (3), **-cussi, -cussum**, to toss up,
fling aloft
sucus, -i (*m*), juice, moisture
sufficio (3), **-feci, -fectum**, to be
sufficient, cope with
suffugium, -i (*n*), place of refuge
summa, -ae (*f*), the sum total of
summoveo (2), **-movi, -motum**, to
thrust aside
summus, -a, -um, greatest, highest, top of,
surface of
summus dies, last day, death
sumo (3), **sumpsi, sumptum**, to take up,
summon up
sumptus, -us (*m*), expense
super (*adverb*), besides that, more than
enough
super (+ *abl.*), over, about, on account of
super (+ *acc.*), above, against
superbus, -a, -um, proud, haughty,
overbearing
superior, -ius, higher up, superior, better,
previous
supero (l), to overcome, defeat, surpass, be
superior to, cross over, climb over
superpono (3), **-posui, -positum**, to
place above, place upon
supersedeo (2), **-sedi, -sessum**, to
refrain from, leave undone \
supersum, -esse, -fui (+ *dat.*), to remain,
be left over, survive, abound, be in
abundance

superus, -a, -um, upper, higher, of the
world above
superi, -orum (*m.pl*), the gods
supra (*adverb*), above
supremus, -a, -um, last
surgo (3), **surrexi, surrectum**, to rise, get
up
suscipio (3), **-cepi, -ceptum**, to
undertake, receive
suscito (l), to rouse, alert
suspendium, -i (*n*), hanging-place
suspendo (3), **-pendi, -pensum**, to hang
suspensus, -a, -um, suspended, hanged,
hanging, strung up
suspicio, -onis (*f*), suspicion
suspicio (3), **-spexi, -spectum**, to
suspect
suspicor (l), to suspect
suspirium, -i (*n*), sigh, breath, breathing
sustento (l), to support
sustineo (2), **-ui, -tentum**, to stand, hold
out, endure, hold off, keep control of
suus, -a, -um, his own, her own, their
own
sui, -orum (*m.pl*), their own people

T

tabella, -ae (*f*), board, tablet
taberna, -ae (*f*), shop
tabernaculum, -i (*n*), tent
tabesco (3), **-ui**, to melt
taceo (2), to be silent
tacitus, -a, -um, silent
taedet me, I am tired (of)
Taenarius, -a, -um, belonging to
Taenarum
Taenarum, -i (*n*), Taenarum, promontory
in southern Greece (now called Cape
Matapan)
taeter, -tra, -trum, foul, loathsome
talentum, -i (*n*), talent (a valuable coin)
talis, -is, -e, such
talis ... qualis ..., exactly as
tam, so
tam ... quam ..., as much as
tamen, however, nevertheless
tamquam, as if, as though
tandem, at length, at last
tango (3), **tetigi, tactum**, to touch
tantum, only
tantundem, just as much
tantus, -a, -um, such, so great
tanto magis, all the more eagerly

tantum (+ *gen.*), so many, such a great number (of)

tantus... quantus..., as much as

tapete, -is (*n*), carpet, rug, coverlet

tardus, -a, -um, slow, sluggish

Tarentini, -orum (*m.pl*), Tarentines (inhabitants of Tarentum in the heel of Italy)

Tartara, -orum (*n.pl*), Tartarus, the Underworld

Tartareus, -a, -um, belonging to Tartarus

tectum, -i (*n*), roof

tego (3), **texi, tectum,** to cover, conceal, hide, protect

tellus, -uris (*f*), land, the earth

telum, -i (*n*), weapon, spear

temerarius, -a, -um, rash

temere, at random, haphazardly

haud temere, not carelessly, carefully

temo, -onis (*m*), pole (of vehicle)

tempero (1) (+ *infinitive*), to refrain (from doing)

tempestas, -atis (*f*), storm, weather

tempestivus, -a, -um, ripening early (earlier)

templum, -i (*n*), temple

tempto (1), to try out, test, sample

tempus, -oris (*n*), time, age

tempora, -um (*n.pl*), temples (of the head)

ad tempus, at a set time

id temporis, at that time

tempori, early, in good time

tendo (3), **tetendi, tensum,** to stretch out, hasten, march, make one's way

tenebrae, -arum (*f.pl*), darkness, night

tenebricosus, -a, -um, shrouded in darkness, shadowy

tenebrosus, -a, -um, dark

teneo (2), **tenui, tentum,** to hold, control, hold back

cursum tenere, to hold one's course

tener, -a, -um, tender

tenuis, -is, -e, thin, fine, delicate

tenuitas, -atis (*f*), thinness

tepefacio (3), **-feci, -factum,** to make warm

ter, three times, thrice

tergum, -i (*n*), back

a tergo, from behind

terga vertere, to take to flight

tero (3), **trivi, tritum,** to rub, wear away

terra, -ae (*f*), earth

terreo (2), to terrify

terribilis, -is, -e, frightening, appalling

terrificus, -a, -um, terrifying

terror, -oris (*m*), fear

tertius, -a, -um, third

testamentum, -i (*n*), will

testis, -is (*m*), witness

testor (1), to call to witness

testudo, -inis (*f*), tortoise, lyre

Teucri, -orum (*m.pl*), Trojans

timeo (2)(+ *dat.*), to fear (for)

timide, timidly

timor, -oris (*m*), fear

tingo (3), **-nxi, -nctum,** to dye, colour

tintino (1), to ring, buzz

titulus, -i (*m*), notice

toga, -ae (*f*), toga

tollo (3), **sustuli, sublatum,** to raise, lift, take on board, grab, remove, take away

tonitrus, -us (*m*), thunder

tormentum, -i (*n*), torture

torpeo (2), to be stiff, be numb, be paralysed

torpor, -oris (*m*), paralysis

torqueo (2), **torsi, tortum,** to poise, brandish

torreo (2), **torrui, tostum,** to dry, bake

torus, -i (*m*), muscle, muscular body; couch, marriage bed

tot, so many

totidem, as many

totidem... quot..., as many... as

totus, -a, -um, all, whole

tracto (1), to treat

tractus, -us (*m*), course

trado (3), **-didi, -ditum,** to hand over, hand on, hand down, surrender, record, relate

tradunt, they say

tragula, -ae (*f*), javelin

traho (3), **traxi, tractum,** to drag, draw, attract, derive, trace

traicio (3), **-ieci, -iectum,** to pierce, transfix

trans (+ *acc.*), across

transabeo, -ire, -ii, to pierce, go right through

transactus, -a, -um, previous, past

transeo, -ire, -ii, -itum, to cross over, pass through

transfero, -ferre, -tuli, -latum, to transfer

transfigo (3), **-fixi, -fixum,** to pierce, transfix

transitus, -us (*m*), way, passage
transmarinus, -a, -um, from across the sea
transmitto (3), **-misi, -missum**, to spend (time)
transporto (1), to carry across
tremendus, -a, -um, dreaded
tremibundus, -a, -um, trembling with fear
tremo (3), **-ui**, to tremble
tremulus, -a, -um, quivering
trepido (1), to be frightened, panic
trepidulus, -a, -um, anxious, agitated
trepidus, -a, -um, fearful, excited
tres, tres, tria, three
tribulatio, -onis (*f*), catastrophe
tribunus militum, tribune of the soldiers
tribuo (3), **-ui, -utum**, to grant, give
triclinium, -i (*n*), dining-room
triduum, -i (*n*), (period of) three days
triennium, -i (*n*), (period of) three years
trifidus, -a, -um, three–forked
triginta, thirty
tristis, -is, -e, sad, sorrowful, miserable, grim, tormenting
tristitia, -ae (*f*), sadness
tritus, *see* **tero**
triumpho (1), to triumph, be given a triumph
trux, trucis, grim
tu, you
tugurium, -i (*n*), hut
tum, then
   tum demum, then and only then
tumultus, -us (*m*), tumult, uproar
tumulus, -i (*m*), hillock, mound, grave
tunc, then, on that occasion, at that time
tunica, -ae (*f*), tunic
turba, -ae (*f*), crowd, throng, band, crew
turgidulus, -a, -um, swollen
turma, -ae (*f*), squadron
turpis, -is, -e, degrading
tussis, -is (*f*), cough
tuto, safely
tutus, -a, -um, safe
tuus, -a, -um, your
   tua opera, thanks to you
tyrannus, -i (*m*), tyrant, ruler
Tyrius, -a, -um, Tyrian, from the town of Tyre, Phoenician

U

ubi, when, where
   ubi primum, as soon as
ubique, everywhere

ullus, -a, -um, any
ulterior, -oris, further, farther
ultimus, -a, -um, last, furthest
ultio, -onis (*f*), revenge, vengeance
ultro, of one's own accord, voluntarily
ululatus, -us (*m*), howling, wailing, shrieking
umbra, -ae (*f*), shadow, shade, spirit, soul (of dead person)
umerus, -i (*m*), shoulder
umor, -oris (*m*), moisture
umquam, ever
   haud umquam, never
una, together, along with, beside
unda, -ae (*f*), wave, water
unde, from where, from which, therefore
undique, from all sides, on all sides
unguentum, -i (*n*), perfume
universi, -ae, -a, all
unus, -a, -um, one, alone
   omnes ad unum, all to a man
urbs, urbis (*f*), city
uro (3), **ussi, ustum**, to burn
ursus, -i (*m*), bear
usquam, anywhere
usque, without a break, all the way, non–stop, without stopping, continually
   usque deorsum, down as far as it can go
usus, -us (*m*), usefulness, benefit, practice
   usui esse (+ *dat.*), to be of use (to)
ut (+ *indicative*), when, as
ut (+ *subjunctive*), in order that, so that
ut (+ *noun*), as
uterque, utraque, utrumque, each of two, either, both
utilis, -is, -e, useful
utinam! would that !
utor (3), **usus sum** (+ *abl.*), to use
utrum... an..., whether... or...
uxor, -oris (*f*), wife

V

vaco (1), to be empty
vacuus, -a, -um, empty of, free from, idle
vae! alas!
vagina, -ae (*f*), scabbard
vagus, -a, -um, wandering
valde, very, very much
vale! farewell!
valeo (2), to be well, be able, get one's way
vallum, -i (*n*), rampart

vallis, -is (*f*), valley
varius, -a, -um, different, ever-
changing
vasculum, -i (*n*), small vessel, small cup
vastitudo, -inis (*f*), huge size
vasto (l), to lay waste
vastus, -a, -um, huge
-ve, or
vecto (l), to carry
vehiculum, -i (*n*), wagon, carriage
veho (3), vexi, vectum, to carry
vehor (3), vectus sum, to be carried, sail,
ride, travel
vel, or
vel... vel..., either... or...
velocitas, -atis (*f*), speed
velociter, swiftly
velum, -i (*n*), sail
velut, such as, as if, just like
veluti, such as, just as, as though
vena, -ae (*f*), vein
venatio, -onis (*f*), hunting, wild beast
show
venator, -oris (*m*), hunter
venatrix, -icis (*f*), huntress
venatus, -us (*m*), hunting
venenum, -i (*n*), poison
venerabilis, -is, -e, revered, respected
venia, -ae (*f*), pardon, permission, leave
venio (4), veni, ventum, to come
venor (1), to hunt
venter, -tris (*m*), belly, stomach
ventito (l), to keep going, keep coming and
going
ventus, -i (*m*), wind
Venus, -eris (*f*), Venus (goddess of love)
venustus, -a, -um, charming, lovable
vepres, -is (*m*), briar-bush
verber, -eris (*n*), whipping, flogging,
blow
verbero (l), to beat, lash, hit, strike
verbum, -i (*n*), word
vere, truly, truthfully
vereor (2), veritus sum, to fear
veritus, -a, -um, fearing
vero, but, now, truly, in truth, indeed
versor (1), to turn
verto (3), verti, versum, to turn
verum, but
verus, -a, -um, true, real, genuine, alive
vera fide, in reality
verutum, -i (*n*), spear

vesanus, -a, -um, mad, insane, love-
crazed
vespa, -ae (*f*), wasp
vesper, -i (*m*), evening
vester, -tra, -trum, your
vestigium, -i (*n*), pad (of a paw)
vestigia, -orum (*n.pl*), tracks, traces,
remains
vestis, -is (*f*), robe, garment, clothes
vetus, -eris, old, of olden times
via, -ae (*f*), way, road
viaticum, -i (*n*), food for a journey
vibro (l), to make to shake, brandish
vicinia, -ae (*f*), neighbourhood, nearness
vicinus, -a, -um, neighbouring
victito (1) (+ *abl*.), to feed (on), live (off)
victor, -oris (*m*), victor, conqueror
victoria, -ae (*f*), victory
victus, -us (*m*), food
video (2), vidi, visum, to see
videor (2), visus sum, to seem, be seen
vigilia, -ae (*f*), watch, wakefulness,
insomnia, lack of sleep
vigilo (l), to lie awake, be sleepless, keep
watch, be on watch
viginti, twenty
vilis, -is, -e, cheap, worthless
vilitas, -atis (*f*), cheapness
villa, -ae (*f*), country-house, villa
vincio (4), vinxi, vinctum, to bind, tie up,
put in chains
vinco (3), vici, victum, to conquer, defeat
vinculum, -i (*n*), bond, knot, chain
vinum, -i (*n*), wine
vina, -orum (*n.pl*), wine-flasks
vir, viri (*m*), man, husband
vires, -ium (*f.pl*), strength
viridis, -is, -e, green
virilis, -is, -e, manly
virga, -ae (*f*), rod, stick
virgo, -inis (*f*), maiden
virtus, -utis (*f*), virtue, courage, bravery,
valour
vis, vim, vi (*f*), force, severity
per vim, violently
viso (3), visi, visum, to visit, see
vita, -ae (*f*), life
vitam agere, to spend one's life
vitalis, -is, -e, life-giving, vital
vitium, -i (*n*), fault, defect (of character)
vito (l), to avoid
vitupero (l), to find fault with

vivo (3), **vixi, victum**, to live, be alive
vix, scarcely, with difficulty
vocalis, -is, -e, giving voice, tuneful
voco (1), to call, beckon
volatus, -us (*m*), flight, flying
Volcens, -entis (*m*), Volcens (Rutulian leader)
volnus = vulnus
volo (1), to fly, fly off
volo, velle, volui, to wish, be willing
volucer, -cris, -cre, winged, swift-flying
voluntas, -atis (*f*), wish, request
voluptas, -atis (*f*), enjoyment, pleasure
volvo (3), **volvi, volutum**, to turn, roll, roll forward, tumble

vomo (3), **-ui, -itum**, to vomit
vos, you
votum, -i (*n*), prayer; (*plural*) good wishes
vox, vocis (*f*), voice, remark, cry, shout
Vulcanius, -a, -um, of Vulcan (god of fire)
vulgus, -i (*n*), common people, public, mob
vulnero (1), to wound
vulnus, -eris (*n*), wound
    adverso vulnere, with wounds on the front of the body
vultus, -us (*m*), face, expression, appearance

PERIOD	HISTORICAL EVENTS	
MONARCHY 753– 510 BC	753 BC 510 BC	**Romulus** founded Rome (according to legend) **Tarquinius Superbus,** the seventh and last king of Rome, was expelled (according to legend)
REPUBLIC 510– 31 BC	500–200 BC 264–202 BC 202 BC 133–122 BC 157–86 BC 138–78 BC 106–48 BC 102 – 44 BC 63 BC 58 – 51 BC 49 BC 48 BC 44 BC 31 BC	Rome extended her power through Italy and the Mediterranean Rome's wars with her main rival Carthage (First and Second Punic wars) Defeat of **Hannibal**, leader of the Carthaginians, at Zama Democratic reforms at Rome. The power of the Senate reduced **Marius,** Roman general, creator of professional Roman army **Sulla:** reforms in law and administration **Pompey the Great:** Roman general who defeated the pirates and made conquests in the Eastern Mediterranean. At first, he was Caesar's ally: later, his rival **Julius Caesar:** conquered Gaul and became dictator in Rome after defeating Pompey **Cicero** was consul and put down the conspiracy of Catiline Caesar's conquest of Gaul and landings in Britain Caesar crossed the River Rubicon and invaded Italy Caesar defeated Pompey at Pharsalus Murder of Caesar **Octavian** defeated **Mark Antony** at Actium
EMPIRE 31 BC– AD 180	27 BC c.4 BC 27 BC– AD 68 AD 64 AD 68 – 69 AD 69– 96 AD 79 AD 96 –180	Octavian became the first emperor of Rome and took the title **Augustus** Birth of **Jesus Christ** The Julio-Claudian Emperors: **Augustus, Tiberius, Caligula, Claudius, Nero** The Great Fire of Rome The year of the four emperors: **Galba, Otho, Vitellius, Vespasian** The Flavian Emperors: **Vespasian, Titus, Domitian.** The eruption of Vesuvius and destruction of Pompeii and Herculaneum "The Five Good Emperors": **Nerva, Trajan, Hadrian, Antoninus Pius, Marcus Aurelius**
THE DECLINE AND FALL OF THE EMPIRE AD 180– 410	AD 192 – 306 AD 313 AD 330 AD 410	In this period there were 33 emperors, many of whom were assassinated **Constantine,** the first Christian Emperor, issued the Edict of Milan allowing Christians to worship freely Constantine founded Constantinople: beginning of the two Empires– Eastern and Western Rome was sacked by Alaric the Goth

	WRITERS – LATIN	WRITERS – GREEK (on Roman subjects)
254–184 BC	**Plautus** (c.20 plays survive)	203– 121 BC **Polybius** (*History of Rome*)
185–159 BC	**Terence** (6 plays survive)	
234–149 BC	**Cato** (*On Agriculture*)	
102–44 BC	**Julius Caesar** (Memoirs of Gallic War and Civil War)	
106–43 BC	**Cicero** (oratory, philosophy, letters)	
84–54 BC	**Catullus** (lyric poems)	
70–19 BC	**Virgil** (epic and pastoral poetry)	
65–8 BC	**Horace** (lyrics, satires)	
59 BC–AD 17	**Livy** (*History of Rome*)	
43 BC–AD 17	**Ovid** (poetry of many kinds)	
4 BC–AD 65	**Seneca** (essays, letters, tragedies)	
?–AD 65	**Petronius** (A novel *The Satyricon*)	AD 46 –121 **Plutarch** (*Parallel Lives of Noble Greeks & Romans*)
AD 35–95	**Quintilian** (*The Education of an Orator*)	
AD 40–104	**Martial** (epigrams)	
c. AD 50	**Curtius** (*History of Alexander*)	
AD 55–117	**Tacitus** (history)	
c. AD 61–114	**Pliny the Younger** (letters)	
AD 65–140	**Juvenal** (*Satires*)	
AD 70–160	**Suetonius** (*Lives of the Caesars*)	
AD 123– c. 165	**Aulus Gellius** (essays)	
AD 340–420	**St Jerome** (Translation of the Bible into Latin)	
AD 354–430	**Augustine** (Christian writings and autobiography)	
c. AD 370	**Eutropius** (history)	